TABLOID JUSTICE

SECOND EDITION

TABLOID JUSTICE

Criminal Justice in an Age of Media Frenzy

Richard L. Fox
Robert W. Van Sickel
Thomas L. Steiger

LYNNE
RIENNER
PUBLISHERS

BOULDER
LONDON

Published in the United States of America in 2007 by
Lynne Rienner Publishers, Inc.
1800 30th Street, Boulder, Colorado 80301
www.rienner.com

and in the United Kingdom by
Lynne Rienner Publishers, Inc.
3 Henrietta Street, Covent Garden, London WC2E 8LU

Library of Congress Cataloging-in-Publication Data
Fox, Richard Logan.
    Tabloid justice : criminal justice in an age of media frenzy / Richard L.
Fox, Robert W. Van Sickel, and Thomas L. Steiger. — 2nd ed.
        p.   cm.
    Includes bibliographical references and index.
    ISBN 978-1-58826-532-6 (pbk. : alk. paper)
    1. Mass media and criminal justice—United States.   2. Criminal justice,
Administration of—United States.   I. Van Sickel, Robert W., 1956–
II. Steiger, Thomas L., 1958–   III. Title.
    P96.C742U63 2007
    070.4'49364973—dc22
                                                            2006103367

British Cataloguing in Publication Data
A Cataloguing in Publication record for this book
is available from the British Library.

Printed and bound in the United States of America

The paper used in this publication meets the requirements
∞ of the American National Standard for Permanence of
Paper for Printed Library Materials Z39.48-1992.

5   4   3   2   1

CONTENTS

TABLES

PREFACE

Prior to publishing the first edition of *Tabloid Justice,* we engaged in endless conversations about the US media's coverage of politics, law, and crime. As dedicated law and politics "news junkies," we found the rancorous debate on the news-talk and commentary programs to be eminently entertaining. Still, the increasingly sensationalistic nature of such programs seemed to trivialize legal news, and this made us wonder about the possible negative effects that such programming was having on public attitudes about the legal system.

After witnessing thousands of hours of programming devoted to the Rodney King events, the O.J. Simpson trials, and the murder of JonBenet Ramsey, we felt that an examination of the social effects of such programming was called for. Our goals for the first edition of *Tabloid Justice* were to present a systematic exploration of the ways that the media had covered high-profile cases during the 1990s and to assess the impact of such coverage on public attitudes toward the justice system. We are grateful for the warm reception that the book received, including its use in numerous university courses in media and politics, criminal justice, and law and society.

Fast-forward to the present. The murder of JonBenet Ramsey is still unsolved, and O.J. Simpson is still making headlines. However, there have been significant changes in the media environment itself. The increasing saturation of the Internet and the blogosphere, the explosion of dramatic law-related fictional television dramas, and the intense media coverage of legal cases such as those involving Scott Peterson, Terri Schiavo, Martha Stewart, and Michael Jackson seemed to us to justify the continued examination of what we termed in the first edition the "era of tabloid justice." In this second edition, we present an updated and expanded book that includes the results of a new national public opinion poll to gauge the potential effects of contemporary media coverage of legal proceedings. As we discuss throughout the text, there have been some significant changes since the 1990s, but the basic approach to media coverage of crime and the legal system established during that decade continues to dominate current programming.

For this second edition we are delighted to welcome Thomas L. Steiger, professor of sociology and women's studies at Indiana State University, as our third author. Tom was incredibly generous in offering, in addition to his own expertise in survey research, the services and funding of the ISU Sociology Research Laboratory to conduct our 2005 national survey. Tom's assistance was invaluable to us in constructing our survey instrument, collecting the data that appear throughout the following pages, and offering consistent and cogent encouragement and insights. This edition would not exist without his contribution. We also gratefully acknowledge the assistance of ISU graduate student Jessica Cenegy and the students from Sociology 280 at ISU who served as callers during the survey.

Hidden within the pages of any scholarly study are the efforts of numerous individuals. Accordingly, we would like to express our gratitude to a number of people who have offered valuable assistance in the completion of this book. We are perhaps most deeply indebted to Stephen Wasby, who was instrumental in helping to shape the final draft of our first edition, and who graciously joined us again for the second edition. He reviewed several versions of the manuscript, and his comments were uniformly helpful, expediently delivered, and relentlessly candid. Professor Wasby has been a great help to us during the writing of both editions of this book.

We are also very thankful for the assistance of Union College student Dan Amira, who fully embraced the spirit of the project and helped us compile much of the research for the second edition. Carol Cichy, the political science department administrator at Union College, assisted us, with good cheer, on many of the time-consuming and tedious tasks that go into producing a finished draft.

A number of other friends, colleagues, and students were of great help in our efforts. The first edition benefited greatly from the guidance, encouragement, and assistance of Richard Neimi, Zoe Oxley, Eric R.A.N. Smith, James Underwood, M. Kent Jennings, Theodore Gilman, Clifford Brown, Terry Wiener, Liam Joynt, Andrew Wininger, Mathew Barry, and Richard E. Rupp. We are indebted to the Union College Faculty Research Fund for generous assistance in funding both of our national polls. Last, we acknowledge the tremendous work of the Brentwood Group, which offered us special consideration in conducting our 1999 survey in an efficient and cost-effective manner.

We would be remiss if we did not thank the folks at Lynne Rienner Publishers, especially Leanne Anderson, who have given us the opportunity to continue working on this exciting project.

Finally, our families and friends were constant sources of support, encouragement, perspective, and friendly criticism. We simply could not have done it without them, and we thus offer our deepest appreciation to Dominique, Lila, Miles, Stephanie, Eli, Naomi, Bill, and Anita.

Introduction:
A Time of Tabloid Justice

The hope of 24/7 television news is that there is so much time to fill that every once in a while something of substance will be uttered or revealed. Alas, experience has shown that not to be the case. . . . The television age has paradoxically left people more informed and more ignorant at the same time.
—*Chicago Sun-Times* columnist William O'Rourke[1]

This trial . . . is the most significant legal event ever to confront America's direct understanding of the legal process.
—law professor Frank Macchiarola, discussing the O.J. Simpson case[2]

Starting around 1990, Americans began to repeatedly focus on lengthy, high-profile, often celebrity-centered criminal and civil trials and investigations. Many of these cases at times resembled something like national obsessions and were associated with extraordinary levels of mass media coverage. Although such "media trials" have occurred episodically at least since the 1920s, recent years have seen an enormous increase in their number. More important, the increased coverage of these legal stories is strongly correlated with a transformation in the way that nearly all legal and political news is presented. Legal news today is dominated by a presentation style that focuses on status, personality, score-keeping, and sex/violence titillation, rather than on legal rules, institutions, processes, and context. In short, the entertainment function of the media has transcended the more important educational function. In the wake of the terrorist attacks of September 11, 2001, the traditional mainstream media have, to a rather limited extent, returned to covering more serious and pressing issues. The cable news stations and Internet sources, however, have continued to devote substantial attention to these legal dramas. We call the years between 1991 and the present the era of *tabloid justice,* and we divide this era into distinct pre– and post–September 11 periods. In this introduction,

1

we delineate the major features of each period and provide a more detailed definition of *tabloid justice*.

Historically, the term *tabloid* has primarily been used to refer to a type of publication. The so-called Yellow Journalism, pulp magazines, and "muckraking" investigative reports of the early twentieth century can be considered examples. Since the 1980s, *tabloid* has taken on a different meaning, as the sensationalistic coverage of earlier publications has been adopted by more mainstream press organizations. In contemporary usage, the term refers most often to a style of coverage rather than a type of publication. The increasing tabloidization of the mainstream press is, broadly speaking, the focus of the present inquiry.

The first period of tabloid justice, lasting from 1991 until the terrorist attacks of September 11, 2001, witnessed an unprecedented explosion of media attention focused on the legal system. The rise of tabloid-style media coverage was driven by the confluence of several newly emerging forces. Among these were a sharp decline in the readership of newspapers and newsmagazines, the advent and expansion of cable television (with its scores of specialized channels), the emergence of the 24-hour news cycle, the increasing popularity of talk radio, and the phenomenal growth of the Internet after 1995. Other trends that encouraged the media shift to sensational and celebrity-centered legal coverage were the relative absence of a major foreign conflict and the presence of a generally healthy national economy. Finally, there occurred an event that, when combined with the preceding trends, created a "perfect storm" leading to the transformation of legal coverage. This, of course, was the murder trial of former star football player and popular celebrity O.J. Simpson. It is important to note, however, that the Simpson case did not create the media's shift to tabloid justice–style coverage of the legal system. The necessary conditions for that change were already well in place by the time that Nicole Brown Simpson and Ronald Goldman were murdered in 1994.

Arguably (beginning with the William Kennedy Smith trial in 1991, certainly reaching a fever pitch during the Simpson trials in 1995 and 1997, and continuing through the largely irresponsible coverage of the Bill Clinton–Monica Lewinsky episode) the public's apparently insatiable appetite for such events steadily rose through the 1990s, as did the media's devotion to their presentation. Perhaps most significantly, in this first period, the mainstream media continually covered legal and political stories in a "tabloid-ized" style.

Other notable cases of the first tabloid justice period involved such figures as Lorena Bobbitt, Lyle and Erik Menendez, Susan Smith, Marv Albert, Timothy McVeigh, Louise Woodward, the Los Angeles Police Department officers who beat Rodney King, Dr. Jack Kevorkian, Elian Gonzalez, Andrea Yates, and Michael Skakel.[3] Even legal cases that never actually made it to the trial stage of the judicial process, such as those involving the seventeen-year hunt for the Unabomber or the murder of six-year-old beauty queen JonBenet Ramsey, also became major, sustained media stories.[4] And the Clinton-Lewinsky matter, which did not even involve an expressly criminal charge in the sense that the preceding cases did, nevertheless seemed to push aside most other political and legal news for all of 1998. This scandal marked a sort of inevitable culmination to the decade's previous media cases in that it involved most of the elements that seem to be predictors of both media attention and public interest: politics, sex, law, crime, gender dynamics, and celebrity participants. As a final twist, once the Clinton-Lewinsky scandal evolved into the Clinton impeachment investigation and Senate trial, the mainstream press seemed ready to assure itself that it was, after all, only covering a profoundly important political development and not merely a tawdry saga of sexual misjudgment by the highest official in the land. Yet throughout 1998, the press covered this high-level legal battle in the very same manner that it had displayed in its coverage of the more expressly tabloid-like cases mentioned earlier.

The second period in the tabloid justice era began following the terrorist attacks of September 11 and continues into the present time. The moment of transformation is evidenced by a temporary (though sharp) decline in coverage of tabloid cases after September 11. In one important example, from June 1, 2001, through September 10, 2001, the three national nightly network news broadcasts aired sixty-three segments about Chandra Levy, the missing congressional intern, and twenty-one segments on Andrea Yates, who stood accused of killing her five children. Over that same time period there were eight segments mentioning Osama bin Laden, none of which identified Al-Qaida, the terrorist organization he headed. After the September 11 attacks, for the remainder of 2001, only one segment mentioned Andrea Yates and three mentioned Chandra Levy, but there were 292 segments mentioning bin Laden. Overall, media coverage in the second era of tabloid justice has been dominated by public debate over the war on terrorism, the US invasions of Afghanistan and Iraq, the Hurricane Katrina disaster, White House and CIA press leaks, the Arab-Israeli conflict, and immigration policy.

There are, therefore, important differences between the first and second periods of the tabloid justice era. Perhaps because of the dominance of public issues like the "war on terror" and all that that concept entails, sensational legal stories have not dominated mainstream news to the same degree that they did during the 1990s. The network nightly news programs and the nation's top newspapers and newsmagazines have devoted less space to high-profile legal proceedings. Gone for now are the days in which the ABC evening news repeatedly devoted a full ten minutes of its half-hour broadcast to the O.J. Simpson trial, or a five full minutes to the JonBenet Ramsey murder investigation. Still, within the mainstream media, though tabloid legal proceedings have taken on a lower profile, they remain a regular presence on all of the major news outlets. Thus, while tabloid justice cases are less likely to be the sustained and pervasive stories they were in the previous period, they have become a "normalized" subject for the news to cover. Among the notable cases of the second era of tabloid justice are Robert Blake, Kobe Bryant, Elizabeth Smart, Mary Kay Le Tourneau, Scott Peterson, Martha Stewart, Michael Jackson, and members of the Duke University lacrosse team. An interesting aspect of the second period of tabloid justice is that in none of the highest-profile cases did the presiding judges permit cameras in the court, a development that made these legal dramas less well suited for sustained television coverage.

Further, the second period has seen an entirely new subgenre of news coverage and talk shows emerge—programs that seem constantly to search for the next "trial of the century," or at least the trial of the year, or even the trial of the month. These new shows include *The Abrams Report* (on MSNBC), *On the Record* with Greta Van Susteren (on Fox), *Nancy Grace* (on CNN Headline News and Court TV), and the short-lived *Celebrity Justice* (on the E! channel). Additional cable news programs that regularly devote significant attention to trials and legal investigations include *Scarborough Country, Countdown with Keith Olberman, The Situation* with Tucker Carlson (later called *Tucker*), *Paula Zahn NOW, Larry King Live, O'Reilly Factor,* and *Hannity and Colmes.*

Finally, one of the most notable developments in the second tabloid justice period has been the phenomenal growth in the number of fictional legal dramas on television. Considering only prime-time network television, for instance, fourteen of the thirty top-rated television programs in 2005 were legal or crime dramas (see Table 3.10). In the spring of 2005, there were four distinct versions of the NBC program *Law & Order* and three different versions of CBS's *CSI: Crime Scene Investigation,* all playing weekly in prime time. And none of this even includes the large number of legal dramas on cable channels, such as *Monk* (on the USA channel) or *The Closer* (on TNT), two of cable television's highest-rated programs. Many of the fictionalized law dramas base their appeal on having a close resemblance to real life. The program *Law & Order* is often promoted with the tag line "ripped from the headlines." In another example, the 2005 legal drama *Close to Home* used actual footage of the Menendez brothers, the BTK Killer, and Scott Peterson in its ad campaign to sell the premise that no one can be sure what lurks behind their seemingly ordinary neighbor's locked doors. Thus, the blending of news and entertainment has continued to increase in prominence during the second period of tabloid justice.

As evidence of the centrality of high-profile legal stories in the lives of citizens, polls have demonstrated that more Americans were able to identify JonBenet Ramsey, a child generally unknown before her death at the end of 1996, than the vice president of the United States. Results from a similar survey revealed that roughly six times as many Americans knew the name of the judge who presided in the Simpson murder trial (Lance Ito) than could identify William Rehnquist, the late chief justice of the US Supreme Court (see Table 4.2). Comparable levels of public awareness exist for acquitted rape suspect William Kennedy Smith, Scott Peterson, and possible murder victim Natalee Holloway.[5] These names, and the alleged or actual illegal conduct associated with them, have become cultural reference points for many Americans. Public knowledge and awareness of these events far exceeds those of subjects that many commentators would deem to be much more important and worthy of national focus.[6]

In both tabloid justice periods, media organizations have been the enthusiastic transmitters of extensive and in-depth coverage of these events, most of which have little public importance. Although stories about criminal trials and legal investigations, and detailed accounts of the personal lives of trial participants, have historically been the stuff of the tabloid press, mainstream print, television, and Internet sources have now joined the act. For instance, *Time* and *Newsweek,* the two highest-circulation newsmagazines in the United States, covered most of the aforementioned cases in great detail. Even the nightly network news broadcasts on ABC, CBS, and NBC, which ostensibly have as their mission the reporting of the most important news in the nation, have given these stories considerable airtime.[7] A number of television network newsmagazines, such as ABC's *20/20* and NBC's *Dateline,* also pay frequent attention to trials and legal investigations around the country. Additionally, the explosion of cable television talk and news stations, such as CNN, MSNBC, CNBC, the Fox News Channel, and Court TV, has provided an outlet that has, perhaps, most fueled the coverage of trials and investigations. Even more "general" cable channels, such as Discovery, the Learning Channel, Arts & Entertainment, and the History Channel, now regularly broadcast shows that deal with crime, criminal justice, and the legal system. Perhaps most telling was E! Entertainment Television's unabashedly voyeuristic coverage of the 2005 Michael Jackson child molestation trial, when that channel actually presented actors reenacting each day's courtroom developments, via that day's official courtroom transcripts.

Further, the phenomenal growth of the Internet has resulted in countless websites that offer coverage and discussion of nearly every aspect of the legal system. At the end of 1998, for example, there remained about 100 websites dedicated to various O.J. Simpson matters, even though Simpson's civil trial ended in early 1997. These sites included a wide array of straightforward news, parodies, discussion groups, jokes, photographs, and games. Similarly, there were more than fifty websites that focused on the investigation of Jon-Benet Ramsey's death, as well as 27,000 individual JonBenet-related Web pages. In late 1998, a cursory search of the key words "Monica Lewinsky" on Yahoo!, a leading Web search engine, resulted in the listing of more than fifty dedicated websites, and an additional 94,000 individual references, including everything from fan clubs to pornographic satire. More recently, and as evidence of the tremendous growth of the Internet since the late 1990s, a 2006 Google search revealed more than 100 Scott Peterson–focused websites and over 26 million individual Web hits.[8]

Defining Tabloid Justice

Aside from the enormous increase in the amount of mass media coverage of the criminal justice process and the legal system more generally, it is the fundamental shift in the style of this coverage that is most interesting—and perhaps most alarming. In this book we argue that the United States has entered a sustained era of *tabloid justice,* in which the mass media, in both their traditional and emerging forms, focus predominantly on the sensationalistic, personal, and lurid details of unusual and high-profile trials and investigations. In short, a great deal of legal news has become a vehicle for entertainment, rather than for public education or for the reporting of breaking events with real public meaning. Throughout this book we employ the phrase "tabloid justice," often referring to tabloid justice cases or tabloid justice coverage. This phrase embodies three important elements.

First, as previously mentioned, the educational function of the press is undermined by its entertainment role.[9] The media focus on legal stories primarily as sources of entertainment, as opposed to opportunities for civic education. In covering the most titillating or personal aspects of a story, present-day coverage often trivializes more important structural and procedural issues. For example, during the period of January through October 1998, the *New York Times* ran at least eighteen stories that mentioned Monica Lewinsky's infamous blue dress, which was found to be stained with President Clinton's "genetic material." In contrast, the *Times* presented only eleven stories that referenced the details of the independent counsel statute under which former judge Kenneth Starr actually derived his power and authority to investigate the scandal. *Newsweek* magazine's coverage showed a similar disparity, with six stories mentioning the blue dress but no articles focusing explicitly on the details of Starr's statutory authority.[10] Similarly, during the 2005 Michael Jackson molestation trial, the *Los Angeles Times,* which ran approximately 317 stories on the case, printed only two pieces focusing on the crucial new California statute that allowed prosecutor Tom Sneddon to introduce evidence of past allegations against Jackson.[11] Much of the *Times* coverage offered almost daily trial updates, which consisted primarily of subjective descriptions of the personal behavior and appearance of the various witnesses and courtroom actors in the case.

The second component of the tabloid justice atmosphere is the frenzy of media activity that envelops a given legal proceeding. The more respected media outlets, as well as the many acknowledged tabloid sources, are deeply involved in the coverage. The story is discussed, dissected, and analyzed by all forms of media. This media frenzy can be illustrated by the veritable army of professional legal reporters and commentators who travel to the location of these trials and investigations. Perhaps the best evidence of a "media frenzy" surrounding high-profile legal cases is the heavy investment in resources and energy that news networks put into covering them. News outlets travel in droves from city to city and courthouse to courthouse, quickly setting down roots and then disappearing just as suddenly once the proceedings are over. During the 2005 Michael Jackson trial, NBC, CNN, Fox, CBS, and Court TV erected large camera towers outside the courthouse, even though the only footage available was that of Jackson briefly entering and exiting the building each day.[12] When basketball star Kobe Bryant faced rape charges during the summer of 2003, veritable media cities were constructed in Eagle, Colorado, to cover his first court appearances. Tents, mobile homes, and platforms were all utilized to cover every development as quickly as possible. CBS and NBC rented office space nearby to serve as their headquarters, and roughly 400 media personnel descended on Eagle for Bryant's first court appearance on August 6, in which the only words he uttered were, "No, sir."[13] The lengths the networks will go to in order to capture even the smallest, most insignificant piece of footage is a testament to the obsessive competition between news outlets.

The third characteristic of the tabloid justice environment is the presence of an eagerly attentive public that witnesses these legal events and to some degree uses them as a means by which to understand and assess the legal system and the judicial process. Public interest, as measured through increased television ratings, publication sales figures, and polling data, spurs continued media focus on these legal proceedings. Without question, the era of tabloid justice has resulted in an enormous increase in the public's basic "awareness" of law. However, the tabloid nature of contemporary coverage may actually result in higher levels of public misinformation about the workings of the system and a corresponding drop in the public's faith in American justice.[14] Further, the polarizing manner in which the media now cover trials, often in terms of blacks versus whites or men versus women or good versus evil, has potentially aggravated some of the most troubling social divisions in US society.

When all three dynamics converge—a legal proceeding presented largely as entertainment, an obsessive media establishment, and an attentive public—the environment of tabloid justice emerges. Within this context, the idealized priorities of the legal system, such as justice and fairness, become secondary to the press's interest in attracting large audiences by presenting titillating images and compelling, personality-centered plots. This is the atmosphere of the tabloid justice era that we examine in this book.

Mass Media Effects on Public Attitudes

Central to our argument that the transition to tabloid-style, entertainment-oriented coverage of legal stories has important consequences for society is the question of whether mass media presentations actually do have important effects on public attitudes and behavior. Most observers fully accept that both factual and fictional media stories help shape the thinking and behavior of the mass public.[15] Scholars also offer propositions about the mass media's ability to influence public opinion and behavior. Many of these academic theories proceed from a perspective of *social constructionism,* or a belief that our reality is composed entirely of the information we gather from social interactions, rather than from any objective, empirical, or socially transcendent knowledge or insight.[16] Intense exposure to media images alters our views of reality. However, exactly how this takes place may be the central conundrum in academic media studies. Many theories of mass media effects assert that heavy exposure to media-generated images may eventually convince consumers that the symbolic reality presented in the media is an accurate reflection of objective social conditions.[17] But to see the world as it is portrayed in the mass media would be to clearly embrace numerous incorrect views. Research shows that many shared misconceptions about occupational pursuits, ethnic groups, racial minorities, the elderly, social and gender roles, and crime and crime rates are at least partly cultivated through exposure to the mass media.[18] It is important to note, however, that such misconceptions may vary widely depending on both the audience and the particular medium conveying the message.

Assuming that the mass media do affect public attitudes and beliefs,[19] it is important to make distinctions among the various forms of media, as many of these differences hinder the construction of a general theory of media effects. For instance, television is a powerful medium for transmitting a sense of realism and emotional appeal.[20] Television's greatest impact is probably derived from its ability to reach millions of viewers simultaneously with the same powerful visual images. Because of the immediate and noncontextual nature of such images, however, research has shown that more than 75 percent of average viewers cannot identify either the specific major facts or the general theses of many television news stories.[21] In contrast, newspapers and magazines do a better job of providing readers with facts than either audio (radio) or visual (television) forms of media.[22] The advent of cable and satellite television and radio, and the presence of video images on the Internet, have complicated matters further by making it difficult to determine what media have what impact.

Despite the various conceptual problems outlined above, three basic models have tended to dominate the academic debate about media effects. Each of these models offers an account of the mass media's effects on the public's notions of social reality.[23]

The first of these approaches has been termed the *hypodermic needle* model.[24] As the term suggests, this perspective assumes that the mass media have a direct and significant effect on the way people perceive social conditions. The public imbibes media coverage like a drug, and the effects are powerful and long lasting.[25] Citizens are thought to be autonomous consumers of media-generated news, to which they turn for answers and from which they adopt beliefs about society and "acceptable" opinions about its various aspects.[26]

A second perspective, standing in contrast to the hypodermic needle model, has been called the *limited effects* model.[27] As with the hypodermic needle idea, this theory posits that a person turns to the media for information and "answers." But this perspective also holds that individuals do far more than simply take in and adopt the "reality messages" conveyed by the media. Rather, individuals assess the accuracy of that information in light of what they already "know" from other sources such as family, school, associations, church, and so on. Thus, although this model is also based on a notion of social constructionism, there is recognition that citizens have preexisting, relatively independent (and often, longstanding) perceptions that condition or blunt the power of new information, such as that emanating from mass media sources. What is more, people from similar backgrounds and experiences are thought to see the world and react to media images in a way that is more alike than different. In effect, they share both the same "symbolic reality" and "experienced reality."[28]

A third perspective has been called *subtle* or *minimal effects*.[29] This model posits that the impact of the mass media is neither total (hypodermic needle) nor significantly mitigated by other factors (limited effects) but somewhere in between. From this perspective, the media's influence can be seen especially in the areas of "agenda setting," "priming," and "framing." Each of these deserves a brief description here.

"Agenda setting" acknowledges that the media choose, for a variety of reasons, to cover a limited and rather predictable range of topics, persons, and organizations in their newscasts and stories.[30] Simply stated, the mainstream press, in effect, tells us "what to think about."[31] For example, when coverage of crime and legal issues so saturates local newscasts that other important topics are pushed to the side, the public will spend much more time thinking about legal proceedings than issues such as health care, US relations with China, border security, poverty, or education. Thus, the agenda-setting function of the media helps determine what citizens perceive as the most important issues of the day. Recent research has examined the relationship between saturation coverage and agenda setting in the Clinton/Lewinsky scandal[32] as well as agenda setting in the post–September 11 period.[33] This research continues to confirm the power of the media to determine the public "agenda," even as the media environment has become more complex.

Closely related to agenda setting, "priming" refers to the idea that when citizens think about people in the news, they will consider individuals in light of the issues and topics covered in the news. Most priming-effect research examines how people assess presidents.[34] In continuing with our example of crime, if crime is covered extensively in the news, then the priming effect would dictate that citizens evaluate the president in terms of how they feel the "crime problem" is being addressed.

The third component in this model, "framing," embodies the notion that the content and format of news coverage may result in citizens adopting particular political attitudes. In the area of crime news, Shanto Iyengar has differentiated between "thematic" coverage, which employs statistics, context, and discussion of general trends, and "episodic" coverage, which employs anecdotal, individualized, and largely superficial legal stories.[35] Iyengar and others have found that the framing of crime news specifically—and legal news more generally—either in episodic or thematic terms, has led citizens to draw somewhat distorted conclusions about the appropriate course of action with regard to crime policy.[36] This finding is particularly important for our analysis, as all of the tabloid justice cases are examples of episodic coverage. In fact, one major feature of our argument that most legal news has become little more than entertainment is the fact that so much of this coverage is now episodic.

Importantly, all of the foregoing theories hold, albeit with significant variations, that mass media images do in fact influence the public's general and specific perceptions of society.[37] Thus, if we accept the premise that media exposure affects how people view the world, then we must explore the question of how the media choose what to cover, as well as the style and approach of that coverage.

What Events Are Deemed Newsworthy?

On the most basic level, we might posit that the news simply exists, it simply happens, in some objective or natural sense, and that the mass media just cover as much of it as possible given their resources. But is the news already "out there," with reporters and news organizations simply going out and "getting the story"? Media scholars would find this assertion far too simplistic. In contrast, perhaps the news is quite simply what the press says it is. In other words, reporters, editors, and producers literally decide what news is.[38] This idea accords with the previously discussed scholars who have ascribed an important agenda-setting function to the media.[39] A substantial body of scholarly research has concluded that the media do enjoy the power of agenda setting, at least to some degree.[40] This makes the focus of the following paragraphs particularly important, as we consider the manner in which the media determine both who and what are worthy of their attention.

In considering what the media cover, it is important to think about the theoretical role the press should play in a democratic society. In the idealized conception of a democratic press, newsworthiness would be determined by the "objective" importance of a story. For the national news media, this might require a primary focus on major questions of public policy, foreign policy, and serious national developments. The media would serve as public educators on issues and stories that are significant to large numbers of citizens, and they would provide sufficient background and context for citizens to make sense of social and political developments of national importance. Additionally, the media would serve as "watchdogs," holding government and other powerful institutions accountable for the exercise of their power. Finally, an idealized conception of the mass media would allow for the free exchange of myriad perspectives and ideas.[41]

When we contrast these idealized notions with the actual workings of the mass media, it becomes apparent that these democratic imperatives are strikingly absent in much of the present news environment. Obviously, the extent to which the media ever conformed to these ideals is debatable. Nevertheless, in the contemporary world of journalism, newsworthiness appears to be determined by the interaction of two factors: competition with other news media, and the internal goals of media organizations, which are often linked to the existence and perceived desires of a specific target audience or market. Portrayals of social reality reflect the subjective judgments of news organizations in their representations of human nature, social relations, and the norms and structure of society.[42] Not surprisingly, in deciding what "news" is, the most self-serving activities and goals of the mass media themselves become nearly as determinative as the actual real-world events that they cover.

Since the 1960s, mainstream news organizations have consistently offered predictable coverage of certain actors and events. In his classic study *Deciding What's News,* Herbert Gans identified three subjects that dominate mainstream news coverage: "known people," "unknown people in unusual circumstances," and a "prescribed set of activities."[43] Known people include all public figures and celebrities, whether they occupy positions of influence or not. Unknown people include protesters, victims (mostly of crime or natural disasters), lawbreakers, voters, and those engaged in highly unusual behaviors. The third category, activities, involves the kinds of "events" on which the media focus—government conflicts, disagreements, decisions, proposals, and personnel changes, as well as protests, crimes, scandals, natural and other disasters, technological innovation, and national ceremonies.[44]

Gans's work remains the classic starting point for mainstream American media analysis. Published in 1979, Gans's study is based on media coverage during the late 1960s and early 1970s. Thus, one might assume his to be an outdated list of characteristics of newsworthiness. Gans's assessment, however, established a framework that still applies today.

Writing more recently, media scholar Richard Davis identified eight factors that journalists and media outlets use to determine newsworthiness: major events, timeliness, drama, conflict, unusual elements, unpredictable elements, famous names, and visual appeal.[45] In comparing the lists of Gans and Davis, one can see a great deal of overlap. Importantly, though, Davis asserts that in the 1990s a new media culture took shape and that standards of newsworthiness evolved accordingly. Similarly, Davis and Diana Owen argue that "entertainment value" is now a central feature in the determination of newsworthiness, as news outlets find themselves in an increasingly more competitive struggle for viewers, readers, and listeners.[46] This competition contributes to the mainstream media's willingness to cover tabloid stories with much more vigor and detail than they had previously. In this book, we actually go beyond Davis and Owen, arguing that "entertainment value," with only a few exceptions, now often trumps most other traditional assessments of newsworthiness.

Since the 1960s, the style, format, and especially the intensity of commercial competition have altered the relative balance and mix of so-called hard news and entertainment that the press presents. For instance, although there has never been a time in US history when a murder case involving a celebrity as well-known as O.J. Simpson would not have been a major media story, past coverage could not have compared to that of today in terms of its sheer volume, immediacy, and pervasiveness.[47] In the 1950s or 1960s, it would have been hard to imagine a scene, such as that which occurred the morning after the murders of Nicole Brown Simpson and Ronald Goldman, in which local network-affiliated news crews jostled one another to broadcast live, graphic video images from the blood-splattered front yard of the infamous Bundy Avenue condominium in California.[48] What has changed since the Gans study is simply the intensity and pervasive nature of today's media coverage, as well as the increased American obsession with the culture of celebrity.[49] In search of any unique angle, journalists and media organizations today are more likely to flock to a sensational story and cover almost every imaginable detail, including the most trivial. For example, cases such as those involving "the Runaway Bride," Scott Peterson, and Natalee Holloway would previously have been afforded far less or no national coverage, and would have been significantly more locally or regionally focused.

Beyond the general standards of newsworthiness identified earlier, the specific selection of stories is further strongly conditioned by the internal goals of the various media outlets themselves. National network news broadcasts, local news broadcasts, and cable news outlets all have different goals and imperatives, and all of them are ultimately beholden to a corporate bottom line. News events are packaged in ways that particular media outlets believe will be of interest to their specific targeted market or audience. Most obviously, Fox News has developed and cultivated a presentation of the news that is designed to appeal to ideologically more conservative viewers. Also, individual programs such as MSNBC's *The Abrams Report* and *Scarborough Country,* Fox News's *On the Record,* and CNN's *Larry King Live* cater to an audience of "scandal junkies," which apparently never tires of repetitive coverage of the latest trial or legal controversy. Clearly, these programs determine newsworthiness based on the niche of consumers they wish to attract. Finally, while not normally known as a news outlet at all, throughout most of 2005 E! Entertainment Television offered daily, extended coverage of the Michael Jackson molestation trial. Obviously, this channel was motivated by the idea that this programming would appeal to Jackson's fan base and to those who normally follow celebrity gossip.

Purpose and Goals

The effects of media coverage and the decisions that news organizations make about what to cover provide a critical foundation in helping to carry out our general aim of explicating and explaining the dynamics of the era of tabloid justice. Throughout this book, two central questions guide our analysis: How have high-profile legal proceedings been covered in the media culture that has developed since 1990? And what impact has this coverage had on the public's knowledge of and attitudes about the legal system? The answers to these questions are necessarily complex, and they depend on particular personalities, stories, cases, and contexts. However, when viewed as a group, the tabloid justice cases have achieved an importance far beyond their existence simply as a new form of entertainment. Because of the public attention that they have received, as well as the public reaction to many of the outcomes of the criminal trials in particular, these stories have potentially broad and important ramifications for the functioning of the legal system in the United States.

In some instances, these tabloid justice stories and the fictional tales presented in the many legal television dramas have highlighted legitimately troubling and controversial aspects of the justice system. At other times, they demonstrate that the legal system is functioning somewhat as intended. But most important, we believe that these stories, and particularly the media's portrayal of them, have played a substantial role not only in exposing a new and irresponsible era of journalistic standards but also in undermining public faith in the justice system in contemporary US society in general. Of course, one could argue that the public would be entirely justified in being skeptical of (or even angry with) the legal system based on many of these proceedings. However, we believe that weaknesses in the system are exploited and sensationalized by tabloid-style coverage. The media emphasis on highly anomalous cases, presented as though they illustrate the everyday workings of the system, presents a highly inaccurate picture of law and justice in the United States.

Beyond explicating the two central questions of this book, an important goal of this work is to answer some of the questions posed by a number of scholars, journalists, and legal professionals such as Susanna Barber, Ronald Goldfarb, Alan Dershowitz, and Anna Quindlen, who have grappled with assessing the benefits of extensive televised coverage of the legal system.[50] Most such writers focus on the need to protect the rights of defendants, and they suggest that increasing the presence of cameras in courtrooms may have the effect of improving the behavior of legal professionals and juries by making certain that they are held publicly accountable for their actions.[51] Often the policy discussion over media coverage of the legal system turns to the debate over whether cameras should be allowed in the courtroom. Using a compelling argument about the need for open examination of judicial proceedings in a democratic political system, most commentators weighing in on the topic support a national law that would allow cameras in all US courtrooms.[52] In 1999 the American Bar Association took a public stand advocating cameras in all federal court proceedings, including those of the US Supreme Court.[53] In contrast, some legal scholars, and most importantly, the US Judicial Conference (the policymaking arm of the federal court system), are adamantly opposed to cameras in courtrooms, arguing that they will distort, cheapen, and in general subvert the sanctity of the legal process.[54]

While the debate over cameras in the courtroom is not something we address specifically in this text, we are able to assess whether more legal coverage and actual footage of the judicial process is a positive development. In considering possible wider public benefits from increased coverage of the justice system, three possible benefits could emerge: (1) civic education about the inner workings of the legal system; (2) greater public assurance of due process, as the media's coverage forces the courts to behave in the fairest possible manner; and (3) increased public confidence in the legal system. While some commentators are skeptical about these potential benefits (especially Barber, Dershowitz, and Quindlen), they tend to assert that any coverage is at least better than no coverage. What is missing in these assessments, as Barber notes, is any broad empirical evidence about the positive effects of trial coverage on public attitudes.[55]

Although the increased tabloid-style media coverage since 1990 has provided an opportunity for the public to learn about the courts and the justice system, we will contend that the tabloid-like nature of even mainstream press behavior has seriously undermined the possibility of broader public benefits. We will argue that this style of media coverage has resulted in lower levels of public confidence while at the same time doing little to increase factual, substantive knowledge about the judicial process. In sum, observers of the legal system may make accurate predictions about the benefits of television coverage in modifying the behavior of lawyers and judges, but for the most part they have underestimated the negative effects of the contemporary media style of coverage on wider public attitudes.

Throughout this book we seek to demonstrate that the media's coverage of various high-profile legal cases has had a negative effect on the way in which Americans perceive the justice system, largely in terms of public confidence toward the everyday workings of that system. We believe that the new style of coverage has led us to a troubling intersection of mass media agenda setting and entertainment programming. The agenda that the media have adopted is now heavily skewed toward a series of legal proceedings that often have little objective importance to the lives of a vast majority of Americans. Further, as coverage of these cases is the dominant mode of conveying the workings of the legal system, the result is that these highly anomalous cases come to be viewed as examples of the typical functioning of the system. Here, we freely admit a basic bias that we harbor. We believe that regular, detailed, factual coverage of public policy, government, international relations, and the legal system is simply more important than stories about individual criminal trials, let alone stories about the personality quirks of defense lawyers, the hairstyles of attorneys, analyses of the president's phone sex preferences, extensive video footage of JonBenet Ramsey's beauty contests, or national press conferences held by lawyers representing college lacrosse players accused of rape.

Tabloid justice–style media coverage, then, has distorted the public's perception of the legal system. For instance, during the coverage of most of the cases we will discuss, the media tend to give the impression that the majority of defendants actually have trials and that they are either found guilty or acquitted after a jury has considered all of the relevant evidence.[56] In contrast, relatively little attention has been devoted to the more prevalent problems of plea bargaining, court bureaucracy, courtroom subcultures, race and gender discrimination, and access to effective legal representation. Thus, the agenda that is set by the media in legal coverage regularly ignores broader, substantive, and longstanding public issues. In sum, the style of media coverage that emerges from these legal proceedings represents a missed opportunity to inform the public about the real workings of the system.

Organization of the Book

In presenting our argument, we divide this book into three parts. Part 1 presents an account of the rise of the media's current obsession with covering high-profile legal cases and of the mainstream media's adoption of a tabloid style of coverage with regard to crime and the judicial process. In Chapter 1 we argue that the period since 1990 has been a unique one, both in terms of the sheer amount of media coverage that legal stories have received and the public's increased interest in legal cases generally. We introduce some of the period's major media cases and offer brief summaries of those involving William Kennedy Smith, Rodney King, the Menendez brothers, Louise Woodward, O.J. Simpson, JonBenet Ramsey, Martha Stewart, Scott Peterson, Terri Schiavo, and Michael Jackson. We assert that these cases have been, arguably, the most dominant ones, both in the levels of media attention they received and in the public interest paid to them. These are also the cases that best illustrate the mass media's behavior in the era of tabloid justice.

In addition, Chapter 1 considers the characteristics that seem to elevate a given legal proceeding to a very high level of national interest. Clearly, an urgent sense of human intrigue is important, but this can take many forms. Violence, especially murder, has always been a predictable draw. In fact, murder accompanied by sex has traditionally been seen as the most provocative of all crime and law stories. After all, popular movie genres such as film noir and courtroom films were built on little else. But other factors, such as race, gender, celebrity, physical beauty, and social class, also appear to be good predictors of the public's (and the media's) interest in particular legal proceedings. In sum, Chapter 1 addresses the media's constant search for the next "trial of the century."

In Chapter 2 we recognize that the mainstream media's attention to such stories began at least as early as the celebrated Lindbergh baby case of the 1930s and has continued through the ensuing decades. However, since about 1990 we have definitely witnessed an exponential increase in both the amount and immediacy of such coverage. We offer empirical evidence of the overall increase in the media's coverage of US courts and criminal justice issues. Also in Chapter 2, we revisit the previous discussion of "newsworthiness" by drawing a distinction between the ways in which the traditional mainstream media and the so-called tabloid or entertainment media have historically defined a good story. We suggest that there have been important changes in the news business since 1990, and that the emergence of television newsmagazines, the growth of cable news-talk, and the tremendously rapid expansion of the Internet have been accompanied by an extraordinary increase in media coverage of law and the judicial process. Perhaps even more significantly, since 1990 there has been a blurring of the lines that have traditionally divided the mainstream and tabloid presses.

In Chapter 3 we discuss the rise of the so-called new media, considering in greater detail phenomena such as cable television news, talk radio programs, the Internet, and fictionalized legal dramas. These media have contributed greatly to the increasing entertainment flavor of political and legal news. In addition, they have blurred the line between the reporting of, and the consuming of, political and legal news. In effect, cable news-talk shows and Internet chat groups and blogs allow the public an opportunity to participate in, as well as to consume, the news. It is also worth noting that it is not at all unusual nowadays for cable news shows, in particular, to devote considerable time to journalists discussing how other journalists are covering particular stories. Media coverage of a story, in some sense, becomes the story itself. This new self-referential mode of coverage comprises yet another aspect of the new era of media behavior.

Part 2 of the book assesses the impact of the new tabloid justice media culture. We emphasize here that our primary concern is that the era of tabloid justice represents an important missed opportunity in which the press has squandered the chance to truly educate the public about the legal system and has instead left citizens with little more than a detailed memory of the personalities involved in these cases. The chapters in Part 2 present the findings from our 1999 and 2005 national polls, each involving more than 1,000 respondents. The 1999 poll focused on six of the most prominent cases in the first period, and the 2005 poll focused on four of the most prominent cases of the second period of the tabloid justice era. (For a full description of our survey methods and a copy of the survey instruments, see Appendix B.)

Utilizing our survey results in Chapter 4, we examine public attitudes toward specific actors and features of the legal system and the current media environment, including the jury system, defense attorneys, prosecutors, judges, and the police. Importantly, we demonstrate that although citizens may now possess more familiarity with some of the basic structural and procedural components of the judicial process, the era's tabloid-style legal coverage has led to unduly negative assessments of the system. Finally, we conclude that the tabloid-like coverage of the law works to undermine the legitimacy and effectiveness of that system. Indeed, a significant number of citizens have begun to worry about their own possible treatment in the legal process as a result of what they have learned in the tabloid justice era.

Chapter 5 considers whether the new media culture has had different impacts on the public attitudes of citizens of different race, education level, income level, gender, age, and political party affiliation. Because divisions among these groups have been central features in many of the cases in our analysis, our goal here is to examine how the media coverage of these issues affects the public's views about them. For instance, did the Simpson and Rodney King cases change or inflame racial attitudes? Did the outcomes of the cases involving William Kennedy Smith, Martha Stewart, and Terri Schiavo have different effects on the views of men and women? We attempt to answer these questions by examining how blacks and whites, women and men, the rich and poor, and Republicans, Democrats, and Independents view the justice system and these specific cases. Ultimately, we focus on race, gender, and class issues, and conclude that tabloid justice coverage has simply reinforced different social groups' existing attitudes, biases, and assumptions about the system, rather than teaching them about the real everyday workings of law in the United States.

Finally, in Part 3, Chapter 6 summarizes our central arguments and findings. We then draw some broad conclusions about what this new era has meant, not only for the future of the legal system but also for the mass media's relationship with that system. We conclude by speculating about what the future holds in terms of this relationship.

Notes

1. William O'Rourke, "TV Has Left People More Informed and More Ignorant at the Same Time," *Chicago Sun-Times,* April 10, 2005, p. 35.
2. Frank Macchiarola, "Finding the Truth in an American Criminal Trial: Some Observations," *Cardozo Journal of International Comparative Law* 5 (Spring 1997): 97.

3. For a discussion of these and other notable trials in US history, see Alan M. Dershowitz, *America on Trial* (New York: Warner, 2004); Edward W. Knappman, ed., *Great American Trials* (New York: Barnes and Noble, 2004); and Gilbert Geis and Leigh B. Bienen, *Crimes of the Century* (Boston: Northeastern University Press, 1998).

4. For an analysis of the Unabomber case, see Robert Graysmith, *Unabomber: A Desire to Kill* (Washington, DC: Regnery, 1997); Alston Chase, *A Mind for Murder: The Education of the Unabomber and the Origins of Modern Terrorism,* (New York: W. W. Norton, 2004). We discuss the Ramsey case further in Chapter 1.

5. Polling information about the public's knowledge of well-known criminal cases was provided by the Pew Research Center. Questions were asked between 1991 and the end of 2005.

6. Although we would ideally hope for expanded coverage of important domestic and international political and social issues, those who have studied the media's portrayal of the electoral process have found that "issue coverage" has been rare and episodic. See Louis Sandy Maisel and Darrell M. West, eds., *Running on Empty?: Political Discourse in Congressional Elections* (Lanham, MD: Rowman and Littlefield, 2004); Thomas Patterson, *The Mass Media Election: How Americans Choose Their President,* 3d ed. (Westport, CT: Praeger, 1988); and Eric R.A.N. Smith, *The Unchanging American Voter* (Berkeley: University of California Press, 1989).

7. For a discussion of how the networks have historically determined what stories to cover, see Herbert Gans, *Deciding What's News: A Study of CBS Evening News, NBC Nightly News, Newsweek, and Time* (New York: Vintage, 1979), chap. 3.

8. Our Web searches for O.J. Simpson, JonBenet Ramsey, and Monica Lewinsky were conducted in November 1998; the Scott Peterson search was conducted in June 2006.

9. Historically, one of the primary arguments made in favor of increased electronic media access to the courts has been the supposed educational function of such coverage. For an effective summary of these arguments, see Susanna Barber, *News Cameras in the Courtroom: A Free Press–Fair Trial Debate* (Norwood, NJ: Ablex, 1987), 54, 94–95.

10. These figures are based on a Lexis-Nexis search conducted on October 6, 1998.

11. Based on an analysis of *Los Angeles Times* articles over the course of the trial, February 25, 2005, through June 14, 2005.

12. Paul Farhi, "A Trying Time for the Media at Jackson Trial," *Washington Post,* February 23, 2005, p. C01.

13. Kevin Brass, "Trial and Error?" *American Journalism Review* 26 (2004): 52–57.

14. Another major argument in favor of increased media coverage of the courts has been that press attention fosters an increased confidence in the system. See, for instance, Barber, *News Cameras in the Courtroom,* 54 ff. As we shall see, this has not been a result of the tabloid era of media coverage of criminal trials.

15. Doris Graber, *Mass Media and American Politics,* 7th ed. (Washington, DC: Congressional Quarterly Press, 2005), 182.

16. Ray Surette, *Media, Crime, and Criminal Justice: Images, Realities and Policies,* 3d ed. (Belmont, CA: Wadsworth, 2006), 31–32.

17. There are considerable methodological problems involved in attempting to measure the effects of media exposure on people's attitudes and perceptions. For good discussions of these difficulties, at least as applied to the study of politics, see Graber, *Mass Media and American Politics,* 205–207; Benjamin I. Page, Robert Y. Shapiro, and

Glenn R. Dempsey, "What Moves Public Opinion," *American Political Science Review* 81 (March 1987): 23–43; and Thomas R. Dye, L. Harmon Zeigler, and S. Robert Lichter, *American Politics in the Media Age,* 4th ed. (Fort Worth, TX: Harcourt Brace, 1992), 106.

18. Albert Bandura, "Social Cognitive Theory of Mass Communication," in Jennings Bryant and Dolf Zimmerman, eds., *Media Effects: Advances in Theory and Research* (Hillsdale, NJ: Lawrence Erlbaum, 1994), 76.

19. Assessing such effects is made yet more difficult when one considers the wealth of research that indicates Americans possess very little real knowledge about politics or the judicial process. See, for instance, John P. Robinson and Dennis K. Davis, "Television News and the Informed Public: An Information-Processing Approach," *Journal of Communication* 40 (Summer 1990): 106–109; L. Harmon Zeigler and William Haltom, "More Bad News About the News," *Public Opinion* (May/June 1989): 50–52; Michael Robinson, "Public Affairs Television and the Growth of Malaise," *American Political Science Review* 70 (1976): 425–430; Dye, Zeigler, and Lichter, *American Politics in the Media Age,* 104–108; and Richard Davis and Diana Owen, *New Media and American Politics* (New York: Oxford University Press, 1998), 165–166.

20. Graber, *Mass Media and American Politics,* 183.

21. See Jacob Jacoby and Wayne D. Hoyer, "Viewer Miscomprehension of Televised Communications: Selected Findings," *Journal of Marketing* 46 (Fall 1982): 12–26.

22. Robinson and Davis, "Television News and the Informed Public," 106–119; and Graber, *Mass Media and American Politics,* 189–190.

23. This discussion is adapted, in part, from Maxwell McCombs, "News Influence on Our Pictures of the World," in Bryant and Zimmerman, *Media Effects,* 1–16; and John R. Zaller, *The Nature and Origins of Mass Opinion* (New York: Cambridge University Press, 1992).

24. Roy Edward Lotz, *Crime and the American Press* (Westport, CT: Praeger, 1991), 40–41.

25. Cecil Greek, "Crime and the Media Course Syllabus and Lectures," http://www.fsu.edu/~crimdo/grade&m.html#lectures (June 12, 1998).

26. Ibid.; Lotz, *Crime and the American Press,* 37–48; and Surette, *Media, Crime, and Criminal Justice,* 33–34.

27. The foundation for this approach is laid out in Shanto Iyengar and Donald Kinder, *News That Matters* (Chicago: University of Chicago Press, 1987), 112–120.

28. Surette, *Media, Crime, and Criminal Justice,* 33–34.

29. The "minimal effects" conceptualization is presented in Iyengar and Kinder, *News That Matters,* 19–33 and 116–120.

30. For good overviews of agenda-setting research and theoretical approaches, see Stefaan Walgrave and Peter Van Aelst, "The Contingency of the Mass Media's Political Agenda Setting Power: Toward a Preliminary Theory," *Journal of Communication* 56 (2006): 88–109; and Everett M. Rogers, William B. Hart, and James W. Dearing, "A Paradigmatic History of Agenda-Setting Research," in Shanto Iyengar and Richard Reeves, eds., *Do the Media Govern?* (Thousand Oaks, CA: Sage, 1997), 225–236.

31. Iyengar and Kinder, *News That Matters,* 2–4.

32. See Bruce A. Williams and Michael X. Delli Carpini, "Monica and Bill All the Time and Everywhere," *American Behavioral Scientist* 47 (2004): 1208–1230; and Julie Yioutas and Ivana Segvic, "Revisiting the Clinton/Lewinsky Scandal: The Convergence of Agenda Setting and Framing," *Journalism and Mass Communication Quarterly* 80 (2003): 567–582.

33. See Matthew D. Matsaganis, "Agenda Setting in a Culture of Fear: The Lasting Effects of September 11 on American Politics and Journalism," *American Behavioral Scientist* 49 (2005): 379–392; and Stefanie Craft and Wayne Wanta, "US Public Concerns in the Aftermath of 9/11: A Test of Second Level Agenda-Setting," *International Journal of Public Opinion Research* 16 (2005): 456–463.

34. For an assessment of how the priming effect influenced voter assessments of President George H. W. Bush, see Joanne Miller and Jon A. Krosnick, "Anatomy of News Media Priming," in Iyengar and Reeves, *Do the Media Govern?* 258–275.

35. Shanto Iyengar, *Is Anyone Responsible? How Television Frames Political Issues* (Chicago: University of Chicago Press, 1991), 13–16, 26–31, and 39–45. This is generally considered the authoritative work on "framing."

36. For sources on how the media frames crime issues, see Carol Stabile, *White Victims, Black Villains: Gender, Race, and Crime News in US Culture* (New York: Routledge, 2006); Robert Entman, "Modern Racism and Images of Blacks in Local Television News," in Iyengar and Reeves, *Do the Media Govern?* 283–286; and Franklin D. Gilliam Jr., Shanto Iyengar, Adam Simon, and Oliver Wright, "Crime in Black and White: The Violent, Scary World of Local News," in Iyengar and Reeves, *Do the Media Govern?* 287–295.

37. Among the other theories of media effects are the "bandwagon effect," which posits that people simply want to be on the winning side. For a discussion of this approach, see Albert H. Cantril, *The Opinion Connection* (Washington, DC: Congressional Quarterly Press, 1991). Another approach examines the "third-person effect" (in which people perceive broad media effects on everyone but themselves). A description of this idea is contained in W. Phillips Davison, "The Third-Person Effect in Communication," *Public Opinion Quarterly* 47 (Spring 1983): 1–15. However, we believe that we have presented the most widely discussed theories here.

38. Kathleen Hall Jamieson and Karlyn Kohrs Campbell, *Interplay of Influence: News, Advertising, Politics, and the Mass Media,* 4th ed. (Belmont, CA: Wadsworth, 1998), 19; and Greek, "Crime and the Media."

39. See, generally, Donald Shaw and Maxwell McCombs, *The Emergence of American Political Issues* (St. Paul, MN: West, 1977), chap. 1; and Iyengar and Kinder, *News That Matters.*

40. For a wide range of works that examine the role of agenda setting, see David L. Protess and Maxwell E. McCombs, eds., *Agenda Setting* (Hillsdale, NJ: Lawrence Erlbaum, 1991); and Bryant and Zimmerman, *Media Effects.*

41. The political functions and idealized role of the mass media are summarized in Dye, Zeigler, and Lichter, *American Politics in the Media Age,* 6–19; Graber, *Mass Media and American Politics,* 92–102; and Kenneth Dautrich and Thomas H. Hartley, *How the News Media Fail American Voters: Causes, Consequences, and Remedies* (New York: Columbia University Press, 1999), 102–104.

42. Bandura, "Social Cognitive Theory of Mass Communication," 75.

43. Gans, *Deciding What's News,* 8–18.

44. Ibid., 16–18.

45. Richard Davis, *The Press and American Politics,* 2d ed. (Upper Saddle River, NJ: Prentice-Hall, 1996), 129.

46. Davis and Owen, *New Media and American Politics,* chap. 1.

47. Gans, *Deciding What's News,* 8–18.

48. Jeffrey Toobin, *The Run of His Life: The People v. O.J. Simpson* (New York: Touchstone, 1997), 68. Toobin's book effectively recounts the media's often offensive behavior both before and during the Simpson criminal trial.

49. For good general accounts of the modern media environment, see Larry J. Sabato, *Feeding Frenzy* (New York: Free Press, 1993); and Thomas Patterson, *Out of Order* (New York: Knopf, 1993). For recent accounts of the increasing prevalence of a celebrity culture, see Su Holmes and Sean Redmond, eds., *Framing Celebrity: New Directions in Celebrity Culture* (New York: Routledge, 2006); and P. Da Marshall, *Celebrity Culture Reader* (New York: Routledge, 2006).

50. For works that have assessed broader public impact of media coverage of the criminal justice system, see Barber, *News Cameras in the Courtroom,* 95–98; Ronald L. Goldfarb, *TV or Not TV: Television, Justice, and the Courts* (New York: New York University Press, 1998), 160–166; Alan M. Dershowitz, *Reasonable Doubts: The Criminal Justice System and the O.J. Simpson Case* (New York: Simon and Schuster, 1997), 129–134, 146–148, and 203–204; Anna Quindlen, "Public and Private: Order in the Court," *New York Times,* July 25, 1994, p. A19; Eileen Libby, "Court TV: Are We Being Fed a Steady Diet of Tabloid Television? No: Tacky or Not, It Helps Bring the Law to Life," *ABA Journal* (May 1994): 47; Ruth Ann Strickland and Richter H. Moore Jr., "Cameras in State Courts: A Historical Perspective," *Judicature* 78 (November/December 1994): 128–135; and Alan M. Dershowitz, "Court TV: Are We Being Fed a Steady Diet? Yes: Its Commercialism Hides Its Potential," *ABA Journal* (May 1994): 46.

51. For a work in this area that focuses on the fair treatment of defendants, see Marjorie Cohn and David Dow, *Cameras in the Courtroom: Television and the Pursuit of Justice* (Lanham, MD: Rowman and Littlefield, 2002).

52. For a sampling of arguments favoring cameras in the courtroom, see "Let the People See the Court," *Chicago Tribune,* May 3, 2006, p. 26; Ellia Thompson, "Courtroom Cameras: Issues Move In and Out of Focus," *The Quill* (September 2004): 7–9; Anna Quindlen, "Lights, Camera, Justice for All," *Newsweek,* January 21, 2002, p. 64; and Philip S. Anderson, "Time to Open the Electronic Eye," *ABA Journal* (June 1999): 85.

53. "Cameras in the Court Gain Support, but Lose in Wyoming Trial," *News Media and the Law* (Spring 1999): 301.

54. See Karen Aho, "TV and the Supreme Court," *Columbia Journalism Review* 42 (September/October 2003): 63; and "Judicial Conference Nixes Cameras in the Courtrooms," *Defense Counsel Journal* 67 (October 2000): 429–435.

55. Barber, *News Cameras in the Courtroom,* 122–123.

56. See Greek, "Crime and the Media."

PART ONE

From Journalism to Sensationalism

ONE

Looking for This Week's "Trial of the Century"

I think the media coverage [of the Scott Peterson trial] is a reaction to what viewers want. I don't think we are creating the interest. We are reacting to the interest.

—Marlene Dann, senior vice president of daytime programming at Court TV[1]

It's a response to public demand in the way that a kindergarten class requests ice cream for lunch instead of basic food groups. Yes, it's what we want . . . but by serving us junk food news, the news industry is creating an illusion of delivering information.

—Matthew Felling, media director for the Center for Media and Public Affairs, discussing coverage of the Michael Jackson case[2]

In March 1997, the prime-time announcement of O.J. Simpson's civil trial verdict came at the same moment that President Bill Clinton was delivering his State of the Union message to Congress and the American people. The mainstream television networks and many cable news channels had exhaustively covered the Simpson drama for more than two years. Would they break into the president's speech to report the jury's verdict? Although CBS and NBC managed to restrain themselves in deference to the state of the nation, ABC printed the verdict along the bottom third of the screen. CNN and MSNBC chose O.J. Simpson over the president's speech.[3] In the end, nine national cable networks, including the sports channels ESPN and ESPN2, offered live coverage of the verdict's announcement. ABC immediately altered its schedule for that night in order to broadcast a two-hour special on the verdict.[4]

A similarly revealing set of events occurred in August 2006, when a suspect in the JonBenet Ramsey murder case was arrested. Although the child beauty queen's murder had taken place nearly ten years earlier, when the media leaked information that John Mark Karr, an American citizen living in Thailand, had confessed to the crime, a news frenzy promptly erupted. The

25

New York Daily News ran an enormous front-page headline exclaiming "Solved," *Larry King Live* was among numerous of the cable news programs that devoted virtually an entire week of shows to the emerging story, and even the evening network newscasts ran the story at or near the top of their programs for several days.[5] The story temporarily displaced the Iraq War, the Israel-Hezbollah war, the aftermath of Hurricane Katrina, and the upcoming midterm congressional elections as the leading news story.

The arrest of John Mark Karr dominated the news for about two weeks. Karr was extradited from Thailand to Boulder, Colorado, for questioning and DNA tests. And although the tenor of media coverage seemed overwhelmingly to accept as a given that Karr had committed the crime, a number of television commentators voiced doubts that Karr had even been in Boulder at the time of the murder. Then, Boulder district attorney Mary Lacy abruptly announced that DNA tests had conclusively proven that Karr could not have been the killer and that circumstantial evidence also indicated that his confession contained numerous holes and inconsistencies. She announced that he was no longer a suspect in the case. Just as quickly as the case had burst back on the national scene, the story faded from the headlines.

As the public's decade-long interest in the JonBenet Ramsey case suggests, it seems as though the latest US pastime is watching trials and legal investigations on television, especially those involving celebrities, murder, sex, racism, child abuse, or police misconduct. Media coverage of such stories is not confined to any particular journalistic format or media outlet. Crime, criminal justice, legal news, and the judicial process now occupy the attention of national network news organizations, prestigious daily newspapers, tabloid weeklies, talk radio, cable television, prime-time dramatic shows, and network morning news shows.[6] The actual participants in these stories also behave in ways that would have seemed extraordinary just a couple of decades ago. For instance, it is now increasingly common for defense attorneys to hold daily news conferences, for well-known defendants to hire public relations specialists to represent them to the press and the public, and for police departments to maintain in-house staffs charged with "image management" and press relations.[7]

In this chapter, we begin by discussing the practices and principles that seem to govern current media coverage of criminal justice and the legal system. We then provide brief summaries of the ten tabloid stories that have received the highest levels of print and television media attention since 1990. For now, we focus primarily on the actual facts of each case and less on the media coverage itself. In our later chapters we will more fully explore the media culture that enveloped—and in some cases continues to envelop—these cases. However, we believe that an overview of the specific facts surrounding the cases is important, because it reveals what the media have deemed to be newsworthy in the recent past, and it allows us to consider whether these cases warranted the high levels of media attention that they received.

Media Coverage of the American Legal System

Historically, US trial courts have been the source of significant media coverage, especially fictionalized stories in film, print, and television. This attention, however, has always been episodic, superficial, and locally focused. For instance, although local television news has always devoted significant attention to crime stories, both the public and the mass media have typically ignored everyday trials and legal developments, and indeed, local politics generally.[8] For the press to report on a given criminal investigation or trial, there needs to be some factor present that is unusual or out of the ordinary, a prerequisite of newsworthiness identified by both Richard Davis and Herbert Gans, among others.[9] For instance, although hundreds of children in the United States are murdered or abducted each year, the JonBenet Ramsey and Elizabeth Smart investigations drew massive attention partly because they involved a six-year-old beauty queen from an extremely wealthy and prominent family, and an upper-middle-class white child from an upscale, seemingly inviolable Salt Lake City neighborhood. In the era of tabloid justice, however, it is not always clear why a particular case grabs public attention and holds the media spotlight. For instance, Laci Peterson was just one of almost 1,500 pregnant women murdered during the tabloid justice era, and Terri Schiavo's case involved painful end-of-life issues that literally thousands of Americans have to confront each year.[10]

In their 1998 book *Crimes of the Century,* Gilbert Geis and Leigh B. Bienen assert that many of the high-profile trials in the twentieth century have had certain common features, such as the geographic setting of the events, the nature of the offenders and victims, and the details of the offense itself. Crimes that rise to the level of media obsession have historically tended to occur in the three major media markets of New York (the Charles Lindbergh baby trial, Alger Hiss, Son of Sam, Marv Albert, Amadou Dialo, Martha Stewart), Chicago (the Haymarket martyrs, Eugene V. Debs, prominent mobsters in the 1920s, Leopold and Loeb), and Los Angeles (the Black Dahlia case, Charles Manson, the Rodney King case, O.J. Simpson, Robert Blake). However, increasing news homogenization, engendered by the growth of the Internet and 24-hour cable news, seems to have altered this pattern, as recent tabloid-type cases have originated variously in Miami, Boston, Boulder, Houston, South Carolina, Montana, and Alabama.

Criminal cases that receive high volumes of media coverage normally involve provocative or titillating offenses, particularly murder (especially involving multiple homicides, sexual brutality, or the killing of children), although cases such as that of Alger Hiss (peacetime espionage), Bill Clinton (perjury and obstruction of justice), and Enron executives (corporate fraud) do not fit neatly into such categories. As far as the identities of the suspects and victims are concerned, the stakes are often raised when the alleged perpetrator is a prominent celebrity or public figure (1920s film star Fatty Arbuckle, William

Kennedy Smith, O.J. Simpson, Marv Albert, Robert Blake, Kobe Bryant, Martha Stewart, or Michael Jackson), or when the victim is a particularly unusual, intriguing, or sympathetic personality (Leopold and Loeb's alleged murder of a teenage girl, Elizabeth Short in the Black Dahlia mystery, Louise Woodward's killing of an infant in her care, or the death of child beauty queen JonBenet Ramsey). Sometimes the offender may not have previously been prominent or well-known but comes to represent or illustrate the public's dissatisfaction with particular aspects of the legal system, as in the case of Rodney King and the Los Angeles Police Department (LAPD), and the LAPD again in the Simpson criminal trial. Similarly, one might interpret the Terri Schiavo story as emblematic of important and emerging legal issues involving questions of guardianship and medical care for those in a state of incapacitation.

In any event, we would argue that it is the nature of the media coverage, rather than the circumstances of the particular case, that characterizes the tabloid justice era. The media's emphasis on the personal, extraordinary, and sensational fosters a number of public misconceptions about the legal system and may lead citizens away from an actual understanding of important issues such as plea bargaining, courtroom subcultures, attorney and judge interaction, prosecutorial mismanagement, and court bureaucracies.[11] Rather than explore these structural and procedural complexities, however, the media tend to focus on the personal, competitive, and dramatic aspects of legal trials and investigations, continually blurring the line between news and entertainment. Plea bargains do not involve the conflict, tension, or visual images that apparently make a story interesting enough to merit significant press attention or to become the focus of television legal dramas. For instance, in a crime reminiscent of the charges against Scott Peterson, Mark Hacking stood accused of murdering his pregnant wife Lori in 2004. The case, also involving an attractive young couple and years of marital deception, grabbed headlines. The story quickly faded from view, however, when Hacking confessed to the murder and accepted a plea agreement.

On balance, the mass media offer a misleading—or at least incomplete—picture of the daily workings of American law. This state of affairs is worsened when we recognize that the types of cases that do receive extended coverage are what criminal justice scholar Ray Surette has called "media trials" and what we term *tabloid justice cases*. Surette effectively characterizes such trials as "court news as miniseries."[12] High-profile media trials become the foci of intense public exposure and audience interest, and ultimately they become part of the lore of popular culture. Many older Americans can recall the names and faces of the participants from previous "trials of the century," such as those involving Sacco and Vanzetti, Julius and Ethel Rosenberg, Sam Sheppard, Charles Manson, and Patty Hearst.[13]

Tabloid justice–type cases, with their potential for drama and pathos, can be seen as the quintessential vehicles for the melding of the previously distinct news and entertainment aspects of the mass media. Since 1990, patterns of development in the news business, analyzed in Chapters 2 and 3, have resulted in far more intense competition for ratings. As the mainstream flagship institutions of the press have sought to maintain their dominance in the marketplace, they have increasingly tended to present hard news within a structure formerly reserved for entertainment and features. In Ray Surette's words, "fast-paced, dramatic, superficial presentations and simplistic explanations [have become] the norm."[14] William Haltom, in a study of how the press covers judicial actions, refers to this as *dramatized normality*. He hypothesizes that the "news media dramatize abnormal cases until, over time, they have normalized dramatic cases."[15]

The increasing visibility of trials and investigations, when combined with the entertainment-based style in which they are presented, has given such events a symbolic importance far out of proportion with their actual number and real significance. This phenomenon has been further highlighted by the prevalence of realistic yet fictional television crime dramas and films that often replicate the story lines of actual recent cases. Because of their prominence, tabloid justice cases have become central to the social construction of "crime and justice reality." That is, they contribute to the formation of public opinion with regard to important legal and political questions.[16] Competing visions of law, justice, and social reality are debated before the citizenry, with greater ramifications than when a relatively small percentage of the public tunes into a presidential speech or congressional debate.

Further, the fact that television is the medium that exposes most Americans to such events holds enormous importance for their effect on the public's legal and political attitudes. TV possesses its own set of imperatives, which encourage the repetitive showing of striking images and the presentation of news in short and dramatic segments, with little or no background or context. Neither of these television-specific characteristics leads to the presentation of legal proceedings in a manner that is conducive to civic education. More important, though, the three characteristics of *serialization, personification,* and *commodification* appear to dominate how tabloid-style cases are covered by television (whether via the news, "reality" shows, or fictional legal dramas).[17]

Criminal trials in particular lend themselves to *serialization,* or the presentation of news as a series of short dramatic events involving a relatively small number of recurring characters with specific roles over an extended period of time. Each day's events in a trial or investigation can be presented in a short, simplified, and catchy news segment. As in the trials of O.J. Simpson and the Rodney King officers, the media received assistance from defense attorneys who, in order to influence that day's news coverage, held frequent news conferences. On days in which little activity took place in the courtroom, coverage often consisted solely of information disseminated by the lawyers in these cases. During the 2006 Duke University rape case involving that school's lacrosse team, accused team members, as well as the prosecutor, repeatedly held news conferences and gave television interviews to national legal news programs like *The Abrams Report* and *On the Record*. The three defendants in the case even appeared in interviews on CBS's celebrated television news program *60 Minutes*.

Personification refers to the presentation of events through a focus on the emotional, personal, human aspects of a story, often at the expense of context, background, structure, and analysis. This is the manner in which television presents virtually all news, but we believe that it is particularly problematic when this style of coverage is used to present images of the judicial process. After all, law is (ideally) intended to ensure objectivity, procedure, stability, predictability, and equality; the emotional states, biases, and personal backgrounds of the participants are not, in theory, supposed to influence the outcome of investigations and trials. And yet, national newsmagazines reported on such things as the changing hairstyle of O.J. Simpson prosecutor Marcia Clark.[18] In the JonBenet Ramsey investigation, the media reported on the cost of JonBenet's beauty pageant outfits.[19] In covering the investigation of President Clinton, ABC National News radio reported that Monica Lewinsky had two blueberry pancakes for breakfast the day independent counsel Ken Starr and members of the House of Representatives questioned her.[20] In a final example, the media relentlessly focused for nearly a week on the fact that on one day during the course of his trial, a disheveled Michael Jackson arrived at the courthouse wearing pajama bottoms. Presenting the legal system through the lens of individual portraits of idiosyncratic participants undermines the educational function of the media.

The commercial imperatives of the television medium also contribute to the *commodification* of trials, as these events are packaged, promoted, and sold much like any other show.[21] Coverage in cases such as those of Louise Woodward, O.J. Simpson, Martha Stewart, Robert Blake, and especially Michael Jackson serve as evidence. All of the networks and major cable news stations presented the Clinton-Lewinsky saga much like a dramatic miniseries, often including a musical theme, logo, tagline, and graphic introductory material. This aspect of television coverage may confuse the public's perception of the legal cases that do, in fact, have important legal or political ramifications. Examples and analysis about the legal system drawn from the cases involving Rodney King, Enron, and Terry Schiavo, as well as the Clinton impeachment and Senate trial, are instructive. These and a few other tabloid justice stories might have proven to be useful vehicles for illuminating broader problems in the legal system and American society. But if arguably important legal developments such as these are presented in a manner that is identical to the even more socially trivial cases of JonBenet Ramsey, William Kennedy Smith, Marv Albert, O.J. Simpson, Robert Blake, and Natalee Holloway, it is not surprising that the public may interpret all such stories simply as undifferentiated human entertainment pieces, to be viewed or ignored as one pleases.

Thus, the decision by consumers whether to follow coverage of the Clinton impeachment and Senate trial simply becomes another in a chaotic panorama of entertainment choices, which are not perceived by the viewer as being in any way related to citizenship or the well-being of the nation. Even though such events offer valuable opportunities for public education about the legal and political systems, the mode of media coverage, combined with the public's apparently uncritical reception of that coverage, undermines this.

The Top Tabloid Justice Cases Since 1990

The rules and norms of media coverage, especially regarding the legal system, have evolved greatly since the 1990s. As a result of the tremendous increase in the mainstream media's coverage of the justice system, a significant portion of the American public has formed, or perhaps *re*formed, its opinions about the judicial system and the role of law in society. It is problematic that anomalous yet highly visible cases have been relied upon by citizens in assessing US law. In recent years, we have unquestionably witnessed a sea change in the amount and style of legal news in the mass media, as well as a corresponding increase in the public's appetite for legally oriented "infotainment." In fact, as previously stated, the merging of the formerly distinct media categories of news and entertainment, especially as applied to coverage of the legal system, is mainly what characterizes the era of tabloid justice. Trials and investigations, most of which do not involve any overarching issues of public policy, international affairs, or, at least overtly, broad social questions, have overshadowed interest in events with obvious and profound international and domestic consequences, such as Medicare and Social Security reform, the spread of nuclear weapons, campaign finance reform, the 2000 presidential election controversy, and at times even the "war on terror."

The numerous trials and legal proceedings that have captivated the public have been "tabloid" in nature in that they have involved personal and intimate details about often bizarre and shocking events that have, frankly, little public importance. For instance, there was the 1994 case of Susan Smith, the South Carolina mother who drowned her own children. Before the bodies were recovered, Smith maintained her innocence, suggesting on national television that a black man had abducted her two sons at gunpoint. A national outpouring of support came her way, but when the true circumstances of the crime were revealed, she was ultimately convicted of murder and sentenced to life in prison. A second example involves the ongoing media fascination with Amber Frey, the woman who was dating Scott Peterson and a key witness in his murder trial in 2004. Even after the trial concluded with Peterson's conviction and death sentence, her life was the subject of regular "updates" on the legal news shows. When she married in mid-2006, over two years after the conclusion of a trial in which she was simply a witness, her wedding was covered on virtually every legal news program as well as on the whole range of morning network news shows.

Or consider the now infamous case of *Bobbitt v. Bobbitt*. In 1993, Lorena Bobbitt was charged with malicious wounding and assault for the "dismembering" of her husband, John Bobbitt. She claimed that she attacked him only after he raped her and should not be held legally responsible for her actions due to a condition of temporary insanity. The defense presented a detailed account of the years of domestic violence and sexual abuse Lorena Bobbitt allegedly suffered. On January 21, 1994, a jury found her not guilty by reason of insanity. She was committed to a mental health facility for observation and treatment for a period of forty-five days and was then released from custody. This case gained widespread notoriety both for its graphic nature (Lorena Bobbitt had severed her husband's penis) and for the example it provided for discussion of the increasingly widespread use of the so-called battered wife syndrome as a defense in domestic violence cases. But coverage of the story went from at least semi-serious to farcical when John Wayne Bobbitt, after undergoing "reattachment surgery," began a new career as an actor in pornographic films. Any further discussion of the battered wife defense was superseded by human interest tales about Mr. Bobbitt's new vocation.

Then there was the investigation of the first set of child sexual abuse charges leveled against pop music star Michael Jackson. A nightly news staple for weeks, the case faded from the public eye when the alleged victim accepted a large cash payment from Jackson (Jackson's second molestation case is discussed at length later in this chapter). A list of high-profile tabloid cases, also from the first period of tabloid justice, might include the rape trial of heavyweight boxer Mike Tyson, the sexual assault case brought against nationally known sportscaster Marv Albert, the investigation into the murder of fashion designer Gianni Versace, the murder trial of the killer of Ennis Cosby (son of entertainer Bill Cosby), the investigation of the assault on Olympic figure skater Nancy Kerrigan (allegedly orchestrated by rival skater Tonya Harding), and the conclusion to the seventeen-year search for the so-called Unabomber (a man accused of sending a series of mail bombs to scientists and business leaders).

In the second tabloid justice period (2001–the present), these legal dramas continued with the conviction of actress Wynona Ryder for shoplifting, the murder trial of Andrea Yates (a Texas woman accused of drowning her five children), the indictment of basketball star Kobe Bryant for rape/sexual assault (the charges were dropped days before the trial was scheduled to begin), the so-called Runaway Bride case (the story of Jennifer Wilbanks, who mysteriously disappeared days before her scheduled wedding, claiming to have been kidnapped), the indictment of Duke University lacrosse players on rape charges, and the murder trial and acquittal of actor Robert Blake. These and other cases have been sources of intense national media coverage.

For the purposes of our investigation, we chose to focus most heavily on the ten cases (we count the criminal and civil trials of O.J. Simpson as one "case") that received the highest volume of media attention in the era of tabloid justice. This determination was based on an analysis of newspaper, network television, and Internet coverage. Six of these cases occurred in the era's first period (1991–2001) and four took place in the second period (2002–2006). Table 1.1 shows the primary individual or individuals involved in the proceeding and the year that each case effectively ended. Five of the cases involve murder allegations (Menendez, Simpson, Ramsey, Woodward, and Peterson), one focuses on a rape charge (Kennedy Smith), one involves police brutality (King), one deals with child sexual abuse (Jackson), one is a "right to die" case (Schiavo), and one involves financial misconduct (Martha Stewart). In referring to these cases as episodes or instances of tabloid justice, we do not mean to trivialize any of the disturbing realities of the facts alleged in each of them.

Because we refer to them extensively throughout this book, the cases identified in Table 1.1 warrant a somewhat more detailed introduction. As we move through the cases, a number of questions must be considered. Are there issues of national importance at stake in each of them? Do they help to educate the public about the legal system? Is the case representative of a normal judicial proceeding? Is it necessary for the public to be informed about many of the details about the participants in the cases? The answers to these questions will vary depending upon the case. However, for the majority of them we would answer no to each of the foregoing questions.

Table 1.1 Top Tabloid Justice Cases, 1991–2005

Trial or Investigation	Year the Main Proceeding Concluded
First period	
Trial of William Kennedy Smith	1991
Trial of the officers in the Rodney King beating	1992
Trial of Lyle and Erik Menendez	1993
Trial of O.J. Simpson (criminal)	1995
Trial of Louise Woodward	1997
Trial of O.J. Simpson (civil)	1997
Investigation into the murder of JonBenet Ramsey	1998[a]
Second period	
Trial of Martha Stewart	2004
Trial of Scott Peterson	2004
Trial of Michael Jackson	2005
Terri Schiavo case	2005

Note: a. The main activity and media exposure of the JonBenet Ramsey case occurred in 1997 and 1998, though because the case was unsolved it has appeared episodically in the news until this day.

William Kennedy Smith: A Kennedy Family
Member Goes on Trial for Rape

It is reasonable to conclude that the trial of William Kennedy Smith, along with the Rodney King case discussed next, ushered in the tabloid justice era of the early 1990s.[22] In many ways, Smith's was the quintessential tabloid justice case. It contained almost all of the typical necessary elements: a wealthy defendant from a famous family, allegations of a violent crime with strong sexual overtones, and a trial certain to involve famous witnesses. Although it was essentially a rape case with little potential impact on public policy or legal reform, it generated unprecedented attention throughout both the mainstream and tabloid media.

The origins of the case involved something of a "he said, she said" scenario, as each side had trouble corroborating its version of the relevant events. Sometime after midnight on a Friday evening, Patricia Bowman, a twenty-nine-year-old Florida woman, met Smith, his cousin Patrick Kennedy, and his uncle, US senator Edward Kennedy, at a Palm Beach nightclub. Bowman agreed to drive Smith back to the Kennedy estate, where she eventually accepted Smith's invitation to stay for drinks and tour the extravagant compound. She claimed that as the evening came to an end, she headed for a set of stairs leading to the swimming pool area. Bowman alleged that Smith essentially tackled and raped her on the lawn near the pool. She then called a friend to take her home, recounted the rape, and telephoned the police soon after. William Kennedy Smith countered that the two merely had consensual sex on the beach.

Prosecutors charged Smith with second-degree sexual battery and first-degree sexual assault. The trial, however, was repeatedly postponed in the wake of extraordinary levels of publicity. Throughout 1991, the media treated the public to virtually daily updates about the case. Because Smith was a member of the famous Kennedy family, albeit previously a very low-profile one, his trial drew an enormous number of reporters to south Florida, including journalists ranging from the *National Enquirer* to the *New York Times*. Many news organizations attempted to portray the trial as a referendum on everything from cameras in the courtroom to the then-emerging issue of date rape to the influence of wealth and celebrity on equal justice to the general state of gender relations. The fact that Senator Edward Kennedy of Massachusetts was slated to testify (former first lady Jacqueline Kennedy Onassis was also rumored to be traveling to Florida for the trial) further sparked media and public interest. The media created what some termed a circus-like atmosphere, made worse when news outlets reported that three other women were prepared to testify that Smith sexually assaulted them in the previous year. The defense then made the first of many claims that the level of pretrial publicity had hopelessly tainted the jury pool. Eventually, a six-person jury was seated, and the long-awaited trial began on December 2, 1991.

Smith's attorney, the well-known defense lawyer Roy E. Black, asserted that Bowman had lied about the encounter because of her fear of becoming pregnant, her anger at Smith when he had called her by the wrong name, and his lack of interest in developing a more serious relationship.[23] Smith's attorneys attacked the woman's credibility, while the prosecution sought to taint the defendant's story by raising the other alleged rapes. Public and media interest intensified. The then-new Court TV offered gavel-to-gavel coverage, CNN devoted large blocks of time to the case, and all three major television networks assigned reporters around the clock.[24] The local NBC affiliate offered daily commentary from famed defense attorney F. Lee Bailey, and most outlets offered insights from a wide variety of legal luminaries, feminist activists, and academic experts on rape and sexual harassment. Local entrepreneurs offered T-shirts featuring caricatures of the Kennedys in a frying pan, as well as ice cream flavors named after each of the major trial participants (the "Teddy" flavor was spiked with Chivas Regal scotch).[25] The William Kennedy Smith matter became what was probably the trial most widely covered by television up to that point in history.

Eventually, Smith was acquitted on all counts. Following a twelve-day trial, the jury deliberated for a total of one hour. Most commentators expressed little surprise at the verdict, noting the largely circumstantial and uncorroborated evidence against Smith. Some observers, however, openly feared that the acquittal would "send the wrong message to the country," symbolizing that women who accused acquaintances of rape exposed their personal lives to detailed scrutiny by the mass media, and risked destroying their reputations.[26] But most experts on rape issues, such as Susan Estrich, Susan Brownmiller, and Vivian Berger, considered this a case in which the evidence to convict was not presented. According to Brownmiller, the author of a book on the history of rape, the case had been weak all along.[27]

Rodney King: Race, Police Conduct, and Justice in Los Angeles

Although the central incident precipitating the Rodney King trials occurred prior to the alleged crime in the Kennedy Smith case, the trial and ensuing trauma occurred several months later.[28] In retrospect, this event may have signaled the beginning of the tabloid justice decade of the 1990s. On March 3, 1991, a late-breaking story interrupted the popular *KTLA News at Ten* broadcast in Los Angeles. Anchorman Hal Fishman introduced what he described as a videotape by amateur cameraman George Holliday, a resident of the nearby suburban San Fernando Valley. Shot the previous evening around midnight, the eighty-one–second tape showed what appeared to be several officers of the LAPD savagely beating a black motorist, later identified as Rodney King, next to his vehicle. The officers could be seen delivering repeated baton blows and kicks as King rolled on the ground, attempting to shield his head with his hands.

In the ensuing days, weeks, and months, these images would be seared into the minds of the nation's—and the world's—television viewers, as edited versions of the videotape were repeatedly broadcast in both real time and slow motion.[29] Legal historian Alfred Knight has called the video the "most widely viewed and evaluated piece of evidence in the history of criminal justice." Knight further notes that the tape made people "certain that the cops were guilty because they had seen the crime itself."[30] Outraged groups in Los Angeles called for the dismissal of the officers, as well as the resignation of Los Angeles police chief Daryl F. Gates. In time, four of the officers, who eventually became the defendants in a criminal trial brought by the city, were removed from duty without pay. The city council appointed a blue ribbon panel to investigate the incident and report to the police commission. Headed by prominent attorney and later secretary of state Warren Christopher, the Christopher Commission eventually concluded that the LAPD was guilty of tolerating racism and rogue cops and called for the resignation of Chief Gates. As tensions mounted and political rhetoric reached a fever pitch, concerns were raised that the pool of potential jurors would be tainted. Still, many were surprised when a state appellate court judge, fearing a biased jury, ordered the trial moved to a new jurisdiction, the conservative white community of Simi Valley in nearby Ventura County.

A lengthy criminal trial followed in which the four officers stood accused of a number of charges including use of excessive force and failing to follow police procedure. The prosecutors argued that the officers violated codes of police conduct by using excessive, racially motivated force. They played tapes that included racial epithets and attempted to demonstrate that racism motivated the police brutality. The defense strategy attempted to persuade the jury that King had been a combative, dangerous suspect who did not comply with the officers' repeated commands. The defense offered into evidence the entire videotape, rather than the roughly nineteen-second edit that had been widely broadcast on television, which showed a more belligerent, uncooperative King. The defense also emphasized that prior to the incident, King, while highly intoxicated, had led the police on an eight-mile high-speed chase through crowded city streets.

After hearing twenty-nine days of testimony and deliberating for one week, the all-white jury acquitted all four officers on all but one count, on which the jury deadlocked. Within hours of the verdict, angry demonstrators burned buildings, looted stores, and assaulted passersby; civic leaders called for calm and restraint. Mayor Tom Bradley announced a curfew and ordered citizens "off the streets," and California governor Pete Wilson dispatched the National Guard. In the worst urban riots since the Civil War, fifty-four people lay dead, 2,000 were wounded, and property damage in Los Angeles exceeded tens of millions of dollars.

Months after the riots, in what seemed to be an insufficient afterthought, federal prosecutors brought a second suit against the officers, charging that they violated the federal civil rights of Rodney King. This time, the trial was held in Los Angeles District Court, and a racially mixed jury found two of the officers guilty. As the verdicts were announced, the city deployed 3,200 police officers—about ten times the normal number. Additionally, the county sheriff's office dispatched 1,400 officers, and the National Guard deployed over 600 guardsmen at local armories.[31] Ultimately, the verdicts resulted in no significant public disorder. Lou Cannon, the author of the definitive recounting of the King trials and riots, wrote that it was as if all of the people of Los Angeles had breathed a sigh of relief.[32] Several months later, Rodney King himself sued the city for police brutality and reached a civil settlement that awarded him more than $1 million.

For a number of reasons it is difficult to consider the Rodney King trials as examples of tabloid justice. The incident, ensuing lawsuits, eventual replacement of Daryl Gates with an African American chief of police, and the riots of March 1992 certainly raised issues of race relations and police brutality. The beating, acquittals by the Simi Valley jury, and differing ways in which the riots were perceived have sometimes supported the notion that the United States remains a deeply racist nation.[33] However, we contend that the media coverage of these events helped to fuel this drama. The repeated airing of the King videotape, well beyond any reasonable attempt to inform citizens about the story, was clearly intended to sensationalize and bring viewers into the story. Noted media scholar Doris Graber has even concluded that "overly extensive" coverage of the King beating "contributed to the frustrations that exploded in the Los Angeles riots."[34] As *Los Angeles Times* columnist Howard Rosenberg pointed out in the aftermath of the rioting, numerous local stations showed footage of the beating immediately after the verdict, which had the effect of inflaming the mounting anger over the jury's decision. Further, the morning after the verdict, with rioting still under way, NBC's *Today Show* aired footage of the beating four times in a forty-five–minute period.[35] The media emphasis on sensational images clearly embraced the principle of entertainment over measured reporting.

The Menendez Brothers: Abuse and Revenge

On August 20, 1989, entertainment executive Jose Menendez and his wife, Kitty, were found slain in their Beverly Hills mansion.[36] The first reports of the crime in the *Los Angeles Times* described a mob-style execution that was likely connected to one of Jose Menendez's many business dealings. Throughout the investigation, the Beverly Hills Police Department refused to divulge any details to the press. Nevertheless, the media reports for several months after the killings continued to speculate about the possibility of vengeful business partners in the entertainment industry. Those following the story, which in the first months of the investigation received little press attention, were shocked when the couple's two sons, Lyle and Erik, were charged with the slayings. A short time after their arrest, the brothers admitted killing their parents. They confessed to shooting their father numerous times in the head as he lay sleeping on a couch in the family den. They also confessed to wounding their mother in the initial shooting, at which time Lyle had gone to the trunk of his car, reloaded his shotgun, and returned to the house, where he fatally shot her.

Preceding the trial there were numerous delays, as attorneys for both sides wrangled over evidentiary issues and an extensive series of motions, some of which raised concerns about the prejudicial nature of the now-extensive media frenzy that had developed around the case. The coverage and footage from the trial were broadcast nationally, as Court TV was permitted to carry the proceedings live. When the trial finally did get under way, more than three years after the arrests, prosecutors contended that the brothers had killed their parents in order to acquire the family's fortune, estimated at more than $14 million. The brothers' defense attorneys countered that the young men had essentially struck back at Jose and Kitty Menendez for a lifetime of physical, sexual, and emotional abuse.

From the outset, the trial centered not on the brothers' guilt, which had been admitted, but rather on the defense's argument that Erik and Lyle should not be held fully responsible for their deeds. The brothers' trials were held at the same time, and both juries initially deadlocked, leading to the declaration of mistrials for both defendants. In a second set of trials, in which Court TV was banned from showing live coverage, both brothers were convicted of first-degree murder and sentenced to life in prison, where they both continue to reside.

The final conviction and sentencing of the Menendez brothers did not occur until April 18, 1996, more than six and a half years after the crime. This was the longest of any of the tabloid justice sagas that we investigated for this book. The attention that the crime and ensuing trials received can undoubtedly be attributed to the Beverly Hills location, the US community perhaps most associated with glamour and wealth. Dominick Dunne, the well-known *Vanity Fair* correspondent who attended the opening days of the first trial, summed up the case this way: "Two pampered and handsome young men, an execution-style killing and the brothers' lavish spending habits in the weeks after the killings."[37] As he waited for opening arguments, Dunne further commented, "I think we're going to be shocked by what we're about to hear. . . . I love covering trials."[38] In addition to Dunne, more than sixty TV and radio reporters were there for opening day to cover one of the most anticipated trials in Los Angeles history. Hector Tobar, a *Los Angeles Times* reporter, compared the scene of the courtroom on opening day to a made-for-television drama. The attention paid to the Menendez case can be considered, up until that point, to have been the clearest presentation of "crime for entertainment."[39] The case simply contained no overriding or broader public issues, and yet, several years later, most Americans are able to recall numerous details from this story.

O.J. Simpson: Media Circus of the Century

The basic facts surrounding O.J. Simpson's criminal trial are familiar to most Americans. Over a period of nearly three years, the media inundated the public with detailed and repetitive coverage of almost every aspect of this story. As evidence of the country's broad level of attention, fully 80 percent of the public either watched or listened to the live announcement of the verdict.[40] This case, which has repeatedly been referred to as the "trial of the century," a moniker that had previously been applied to many other cases,[41] centered on a brutal, although not uncommon crime.

On the night of June 12, 1994, Nicole Brown Simpson, the ex-wife of football legend O.J. Simpson, and Ronald Goldman, a waiter and aspiring actor, were found murdered in the wealthy Southern California community of Brentwood. The murders took place outside Nicole Brown Simpson's condominium, where her two children slept upstairs. She died from a knife slash to her throat; Goldman died from sixty-four separate stab wounds.[42] The story broke modestly, with a small front-page article in the *Los Angeles Times* reporting the death of "football great O.J. Simpson's former wife and a 26-year-old man."[43] From these early reports, though, the story catapulted to heights of media coverage that surely could not have been predicted, and which were only exceeded by the coverage of the Clinton-Lewinsky scandal and impeachment trial.

Four days after the murders, the Los Angeles Police Department ordered O.J. Simpson to turn himself in, informing him that he would be arrested and charged with both murders; Simpson agreed to turn himself in by 11 AM on Friday, June 17, but the deadline for Simpson to surrender passed with his whereabouts unknown. Simpson apparently fled. In a public announcement, Simpson's lead attorney at the time, Robert Shapiro, urged Simpson to turn himself over to the police. Robert Kardashian, a friend of Simpson's, read a letter written by Simpson, which sounded to many people like a suicide note.[44]

The following hours produced a media spectacle. O.J. Simpson, accompanied by his longtime friend Al Cowlings, was spotted traveling on a Los Angeles freeway. Simpson and Cowlings led police on what the *Los Angeles Times* called "the most spectacular pursuit in Los Angeles police history."[45] All of the major television networks provided live coverage of the chase; NBC even interrupted coverage of the National Basketball Association finals. Ultimately, Simpson drove back to his home and surrendered to police. Although the drama of the Bronco chase had come to an end, the legal odyssey, which would end 474 days later with a jury's decision to find O.J. Simpson not guilty of the slayings, was only just beginning.

Simpson assembled what the media labeled a legal "dream team," which included Johnnie Cochran, a prominent Los Angeles lawyer; F. Lee Bailey, who had made his name, in part, by winning the release of Sam Sheppard in the 1960s[46]; and Alan Dershowitz, a Harvard law professor who won the release of

Claus von Bulow in a celebrated case of the 1980s.[47] The Los Angeles District Attorneys' office assigned longtime prosecutors Marcia Clark and Bill Hodgman to lead an unusually large group of prosecutors. Christopher Darden later joined the team, in effect replacing Hodgman in the courtroom.

Both inside and outside the courtroom, the Simpson trial made for great theater. In terms of trial strategy, the prosecution built its case on DNA and blood evidence, which the district attorney's office believed proved conclusively Simpson's guilt. The defense team sought to show that the prosecution's case was built on sloppy, unreliable police work. Moreover, the defense argued that certain officers involved in the case were overzealous and racially motivated in their pursuit of Simpson as the lone suspect. The actual trial, which lasted almost nine months, was a collage of skirmishing lawyers, expert witnesses, lengthy and often dull descriptions of scientific evidence, aggressive cross-examinations, daily defense team press conferences, and judicial posturing. In describing this spectacle, veteran trial reporter Theo Wilson asserted that the media presentation in the Simpson case was all "flash and trash," with the important legal and evidentiary questions often taking a backseat to the tabloid-style coverage of the case outside of the courtroom.[48] Wilson notes, for example, that both Marcia Clark and Johnnie Cochran were the subjects of extensive and often humiliating tabloid news stories about their personal lives.[49]

The Simpson saga did not end with the not-guilty verdict in the criminal trial. The parents of Ronald Goldman spearheaded a wrongful death civil suit against Simpson. Although the actual legal proceeding was quite different, with different rules of evidence, no camera in the courtroom, the mandatory testimony of O.J. Simpson, and so forth, the civil proceeding perpetuated further rumination and discussion about the Simpson criminal case. Much of the media apparatus focusing on the criminal trial continued to cover and analyze the civil case. In March 1997, the jury in the civil suit found Simpson "responsible" for the deaths of Nicole Brown Simpson and Ronald Goldman, and he was ordered to pay more than $33 million in damages. This brought the legal saga to its conclusion, although many citizens found themselves wondering about a legal system that would find someone responsible for the murder of two people yet not require that same person to serve any jail time.

What factors made the Simpson cases so extraordinary? Why did they become a national obsession? A convergence of many factors, both large and small, catapulted the first trial into the public spotlight. Foremost, the crime involved a popular and wealthy celebrity whom many Americans considered a hero. Much commentary suggested that Simpson's ability to fight his criminal prosecution was clearly an example of a very rich man simply "buying an acquittal."[50] Further, the crime involved a black defendant and white victims, a circumstance that ignited many deep-seated passions about race and the law. In addition to this racial angle, the Simpson case provided a venue for raising public awareness of important gender dynamics in society. O.J. and Nicole Brown Simpson's violent marital relationship, marked by almost ten years of documented violence by the defendant, raised questions about how the legal system deals with husbands who abuse their wives.[51]

Thus, the trial of O.J. Simpson tapped into many of the most divisive social fault lines in US culture. Coupled with some of the more mundane and logistical components of the case, such as the presence of cameras in the courtroom, the length of the criminal trial, and the expanding role and presence of cable TV, these notable class, racial, and gender overtones produced a recipe for a national drama of unprecedented proportions.

Louise Woodward: Murderous Nanny or Accidental Death?

The media machinery that developed over the course of the Simpson trials undoubtedly spurred the coverage of the Woodward murder trial.[52] This coverage began to intensify after the verdict in the Simpson civil trial. Louise Woodward, a teenaged British nanny, was accused of first-degree murder for allegedly shaking to death eight-month-old Matthew Eappen, the infant she baby-sat. Prosecutors said that Woodward became so impatient with Matthew's crying that she shook him violently to quiet him. Woodward then allegedly slammed the infant against a hard surface to silence him. State medical examiners said Matthew hit the floor with the "force equivalent to a fall from a second-story window." Matthew suffered a fractured skull and later died from his injury. Woodward's defense team claimed that some prior incident, or a genetic defect, contributed to the baby's skull fracture. The defense also claimed that the Eappens' two-year-old son, Brendan, who was the only other person at home at the time, could have caused the fatal injury.

Woodward was imprisoned without bond after the incident, which caused considerable controversy. Her supporters, in both Massachusetts and Great Britain, argued that she should not be kept in a state women's prison with hardened criminals. They also claimed that Woodward did not understand the US justice system and should have been released on bail. Prosecutors countered that Woodward would likely leave Massachusetts if released from custody.

Toward the end of the long, divisive, technically complex, media-saturated trial, the prosecution filed a motion asking Judge Hiller Zobel to allow the jury to consider charges of voluntary and involuntary manslaughter, in addition to the first-degree murder charge it had originally requested. The prosecutors proposed that the jury have the option of convicting Woodward on one of these lesser charges. Defense attorneys sharply objected, wanting the jury only to have the more narrow option of convicting Woodward on either first- or second-degree murder or acquitting her altogether. Judge Zobel sided with the defense, allowing the jury only the narrower set of options. Upon immediate review by the Supreme Judicial Court of Massachusetts, the ruling was upheld.

In what came as a surprise to many observers, and certainly to the judge and the defense attorneys, the jury returned a conviction of second-degree murder, which carried with it a mandatory prison sentence of fifteen years. During the sentencing phase of the trial, the defense requested that Judge Zobel set aside the conviction and dismiss the case entirely, set aside the verdict and hold a new trial, or reduce the conviction to manslaughter. In a stunning development, Judge Zobel agreed with the defense, dismissed the jury's verdict, and reduced the conviction to involuntary manslaughter. He sentenced Woodward to 279 days in jail, which was "time already served," and released her from custody immediately. The ruling was not only unusual but was also delivered in an unorthodox fashion—the judge posted the decision and his full opinion on the Internet and presented considerable legal and historical support for his right, even his duty, to overturn what he believed to be a fundamentally unjust conclusion to the trial. He stressed that the decision should not be construed as a criticism of the jury, because he had not even given jury members the option of convicting on the involuntary manslaughter charge. However, Zobel explained that "a judge is a public servant who must follow his conscience."[53]

The judge's actions, which seemed to undermine the premises of the jury system, stunned prosecutors and law enforcement officials as well as many outside legal observers. Nevertheless, the Massachusetts high court upheld Zobel's decision. Woodward returned home to England, and the Eappen family filed a wrongful death civil suit against her. Woodward continued to maintain her absolute innocence but defaulted, claiming that she could not afford the costs of a prolonged civil trial.

There have been numerous trials with defendants being charged with the murder of an infant who was in their care, but none of these trials has reached the national audience. What are the factors that explain the rise of this case to national prominence? *Boston Globe* reporter Mark Jurkowitz, who covered the Woodward trial, has identified a formula for high-profile trials that appears to fit the facts of the Woodward case quite well. First, the case must be seized upon early by active local news media. This occurred through extensive coverage provided by the *Boston Globe* and *Boston Herald*. In addition, the presence of cameras in the courtroom allowed the local Boston affiliates to show the case live and give it extensive coverage on the local newscasts. And finally, a national audience becomes attracted to the case through the exposure on Court TV. Once these factors fell into place, the trial garnered extensive national attention and became the most watched trial since the Simpson events.[54]

The JonBenet Ramsey Investigation: Murder of a Child Beauty Queen

More than three years after the death of six-year-old JonBenet Ramsey, a grand jury investigation of the child's murder disbanded without prosecutors having charged a suspect.[55] The case had begun when Patricia Ramsey, JonBenet's mother, telephoned police early on December 26, 1996, to report that her daughter, a child beauty pageant champion, was missing from their Boulder, Colorado, house. She claimed to have found a ransom note demanding $118,000 for JonBenet's safe return. Patricia Ramsey reportedly found the handwritten ransom note on a back stairway in the family's home. The writer of the note claimed to represent a "foreign faction." Police arrived at the Ramsey house shortly before six in the morning, with Boulder detectives arriving by eight, as all parties expected imminent contact from the kidnappers. Police also searched the home but found no sign of the missing child. Eight hours later, after police had searched the house, JonBenet's father, John, found his daughter's body in a small, secluded basement closet that the police had inexplicably failed to search. Wrapped in a blanket, with her wrists tied above her head, her mouth covered with tape, and a nylon cord wrapped around her neck, JonBenet had been beaten, bound, and strangled. An autopsy showed that she had suffered a severe blow to the head and died by strangulation from the nylon garrote. Thus, what had hours earlier been considered a kidnapping case became an intensive murder investigation.

A month later, Boulder district attorney Alex Hunter announced that JonBenet's parents were "the obvious focus of the investigation." The Ramseys vehemently denied any involvement in their daughter's murder. A year later, Hunter said that the Ramseys, who continued to maintain their innocence, remained "under an umbrella of suspicion." Theories about JonBenet Ramsey's death abounded: the kidnap note was real, and an intruder murdered the child; one or both parents killed their daughter and wrote the ransom note themselves; the parents were covering for a relative or friend who had killed the girl; JonBenet and her parents were involved in a child pornography ring operating on the edge of the child beauty pageant subculture. Investigators asked numerous immediate and extended family members for fingerprints, palm prints, and DNA samples.

Eventually, the police and district attorney themselves came under fire. In September 1998, for example, Detective Lou Smit resigned from the district attorney's office, convinced of the Ramseys' innocence and of Hunter's irrational determination to prosecute them. Also in late 1998, Detective Steve Thomas, a Boulder police investigator, left the force, accusing Hunter of protecting the Ramseys. The district attorney also drew intense criticism for failing to indict the parents in the face of supposedly overwhelming circumstantial evidence.

Meanwhile, John Ramsey started a new computer business in Atlanta, and the couple's son, Burke, enrolled in a private school there. The governor of Colorado suggested that he might appoint an independent prosecutor to expedite a resolution to the case and minimize political infighting among the public officials involved, but he never followed through on this. Eventually, public and media interest began to fade. In early 2000, the grand jury in the case was dismissed, and although the murder remained formally under investigation, there was never an arrest in the case. In June 2006, Patricia Ramsey, JonBenet's mother, died in Georgia after a long battle with cancer. At that time, there still remained hundreds of Internet sites devoted to JonBenet's life, her murder, and the legal investigation itself.

Then, in August 2006, nearly ten years after the murder, media leaks revealed that Boulder prosecutors were investigating John Mark Karr, an American citizen living in Thailand who had allegedly confessed to the crime. As discussed earlier, a true media frenzy ensued, with virtually wall-to-wall coverage of the case, especially on cable television news. But just two weeks after this development, Boulder district attorney Mary Lacy announced that both DNA and circumstantial evidence conclusively demonstrated that Karr's story had been fabricated. The media dropped its coverage as abruptly as it had begun. The story again faded from the headlines, and as of early 2007 there had still never been a credible arrest in the decade-long investigation.[56]

The reason that the Ramsey case became national news is not entirely clear. Some have suggested that the eerie and somewhat startling pictures of JonBenet Ramsey wearing adult outfits and heavy makeup while performing in beauty pageants provided intriguing images that captured public attention. In much the same style as with the Rodney King video, many media outlets have repeatedly shown the photos of JonBenet Ramsey in her pageant outfits even when there were no developments in the story. Another possible reason for the ascension of this story was the newspaper rivalry in Denver between the *Denver Rocky Mountain News* and the *Denver Post,* one of the last major metropolitan areas with two competing newspapers. As these papers battled for readers, they may have helped to propel the case forward as both jostled to break the next big development in the case.[57] Regardless, several media commentators posited that if there was ever a trial in this case, it would unquestionably become the next "trial of the century."

Scott Peterson: The Murder of a Young, Beautiful (and Pregnant) Wife

On Christmas Eve 2002, Laci Peterson, a young Modesto, California, housewife and recent college graduate, was reported missing by her husband, Scott Peterson.[58] The community mobilized, holding candlelight vigils, posting flyers, and placing ads in all of the regional newspapers. Within a week, police began to suspect foul play. Thus began a criminal investigation that inevitably focused on Laci's husband, and an inquiry that grew into a legal story that would become one of the most heavily covered of the new millennium.

The exact date and cause of Laci's death were never conclusively determined, but Scott Peterson was found guilty of murdering her and their eight-month-old male fetus on about December 23, 2002, having dumped her body into the San Francisco Bay near the Berkeley marina. The case somewhat inexplicably drew almost immediate national media attention. Peterson claimed that he had been by himself on a fishing trip near Berkeley and that Laci had remained at their home in Modesto, about two hours away in California's San Joaquin Valley. He held a number of press conferences pleading with the public to come forward with any information that might shed light on his wife's disappearance, and for a short period he was apparently not considered a serious suspect in the case.

The initial support that Laci's family and friends had shown for Scott began to crumble when it was revealed that he was involved in an ongoing affair with a Fresno massage therapist named Amber Frey. Police questioning of Frey revealed that Peterson had repeatedly lied to her, including telling her that his wife had died a year earlier. Frey agreed to cooperate with the police, who began to record her conversations with Peterson. During the investigation, Peterson granted a high-profile interview to Diane Sawyer of ABC, in which he claimed that Laci knew about the affair, that the relationship with Frey had ended much earlier that year, and that his marriage was a strong and loving one. Although Peterson never confessed to Frey in any of the taped phone conversations, he was caught in numerous inconsistencies between these conversations and what he had previously told police and the press. It was also made public that Peterson had recently purchased a $250,000 life insurance policy on Laci.

On April 14, 2003, a male fetus washed ashore in the Bay near Richmond, about three miles from where Peterson had supposedly been "fishing," and within days, the badly decomposed body of a young woman was also found. Although the condition of the woman's body made determining a cause of death impossible, police were able to use DNA tests to determine that it was the body of Laci Peterson. Making matters even more dramatic, Peterson himself was now missing. Following a short search, he was located in La Jolla, just north of his hometown of San Diego. In shades reminiscent of the O.J. Simpson getaway attempt years earlier, Peterson had in his vehicle $15,000 in cash (the maximum amount of currency one can legally transport across the nearby Mexican border), four cell phones, camping equipment, a gun, and his brother's driver's license. Shortly thereafter, he was arraigned in Modesto for the murders of Laci and their unborn son, as California law holds that a fetus of just seven weeks' development can legally be considered a crime victim. Because of growing public hostility in Modesto, the trial was moved to Redwood City, just south of San Francisco in San Mateo County.

Peterson retained the services of high-profile Los Angeles defense attorney Mark Geragos, who had previously represented Whitewater scandal suspect Susan McDougal and actress Winona Ryder, and who would eventually become Michael Jackson's original counsel in his 2005 trial. Further heightening the media circus that developed, Amber Frey, although only a witness in the case, hired celebrity feminist attorney Gloria Allred, also a regular presence on all of the legal news programs as well as the host of her own syndicated radio talk show. For reasons that never became clear, even Frey's father retained a criminal defense lawyer.

The trial began on January 26, 2004, and lasted until November 12. It was characterized by press conferences by both sides as well as numerous media leaks that resulted in the dismissal of two jurors. Although the prosecution's case rested largely on circumstantial evidence, the defense was never able to successfully rehabilitate Peterson's countless inconsistent statements, especially to Amber Frey and in the media. In the end, the jury convicted Peterson of first-degree murder in Laci's death and second-degree murder in the case of the fetus. Hundreds of spectators assembled outside the courtroom, and a live audio feed was sent to banks of outdoor loudspeakers when the verdict was announced. Numerous media outlets interrupted their regular programming to cover the verdict live.

The penalty phase of the case was short but dramatic, with Peterson being sentenced to death on December 13. While awaiting the results of automatic appeals processes, Peterson now sits on death row in San Quentin prison. He maintains a regular correspondence with numerous women and has reportedly received several marriage proposals, including one from a former member of the jury that convicted him.

In terms of sustained media coverage, the Peterson case constitutes the second-most-covered investigation and trial of the second period of tabloid justice (after the Michael Jackson case, discussed shortly), as it was a top story in news headlines for nearly two years. Though the case really contained no issues of national importance, it did contain a number of the previously mentioned factors that seem to trigger intense media scrutiny (murder, adultery, the death of a fetus, etc.). Perhaps in the year after the World Trade Center attacks the media had developed an appetite for something other than the relentless drumbeat of terror warnings and the run-up to the Iraq invasion. Perhaps it was because Scott and Laci Peterson were an attractive, popular couple, variously described as "handsome" and "vivacious"[59] and living what appeared to be a dream life in the glamorous setting of California's Bay Area. Perhaps it was the particularly gruesome circumstances of a badly decomposed pregnant woman and her fetus washing ashore in the San Francisco Bay. Or perhaps it was the fact that several trial participants were represented by high-profile Los Angeles attorneys. Whatever the reasons might have been, the Peterson case dominated legal news from late 2002 until 2004.[60]

Martha Stewart: The Homemaking Maven
Caught in a Stock Scandal

Martha Stewart has been a prominent public personality for nearly thirty years.[61] Following graduation from Barnard College in the mid-1970s, she worked initially as a stockbroker and fashion model before opening a successful catering business operated out of her home in Connecticut. The success of this business led to the publication in 1977 of her first book, *Entertaining,* which became a *New York Times* bestseller, the first cookbook to do so since Julia Child's *Mastering the Art of French Cooking* twenty years earlier. Following the publication of several more cooking and homemaking books, in 1987 Stewart signed a lucrative agreement with K-Mart, launching the enormously successful *Martha Stewart Everyday* line of housewares. Her book *Weddings,* the publication of her own magazine, *Martha Stewart Living,* and a syndicated television program with the same name soon followed. In short, by the late 1990s Stewart was one of the most recognizable public figures in the United States. In 1999 the Martha Stewart Living Omnimedia Corporation went public on the New York Stock Exchange, and the initial public offering made Stewart a billionaire almost overnight.

However, beginning in 2002, Stewart's empire was rocked by her involvement with a pharmaceutical company called ImClone. ImClone had applied for federal government approval of a new and experimental cancer treatment drug to be called Erbitux, but on December 28 it was revealed that federal approval of the medicine had been denied. Within a month, the company's stock plunged over 70 percent. Shortly thereafter it was revealed that ImClone founder Sam Waksal had been tipped about the government's decision, and that both he and his daughter had sold large amounts of company stock just before the announcement had been made public. Similarly, Waksal's good friend Martha Stewart had also sold nearly 4,000 shares of stock the day before the government had formally denied approval of the new cancer drug, thereby avoiding an approximately $46,000 loss in the stock's value.

On June 4, 2003, a federal grand jury in New York indicted Waksal, Stewart, and Stewart's broker Peter Bacanovic on several alleged violations of the US Securities and Exchange Act. These charges included securities fraud, obstruction of justice, perjury, and conspiracy. In essence, Stewart was accused of illegal insider trading, lying to investigators, and engaging in a plan with others to use illegal information for financial gain. Additionally, as an actual board member of the New York Stock Exchange itself, Stewart's alleged activities were an embarrassment to the Exchange in a more general sense. Stewart pleaded not guilty, claiming that she had previously given her broker a standing instruction to sell her ImClone shares whenever they might drop below a value of $60/share, and that she had been unaware of the chain of events that had supposedly occurred. Although her reasoning was unclear, she attempted to appeal to the public by purchasing a full-page ad in *USA Today* and developing a website devoted to telling her side of the story. And, of course, she granted extensive interviews to journalists from both television and print media sources.

Nevertheless, even before her trial began, the allegations had a significant impact on the Martha Stewart brand and on Stewart herself. She resigned her position as CEO and chairperson of the board of directors of her corporation, and her various magazines suffered considerable drops in advertising revenues. K-Mart accused her of accounting irregularities and threatened to sever its ties with its Stewart brand, although they eventually reconciled, signing a deal that would continue the relationship through 2009.

In a trial that lasted a relatively short five weeks, prosecutors successfully demonstrated that Stewart had lied to investigators about this and other matters, though they ultimately dropped the more serious insider trading charges. On March 5, 2004, she was convicted of conspiracy, obstruction of justice, and two counts of making false statements. Stewart was sentenced to five months in federal prison, five months of "supervised release" (which included the wearing of a mandatory ankle bracelet), and two years' probation. And although District Court judge Miriam Cedarbaum offered to allow Stewart to remain out of prison while she pursued an appeal, Stewart expressed a desire to begin her incarceration as soon as possible. She then served a five-month sentence at Alderson Federal Prison Camp, a minimum-security facility in West Virginia. This facility has no security fences, and inmates are relatively free to walk the grounds unescorted. Stewart served her sentence and was released in spring 2005.

Stewart's public rehabilitation has included some setbacks, as her daytime television talk show was cancelled, her new program, *Martha Stewart: The Apprentice* ran for only a single season, and her magazines have continued to lose circulation. There have been at least two fairly popular television movies based on her life—*Martha: Behind Bars* and *Martha Inc.: The Story of Martha Stewart,* which have kept her name in the public consciousness. In addition, her K-Mart products remain highly successful, and she has also entered an agreement with Sears stores to offer a line of housewares. In sum, she remains an icon of American popular culture, albeit with an image that is a bit more tarnished than previously.

So, what can we make of the Martha Stewart case and its place in the era of tabloid justice? Clearly, the story contains virtually none of the factors that typically trigger a tabloid justice media frenzy. There is no murder, no sexual misconduct or deviance, no graphic violence, political intrigue, or public policy controversy. Rather, the public and media attention that this story garnered must be seen as almost totally a function of Stewart's celebrity status in contemporary American culture. Indeed, it is hard to imagine how her case involves a single shred of public importance, and yet it is among the four or five most-covered legal stories of the new millennium.

Terri Schiavo: A Tragic Battle Involving End-of-Life Policy Questions

Like the Rodney King incident more than a decade earlier, and unlike the vast majority of major legal stories in the era of tabloid justice, the tragic saga of

Terri Schiavo arguably involves some significant and timely ethical, legal, and public policy questions.[62] Unfortunately, the media machinery and journalistic approach that now dominate legal coverage were simply transferred or super-imposed on the facts of the Schiavo case. Thus, rather than seizing an opportunity to educate the public about the constitution, federalism, judicial structure, trials and appeals processes, privacy rights, and the need for living wills, Americans were presented with interest-group news conferences, grandstanding by politicians (including Congress and the president of the United States), and endless, repetitive video clips of Schiavo lying helpless in a Florida hospital.

Terri Schiavo was born on December 3, 1963, near Philadelphia. By the time she graduated from high school, she had developed problems with her weight. She experimented with a series of intensive diets, and by the time she entered community college in 1982, she had lost about sixty pounds. After marrying her college classmate Michael Schiavo, by 1989 she weighed less than 120 pounds. Many friends and family members believed that she was suffering from an eating disorder, although this was never conclusively established. On a February morning in 1990, Schiavo, who was then living in St. Petersburg, Florida, collapsed on her apartment floor. When paramedics arrived, she had no pulse and was not breathing, and after being taken to a local hospital, she lapsed into a coma that lasted for nearly three months. As with speculation about her eating disorder, the exact cause of Schiavo's collapse was never confirmed.

When she emerged from the coma, Schiavo was able to breathe on her own but had no consciousness of herself or her surroundings and no control over any of her bodily functions. Most significant, she had suffered severe brain damage due to the prolonged period she had spent without oxygen. Her doctors were forced to provide her with nourishment by means of a "feeding tube" inserted into her abdomen, and they considered her condition to be that of a "persistent vegetative state." Examined by numerous doctors, she was given little or no chance of recovery. In 1992 Michael Schiavo filed a malpractice suit against Terri's personal physician, claiming that he had failed to diagnose and treat Terri's bulimia. The case was settled for $1 million. Also in the early 1990s, Michael trained to become a respiratory therapist and emergency room nurse in order to better assist in Terri's treatment. He also began seeing another woman, with whom he would eventually have two children. He refused to divorce Terri, however, as this would have forfeited his rights as her legal guardian under Florida law.

In 1994 Michael sought a court order allowing the removal of Terri's feeding tube, testifying that it would not have been her wish to be kept alive "artificially," especially in her current condition. Although Terri had no living will, a total of eighteen friends and family members testified in support of Michael's request. Significantly, these supporters did not include Terri's parents, Robert and Mary Schindler. They countered that as a devout Roman Catholic, Terri would never violate the church's teachings on euthanasia and the sanctity of life. The Schindlers then attempted to have Michael legally removed from his status as Terri's legal guardian, but the court ruled that Michael had acted appropriately and attentively toward his wife. This began over a decade of legal battles between Michael Schiavo and the Schindlers. Significantly, for most of this period the story received virtually no media attention outside the state of Florida.

In 1998 Michael petitioned a Florida court to have Terri's feeding tube removed. The Schindlers filed an opposing petition, but after nearly eight months of deliberation, the court ruled that Terri's feeding tube could be removed. However, the judge stayed this order while the Schindlers pursued various appeals, including an unsuccessful request for a *writ of certiorari* from the US Supreme Court. This was to be the first of four attempts by the Schindlers to convince the Court to hear their case. Between 1998 and 2003 there were numerous such legal battles between the parties, with one of the cases reaching the Florida Supreme Court. One such battle featured the bizarre spectacle of the feeding tube being removed in accordance with a court order, only to be reinserted through another court's demand two days later. One three-month legal episode involved the Schindlers claiming that more than a dozen doctors had been incorrect in their diagnoses and that Terri was not in fact in a persistent vegetative state. Rather, they argued, she should legally be designated as "minimally conscious," which would apparently preclude the removal of her feeding tube. Again the Schindlers lost in court. Significantly, the case still had not caught the attention of the national mass media.

In 2003, having exhausted their state-level legal remedies, the Schindlers sought to pursue their case (i.e., that Michael should be removed as Terri's legal guardian, and that she be designated as being in a minimally conscious state) in the federal courts. By this time, Terri's case had become a political lighting rod, at least in Florida, with state Republicans, including Governor Jeb Bush, declaring his public support for the Schindlers and filing an *amicus* brief in the federal case. The federal district court ruled that it had no jurisdiction in the case, but by this time the political aspects of the case had begun to overshadow the legal details involved. The case was rapidly becoming a policy debate between prolife forces on one side and right-to-die advocates on the other. In 2003 the Schindlers designated Randall Terry, the militant leader of the Operation Rescue antiabortion organization, as their public spokesman, guaranteeing that the debate would now take place in the media as well as in the courts. The national press began to take notice at this point.

On October 15, 2003, Terri's feeding tube was finally removed. Having exhausted their options in the Florida judicial system, the Schindlers' cause was taken up by the Florida legislature and Governor Bush, which within a week had passed and signed "Terri's Law," authorizing the governor to personally intervene in this particular case. Bush immediately ordered the Florida

Department of Law Enforcement to take Terri from her hospice to a hospital and to have the feeding tube reinserted. There ensued another round of appeals (the American Civil Liberties Union was now assisting Michael Schiavo), which culminated in the Florida Supreme Court declaring Terri's Law unconstitutional under both the Florida and US constitutions. For the next two years, numerous interest groups and public figures entered the fray, holding press conferences, soliciting donations, mailing newsletters, and lobbying the US Congress. The House of Representatives took particular interest in the case, as the Republican-controlled leadership was able to suspend its own rules in order to pass its own "Terri's Law," a statute that would only apply to the person of Terri Schiavo and not a single other citizen. The US Senate more narrowly passed the bill as well, and President George W. Bush, on vacation in Texas, hastily returned to Washington to sign the bill into law on March 21, 2005. The Florida Supreme Court quickly ruled the law to be a violation of the US and Florida constitutions.[63]

The president used the signing ceremony to advocate a "culture of life" and to argue that the legal system should always "err on the side of life." The Schindlers claimed in interviews that Terri could understand their words to her; the family produced a carefully edited videotape that purported to show Terri making faces of recognition and attempting to speak one-syllable words. Sympathetic politicians began referring to Terri as "Terri Schindler" or "Terri Schiavo-Schindler," names she had never used during her marriage. Texas congressman Tom Delay asserted that Terri had been seen "talking and laughing . . . expressing happiness and discomfort." A Florida businessman reportedly offered Michael Schiavo $1 million to stop his attempts to have the feeding tube removed. Perhaps most disturbingly, Michael Schiavo is said to have received a number of death threats.

Despite this bewildering array of legal and political maneuvers, in the end the Schindlers won only a single judgment, losing in court approximately twenty-five times. A federal judge ruled that even if the federal Terri's Law eventually proved to be constitutional, the Schindlers had shown no reasonable evidence that they would prevail in court. A US Circuit Court then rejected the Schindlers' final appeal. At last, Florida District Court judge George Greer ordered Terri's feeding tube removed. Terri Schiavo died thirteen days later, on March 31, 2005.

Media attention to the Schiavo story, which had been virtually nonexistent for over a decade, and which for the most part never focused on the important policy questions at work in her story, quickly built to a fever pitch in 2004 and early 2005. In just the last month of her life, her case so dominated the media environment that her story became the third-most-covered legal story— on both television and in print media—for the entire second period of the tabloid justice era.

Michael Jackson: The "King of Pop" Endures Yet Another Legal Battle

What can one say about Michael Jackson, his lifestyle, and his legal battles that hasn't already been said?[64] In the contemporary American cult of celebrity, Jackson's every move has been chronicled for nearly three decades. His personal eccentricities have provided both tabloid and mainstream media outlets with an endless supply of material, ranging from stories about his marriages, his cosmetic surgeries, and his burn injuries (sustained while filming a Pepsi commercial), to coverage of activities at his Neverland Ranch in California, and the numerous allegations of child molestation that have hounded him since the early 1990s. Yet, the coverage afforded these aspects of his life would pale next to the attention given to his 2005 criminal trial for child sexual assault. In fact, this trial eventually became the most covered legal story in the second period of the tabloid justice era, garnering more media attention than any legal case since the trials of O.J. Simpson nearly ten years earlier.

As previously mentioned, the 2005 trial did not mark the first time that Jackson had been accused of sexual misconduct with children. In August 1993, while Jackson was on a worldwide concert tour, Los Angeles police launched a criminal investigation against him. A thirteen-year-old boy, who had been a "friend" of Jackson's and who had been seen many times in public with the pop star, had disclosed to his psychotherapist that Jackson had molested him, and as required by law the therapist had reported the allegation to police. The boy's family also filed a civil lawsuit against Jackson, accusing him of sexual battery, negligence, and fraud. Upon his return to Southern California, Jackson was taken into custody, questioned, and extensively photographed. The singer gave a number of television interviews claiming that the police had humiliated him, even to the point of taking photographs of his genitals.

Leading the criminal investigation was Santa Barbara County district attorney Thomas W. Sneddon, who would prove to be a tenacious adversary of Jackson. Grand juries were convened in both Los Angeles and Santa Barbara, but these inquiries were short-circuited when the boy agreed to settle the civil suit and to refrain from making any public statements about the matter, and refused to testify in the criminal investigation. Most media sources believed the settlement to be somewhere between $15 and $20 million. Without his central witness, prosecutor Sneddon stated that the case against Jackson was still "open but inactive."

In an apparent effort to rehabilitate his damaged public image, in 2003 Jackson granted British journalist Martin Bashir unprecedented access to Neverland Ranch and agreed to an extensive interview. The resulting program, *Living with Michael Jackson,* was shown worldwide and generated considerable controversy and discussion. In the documentary, Jackson was seen holding hands with two young boys, and talking about his habit of sharing his bed with these and other young "friends." The singer claimed that there was nothing remotely sexual in this practice, and that it was a natural part of adult-child friendship. One of the boys seen in the documentary, Gavin Arviso, who was at that time thirteen years old, would later be the person who prompted the arrest and trial of Jackson for sexual molestation. However, even though the documentary prompted child welfare officials to contact the children seen in the program, at that time Arviso denied that he had been mistreated in any way by Jackson. Nevertheless, in anticipation of possible legal fallout from the documentary, Jackson hired celebrity defense attorney Mark Geragos.

All of the preceding events form the backdrop to Jackson's 2005 criminal trial. In June 2003, a Los Angeles psychologist contacted police to inform them that Gavin Arviso had divulged that he had in fact been sexually molested by Michael Jackson on numerous occasions and had also been given alcohol and encouraged to view pornography while staying at Neverland. Prosecutor Thomas Sneddon then launched another criminal investigation, which included a massive, fifteen-hour search of the Neverland property in November 2003. With news crews hovering overhead in helicopters and amassing outside the gates of the ranch, sheriff's deputies seized truckloads of computers, films, books, and other materials. The search dominated national news for two days.

Several days later Jackson was booked in Santa Barbara on suspicion of child molestation but was freed on a $3 million bond that same day. Following grand jury testimony, the pop star was formally charged with seven criminal counts, including child molestation, furnishing alcohol to a minor, conspiracy to commit child abduction, false imprisonment, and extortion. Jackson pleaded not guilty, and replaced his attorney Mark Geragos (who was still busy with the Scott Peterson case) with well-known Los Angeles defense attorney Thomas Mesereau. Following nearly a year of legal maneuvering by both sides, Jackson's trial began in February 2005. The proceedings were held in the courthouse in the small city of Santa Maria in northern Santa Barbara County, about a thirty-minute drive from Neverland.

The proceedings lasted approximately five months and received wall-to-wall media coverage. Although Judge Rodney Melville refused to allow cameras in his courtroom, both sides in the case opted to hold almost daily news conferences. Countless television, radio, and print journalists set up camp outside the county courts building, and the trial dominated legal news coverage throughout the spring and summer. As with most trials, there was little in the way of significant daily developments, and so media coverage tended to predictably focus on the personality quirks and celebrity status of the various witnesses who were called to testify. Judge Melville did release a written transcript of each day's events, and this transcript would provide material for one of the strangest television programs in memory.

E! Entertainment Television, a channel normally devoted to celebrity gossip, fashion, and reruns of shows like *Saturday Night Live,* began running a nightly "reenactment show," in which actors recreated each day's events in the courtroom based on daily transcripts released to the press. Then, a panel of actual attorneys provided analysis and discussion of what viewers had just seen. At times, it was confusing as to whether the analysts were commenting on the performance of the actors portraying the trial participants, or what the transcript of the day's events actually said.

The prosecution's case was premised on two main fronts. First, the testimony of Gavin Arviso and his mother were central to Sneddon's strategy. Second, in accordance with a 1995 California law, Sneddon intended to introduce as much evidence as possible regarding Jackson's past alleged sexual misconduct and child endangerment. The prosecution claimed that there were at least five such previous offenses. In what most observers thought might prove to be a serious blow to Mesereau's defense, Judge Melville ruled that Sneddon would be allowed to call witnesses to such alleged prior offenses, although in the end only one such young man ended up testifying. In the other cases, third parties or family members gave testimony, which Mesereau argued amounted simply to hearsay evidence.[65]

Jackson's defense team employed a strategy that centered on challenges to the basic credibility of the accuser, and especially of the accuser's mother. Mesereau sought to portray the mother as a grifter who had been involved in previously controversial civil claims against two department stores, had been investigated for welfare fraud, and was now simply seeking to take advantage of Jackson's kindness to the family by extorting money from him. Mesereau's team was completely open about its strategy (conducting numerous interviews in the press and addressing the media each day outside the courtroom) and at one point was chastised by Judge Melville for trying to make its case in the mass media as much as in the courtroom.[66]

After three months of proceedings the prosecution rested its case, having called nearly ninety witnesses and introduced over 500 pieces of evidence. Most of the prosecution's witnesses proved unhelpful, and although Gavin Arviso's testimony was touching and at times compelling, his mother's bizarre and erratic behavior on the stand was considered highly damaging to Sneddon's case. The defense presented numerous witnesses, including celebrities such as Macaulay Culkin, Chris Tucker, and Jay Leno, who, in addition to providing temporary diversion and some levity to the proceedings, appeared far more credible than most of the prosecution's witnesses. Although the defense team consistently hinted that Jackson himself would take the stand, in the end he did not. Many observers believed that his eccentric personality could only have hurt his own case.

After a four-month trial, the jury deliberated for seven days before reaching its verdict. Michael Jackson was found not guilty on all counts against him.

It was a devastating blow to Thomas Sneddon, who many believed had "been after" Jackson for nearly a decade. Hundreds of fans had assembled outside the courtroom, and cheers and celebrations were widespread. Jackson boarded a waiting limousine and returned to Neverland, with several news helicopters flying overhead for the entire thirty-minute drive to the ranch. Court TV and MSNBC covered the entire drive live, never cutting away for commercials. Dozens more well-wishers greeted Jackson at the gates of the ranch, as did scores of additional reporters. All of the daytime news programs broke away from their regular coverage to discuss the verdict, as did several of the networks and other channels such as E! Entertainment Television, VH-1, MTV, and BET. But after a day of completely saturated media coverage, the story abruptly disappeared from the headlines. The news media were ready for a new tabloid installment.

Conclusion

This chapter has introduced several major tabloid justice news stories from 1991–2006 and presented summaries of the cases that we will return to throughout the remainder of this book. Although these investigations and trials share a number of important characteristics, there are also significant differences among them. Two of the cases, the Rodney King–related trials and the Terri Schiavo case, might actually have presented legitimate and important issues of national concern. Questions of police brutality and racism obviously warrant significant media exposure, and end-of-life issues involve increasingly important policy questions as medical technology continues to advance. However, despite the obvious merit and relevance of such issues, much of the press coverage of these cases was sensationalistic, superficial, personalized, commodified, and in no sense really "educational." Furthermore, we would argue that the rest of the preceding cases did not present issues of national significance that would warrant the extensive national media attention they received. They were simply trials involving individual tragedies and traumas.

In reflecting on the cases that we have just presented, we can draw several conclusions. First, because of the lack of national importance of most of them, it is clear that the media have used these cases mostly as a means of entertainment and enhanced ratings rather than as vehicles for public education. The *commodification* of television trials identified by Ray Surette has been strikingly evident in the tabloid justice era. Second, presentation of trials as a new form of entertainment makes it difficult for citizens to distinguish issues of real public importance. For instance, the King and Schiavo cases could have raised important legal, ethical, social, and political issues. However, when cases such as these receive virtually the same style of media treatment as the Simpson murder case or the Jackson molestation trial, the media do not offer any way for the public to gain perspective and context. The lines between assessing what is important and what is merely interesting become blurred.

In Chapter 2 we turn to an exploration of changes in the news business that have contributed to this blurring of the line between news and entertainment. We also discuss how this process has led to the tabloid justice coverage that now dominates almost all law and justice stories.

Notes

1. Quoted in William Booth and Kimberly Edds, "Forget Bush-Kerry. What About Scott-Laci? A Trial Galvanizes, and Polarizes, the Media," *Washington Post,* November 2, 2004, p. A1.

2. Quoted in Lynn Vincent, "The O.J. Decade," *World Magazine,* June 26, 2004, http://www.worldmag.com/articles/9090 (accessed July 15, 2006).

3. Jonathan Alter, "Reversal of Fortune: The O.J. Legacy," *Newsweek,* February 17, 1997, p. 24.

4. Neil Gabler, *Life: The Movie* (New York: Alfred Knopf, 1998), 82.

5. See, for instance, "Without Karr, the Mystery Remains in JonBenet Ramsey Case," *USA Today,* September 9, 2006, http://www.usatoday.com/news/nation/2006-09-03-ramsey-case_x.htm (accessed October 3, 2006); and Andrea Marks, "Why Cable News Pursues the JonBenet Ramsey Case," *Christian Science Monitor,* August 8, 2006, http://www.csmonitor.com/2006/0821/p03s01-ussc.html (accessed October 3, 2006).

6. See Richard Davis and Diana Owen, *New Media and American Politics* (New York: Oxford University Press, 1998), 11.

7. Philip Schlessinger and Howard Tumber, *Reporting Crime: The Media Politics of Criminal Justice* (Oxford: Clarendon, 1994), 13, 51–52.

8. See, for instance, Doris Graber, *Crime News and the Public* (Westport, CT: Praeger, 1980), xvii; and Gregg Barak, "Media, Society, and Criminology," in Gregg Barak, ed., *Media, Process, and the Social Construction of Crime: Studies in Newsmaking Criminology* (New York: Garland, 1994), 3–45.

9. See Richard Davis, *The Press and American Politics,* 2d ed. (Upper Saddle River, NJ: Prentice-Hall, 1996), 129–130; Herbert J. Gans, *Deciding What's News: A Study of CBS Evening News, NBC Nightly News, Newsweek, and Time* (New York: Vintage, 1979), 11–12; and Gilbert Geis and Leigh B. Bienen, *Crimes of the Century* (Boston: Northeastern University Press, 1998), 3–11.

10. For a study and analysis of the number of pregnant women murdered in the United States since 1990, see Donna St. George, "Many New or Expectant Mothers Die Violent Deaths," *Washington Post,* December 19, 2004, p. A01. For a description of the frequency of end-of-life decisions made by families and doctors, see David B. Caruso, "Decision to End Life Support a Common One," Lancaster Online, March 18, 2005, http://ap.lancasteronline.com/4/withdrawing _life_support (accessed July 2, 2006).

11. For more on this argument, see Cecil Greek, "Crime and the Media Course Syllabus and Lectures," http://www.fsu.edu/~crimdo/grade&m.html#lectures (accessed June 21, 1998); and David L. Altheide, "TV News and the Social Construction of Justice," in Ray Surette, ed., *Justice and the Media* (Springfield, IL: Charles C. Thomas, 1984), 292–304.

12. Ray Surette, *Media, Crime, and Criminal Justice: Images, Realities, and Policies,* 3d ed. (Belmont, CA: Wadsworth, 2007), 22–23. Also see William Haltom, *Re-*

porting on the Courts: How the Mass Media Cover Judicial Actions (Chicago: Nelson-Hall, 1998), 186–189.

13. See Edward W. Knappman, ed., *American Trials of the 20th Century* (Detroit: Visible Ink, 1995).

14. Ray Surette, *Media, Crime, and Criminal Justice: Images and Realities,* 2d ed. (Belmont, CA: Wadsworth, 1998), 22–23.

15. Haltom, *Reporting on the Courts,* 186; and Paul Thaler, *The Watchful Eye: American Justice in the Age of the Television Trial* (Westport, CT: Praeger, 1994), xx–xxi.

16. See Doris Graber, *Mass Media and American Politics,* 7th ed. (Washington, DC: Congressional Quarterly Press, 2005), 99–101, for a discussion of how violence can be exaggerated in crime reporting.

17. In support of this argument, see Barry Brummett, "Mediating the Laws: Popular Trials and the Mass Media," in Robert Hariman, ed., *Popular Trials: Rhetoric, Mass Media, and the Law* (Tuscaloosa: University of Alabama Press, 1990), 179–193.

18. For an example of this type of coverage, see Kendall Hamilton, "Marcia Clark Goes Straight," *Newsweek,* April 24, 1995, p. 72.

19. For an example of such coverage, see Bill Briggs, "Talk Swirls About Merits of Child Beauty Pageants," *Denver Post,* January 12, 1997, p. A4.

20. Reported on the ABC National News radio broadcast of January 24, 1999.

21. Further, the growing competition among news sources and the selling of news stories much like other commercial products has been commented on in both journalistic and scholarly settings. For instance, see Jonathan Alter, "In the Time of the Tabs," *Newsweek,* June 2, 1997, p. 32. For an earlier discussion of the effects of competition on print media, see Robert Entman, *Democracy Without Citizens* (New York: Oxford University Press, 1989), chaps. 5 and 6.

22. Where not otherwise cited, the facts of the William Kennedy Smith case are drawn from *Boston Globe* coverage of the case between April and December 1991. The case was covered extensively in the Boston media because of the Kennedy family's connections to Massachusetts. We also consulted the Court TV website, http://www.courttv.com/casefiles; Timothy Clifford, "Curtain Goes Up on Palm Beach Trial," *Newsday,* December 1, 1991, p. 5; Larry Tye, "Lights, Action as Smith Trial Opens Today," *Boston Globe,* December 2, 1991, p. 1; Steve Wick, "Rape Experts Look to Future Trials," *Newsday,* December 12, 1991, p. 7; and Marvin Kitman, "The Trial: Dat's All, Folks," *Newsday,* December 16, 1991, p. 45.

23. Clifford, "Curtain Goes Up on Palm Beach Trial," p. 1.

24. Tye, "Lights, Action as Smith Trial Opens Today," p. 1.

25. Ibid.

26. Wick, "Rape Experts Look to Future Trials," p. 7.

27. Ibid.

28. The facts of the Rodney King–related trials, where not otherwise cited, are based on accounts presented in the *Los Angeles Times* between March 1991 and April 1993.

29. Richard A. Serrano and Tracy Wilkinson, "All Four in King Beating Acquitted," *Los Angeles Times,* April 30, 1992, p. A1.

30. Alfred H. Knight, *The Life of the Law: The People and the Cases That Have Shaped Our Society, from King Alfred to Rodney King* (New York: Oxford University Press, 1996), 244.

31. Lou Cannon, *Official Negligence: How Rodney King and the Riots Changed Los Angeles and the LAPD* (New York: Times, 1997), 485.

32. Ibid., 486.

33. Lori Leibovich, "Rethinking Rodney King," *Salon Magazine,* March 13, 1998, http://www.salon.com/news/1998/03/13news.html (accessed September 23, 1998).

34. Doris Graber, *Mass Media and American Politics,* 5th ed. (Washington, DC: Congressional Quarterly Press, 1997), 152.

35. Howard Rosenberg, "TV's Double-Edged Role in Crisis," *Los Angeles Times,* May 1, 1992, p. F1.

36. The basic facts of the trials for Lyle and Erik Menendez, where not otherwise cited, are based on the detailed summaries that can be found in Court TV's case files section at http://www.courttv.com/casefiles.

37. Hector Tobar, "Disorder in the Court as Trial Starts," *Los Angeles Times,* July 21, 1993, B1.

38. Ibid.

39. Ibid.

40. *The Gallup Poll Monthly,* Gallup Organization, October 1995, p. 35.

41. Two recent books have devoted attention to the phrase "trial of the century." See Knight, *The Life of the Law,* epilogue; and Ronald Goldfarb, *TV or Not TV: Television, Justice, and the Courts* (New York: New York University Press, 1998), chap. 1.

42. This description comes from prosecutor Christopher Darden's posttrial memoir (cowritten with Jess Walter), *In Contempt* (New York: ReganBooks, 1996), 118.

43. Eric Malnick and David Farrell, "O.J. Simpson's Ex-Wife Found Stabbed to Death," *Los Angeles Times,* June 14, 1994, p. A1.

44. For an analysis of the letter, see Sheryl Stolberg, "Picture of a Lost Person," *Los Angeles Times,* June 19, 1994, p. A14.

45. Jim Newton, "'I'm Sorry for Putting You Guys Out': Simpson Collapsed in Officers' Arms; Details of Bizarre Day Are Revealed," *Los Angeles Times,* June 19, 1994, p. A1.

46. For useful information on the Sam Sheppard case, see F. Lee Bailey with Harvey Aronson, *The Defense Never Rests* (New York: Stein and Day, 1971).

47. For a description of the Claus von Bulow case, see Alan Dershowitz, *Reversal of Fortune* (New York: Random House, 1986); and William Wright, *The Von Bulow Affair* (New York: Delacorte, 1983).

48. Theo Wilson, *Headline Justice* (New York: Thunder's Mouth, 1997), chap. 1.

49. Ibid.

50. Polling data reveal this to be the widespread perception of the public. See *The Gallup Poll Monthly,* October 1995, p. 34.

51. The level of domestic violence in the Simpson marriage is in some dispute. In Simpson's civil trial he denied ever striking Nicole Brown Simpson. However, prosecutor Chris Darden's book *In Contempt* carefully chronicles the many documented episodes of domestic violence at the Simpson household.

52. Information about the Louise Woodward trial, where not otherwise cited, is based on the *Boston Globe*'s coverage between February and November 1997. The case was covered extensively in the Boston media. We also consulted Court TV's case files at http://www.courttv.com/casefiles.

53. A complete transcript of Judge Zobel's ruling can be found online at http://www.courttv.com/casefiles.

54. Mark Jurkowitz, "A Nation of Jurors Has Arisen: The Woodward Ruling," *Boston Globe,* November 12, 1997, p. A1.

55. The facts involved in the Ramsey murder investigation, where not otherwise cited, are based on coverage of the story in the *Denver Post* and the *Denver Rocky Mountain News.* Both of these papers have devoted extensive coverage to the investi-

gation. Also consulted in this summary was "JonBenet Ramsey Case Still Unsolved After Two Years," *CNN Interactive,* December 26, 1998, http://www.cnn.com/US/9812/26/jonbenet (accessed January 18, 1999). For additional material, see the CNN website at http://cnn.com, which maintains an extensive archive of JonBenet-related materials.

56. See Dante Chinni, "Overexposure: When Media Coverage Blocks Out the Sun," *Christian Science Monitor,* August 22, 2006, p. 9.

57. For a discussion of media coverage in the Ramsey investigation, see Lynn Bartels, "Professor Lambastes JonBenet Coverage," *Denver Rocky Mountain News,* July 5, 1998, p. 4A; and Howard Rosenberg, "A Clear Case of Media Mayhem," *Los Angeles Times,* September 28, 1998, p. F1.

58. Where not otherwise noted, this summary of the Scott Peterson case is adapted from the coverage of CNN, MSNBC, Court TV, and the *New York Times.*

59. "From the Start, Suspicion Falls on Peterson," CourtTVNews, http://www.courttv.com/trials/peterson (accessed February 10, 2006).

60. The Internet still teems with Peterson-related sites. Where not otherwise noted, our summary of the case relies on the coverage of Court TV, the *San Jose Mercury News,* CNN, and MSNBC.

61. Where not otherwise noted, this summary of the Martha Stewart case is adapted from the coverage of CNN, MSNBC, Court TV, and the *New York Times.*

62. Background material in this section, where not otherwise noted, is adapted from coverage in the *New York Times,* CNN, Court TV, MedLawPlus (http://www.medlawplus.com/library/legal/schiavo.htm), PBS (http://www.pbs.org/newshour/bb/media/jan-june05/schiavo_3-34.html), and PollingReport.com. For an excellent essay on the implications of the Schiavo case, see Joan Didion, "The Case of Theresa Schiavo," *New York Review of Books* 52 (June 9, 2005), http://www.nybooks.com/articles/18050 (accessed January 5, 2006).

63. Laurie Cunningham, "Fla. Supreme Court Declares 'Terri's Law' Unconstitutional," Law.Com, September 9, 2004, http://www.law.com/jsp/article.jsp?id=1095434458246 (accessed June 14, 2005); the Florida Supreme Court's opinion can be found at caselaw.lp.findlaw.com/data2/floridastatecases/9_2004/sc04-925.pdf.

64. Where not otherwise noted, this summary of the Jackson case draws upon coverage by CNN, the *Los Angeles Times,* Court TV, and E! Entertainment Television.

65. See Marci Hamilton, "Give Laws Strength to Take Down Child Molesters," CNN.com Law Center, January 1, 2005, http://www.cnn.com/2005/LAW/06/16/hamilton.child.support/index.html (accessed May 15, 2005); and Mark H. Allenbaugh, "The King of Pop Faces the Music," Findlaw Legal News, December 12, 2003, http://writ.news.findlaw.com/allenbaugh/20031204.html (accessed May 15, 2005).

66. "Michael Jackson's Defense Strategy," CBS News, February 25, 2005, http://www.cbsnews.com/stories/2005/02/25/entertainment/main676661.shtml?CMP=ILC-SearchStories (accessed July 15, 2006).

Two

The Mainstream Media Go Tabloid

If we were doing O.J. every night, I think our ratings would be soaring. It's tempting. But we'd be giving up our moral high ground.
        —Ted Koppel, host of *Nightline*[1]

So why do we find ourselves subjected to an overload of supposed news about the decade-old Boulder murder? Network news executives surely know this story doesn't deserve to lead a serious newscast, or even occupy a prominent place in one. . . . It's hard to avoid the conclusion that their bottom-line judgment amounts to this: Many of our viewers can't separate the important from the trivial—and they will change the channel if we do that for them.
        —Scot Lehigh, *Boston Globe* columnist writing about the resurgent
        coverage of the JonBenet Ramsey murder investigation in 2006[2]

Criminal trials and legal investigations make for fascinating news stories. They are filled with suspense, human tragedy, violence, and, occasionally, titillating sexual behavior. They can surpass the drama of Hollywood's best-scripted police or courtroom thrillers. Of course, at present the television networks and filmmakers are certainly attempting to duplicate the popularity of celebrity and notorious legal cases, in everything from dramatic TV shows like *Law & Order* and *CSI* to films like *The Black Dahlia*. In some ways, however, because they are filled with real people and events and their outcomes are presumably unpredictable, real-world trials and investigations may have even more entertainment value than television programs or motion pictures. The trials of O.J. Simpson, the Menendez brothers, Louise Woodward, and Scott Peterson, and the Terri Schiavo political firestorm have all made for engrossing and intriguing television, even if not for particularly enlightening civic education.[3] In a 1994 poll, conducted early in the tabloid justice era, 60 percent of the American public said that following the Menendez trial was as interesting as or more interesting than watching crime dramas on TV. More than 50 percent said the same thing about the Bobbitt trial.[4] In 2006, within days after it was reported that John Mark Karr had been arrested for the murder of JonBenet Ramsey, a Gallup Poll found that 87 percent of respondents across the country had already formulated an opinion about whether Karr was the real killer.[5]

This is not to say that Americans' fascination with crime and justice stories is anything entirely new. Sensational legal cases have long captured the attention of the public and the media.[6] From the bizarre murder trial of Leopold and Loeb in 1924 to the trial concerning the kidnapping and murder of the Lindbergh baby in 1935 to the two murder trials of Sam Sheppard in 1954 and 1966, Americans have always closely followed sensational court dramas.[7] During the twentieth century, these and several other cases were dubbed the "trial of the century."[8] Legal reporter Theo Wilson has observed that the drama and human tragedy involved in these cases gives them a theatrical quality equal to a performance of *Hamlet* or *Macbeth*.[9]

This book is not a history of famous criminal trials or other legal proceedings; hence, we do not delve extensively into the many high-profile law and crime stories of the twentieth century. This is because we believe that, though intensive media coverage of the occasional "trial of the century" is nothing new in US history, these cases have occurred with greater frequency since the 1990s, and the almost total cultural immersion accompanying such events as those involving Rodney King, O.J. Simpson, JonBenet Ramsey, Scott Peterson, and Terri Schiavo represents a new phenomenon. Even before a case goes to trial, journalists now quickly spin out supermarket-quality books telling true crime stories in explicit and graphic detail.[10] Tellingly, two television movies were produced that focused on Martha Stewart—one of which actually aired prior to her conviction and sentence. Tabloid outlets such as the *National Enquirer,* the *Star,* the *Globe,* and others swarm to these stories, and television programs like the 1990s show *Hard Copy* and the long-running *A Current Affair* and *Inside Edition* rush to provide coverage.[11] The tabloids have treated us to stories about the love life of O.J. Simpson prosecutor Marcia Clark, described the rumored "sex shows" that Monica Lewinsky performed for President Clinton, have speculated about JonBenet Ramsey's incestuous experiences with her older brother, and have described in graphic detail the seduction of male high school students by their attractive women teachers. In some sense, by providing salacious coverage of intimate, personal topics, the tabloid press now does what scandal sheets have always done. The distinguishing feature of the present media culture is the alarming regularity with which mainstream media sources now focus on these same personalized law stories.

Material formerly relegated to the tabloid press now pervades the mainstream press as well. News stories once covered only by the tabloids have found their way into journalism's most respected sources of "hard news" in the United States: CBS, NBC, and ABC, along with the nation's most esteemed newsmagazines and newspapers. *Time, Newsweek, US News and World Report,* the *New York Times,* the *Washington Post,* and the *Los Angeles Times* have become regular purveyors of tabloid-type stories. Moreover, the mainstream national press now exploits crime stories that have little or no bearing on anyone other than the immediate participants in the case. The media regularly use legal investigations and trials as entertainment fodder for attracting viewers. As television journalist Geraldo Rivera, who has worked in both the hard news and tabloid media, suggests, "The difference between a program like *Dateline NBC,* for example, and one of the tabloid shows—say, *Hard Copy* or *Inside Edition*—is in degree, not substance."[12]

In his 1998 book, *Life: The Movie,* Neal Gabler argues that the mass media now present "real life as entertainment."[13] The lines separating actual tragedy, important public events, and dramatic entertainment have become blurred, as have the differences between personalized tabloid titillation and substantive legal and political information. Our analysis of recent high-profile cases reveals clear evidence of this phenomenon. During 1997, for instance, the civil trial of O.J. Simpson received significantly more attention from television news than did issues such as poverty, health-care reform, welfare reform, and mass suffering in Africa.[14] Even the 1997 sexual assault trial of sportscaster Marv Albert, a case totally lacking in societal importance, made its way to the front page of the *New York Times,* the most esteemed media institution in the nation.[15] The *Times* also ran a lengthy front-page story on three Duke University lacrosse players who faced rape charges.[16] In a final example, the 2005 story of Natalee Holloway, an Alabama teenager who went missing on a trip to Aruba, regularly received more attention on network newscasts than many more relevant and important events. On the *CBS Evening News* on June 11, 2005, a segment on Holloway lasting four and a half minutes led off the newscast, ahead of stories such as the G-8 international economic conference, fighting in Iraq, and Mad Cow disease. On June 4, 2005, *NBC Nightly News* spent two minutes and thirty seconds on the Holloway disappearance, while committing just fifty seconds total to American deaths in Afghanistan, military operations in Iraq, and President Bush's address on the economy. Coverage of these and other similar cases suggests an important shift: the mainstream media have abandoned many of their self-imposed standards for avoiding tawdry and sensational topics.[17]

In this chapter we argue that the mainstream media—the traditionally trusted distributors of hard news—now focus an unprecedented and inordinate amount of attention on legal stories that previously might have been fodder only for tabloid media outlets. We consider, from a legal, political, and educational standpoint, whether the entertainment value of such stories has overshadowed their newsworthiness. In other words, have the media chosen to focus so heavily on tabloid justice cases because of their appeal as entertainment, as opposed to their objective importance as hard news? Also, we begin to delineate how, rather ironically, this shift in media attention has given the mass public the closest and most detailed view of the legal system it has ever seen. However, we note that media representations of the legal system viewed in the context of these highly anomalous cases may actually distort the public's view of that system, an idea we develop throughout our remaining chapters. In sum, we believe that a strange condition now exists in which the public knows both "more" and "less" about the American legal system.

To examine this transformation, we have divided this chapter into three sections. The first section specifically describes the mainstream press and the standard journalistic practices of mainstream media organizations. The second briefly discusses changes in the dynamics of the news and information business during the decades preceding the 1990s. Finally, we examine more closely recent newspaper, print magazine, television news program, television newsmagazine, and network morning show coverage of tabloid legal proceedings.

Identifying the Mainstream Media

Americans normally associate the mainstream media, or hard news outlets, with the reporting of serious national issues.[18] One media scholar has defined *hard news sources* as those to which people turn for late-breaking reporting on the most important stories of the day.[19]

Because national news sources play a critical role in establishing the news priorities of local news organizations throughout the country, they are the outlets with which we are primarily concerned.[20] These news outlets have increasingly focused their attention on crime, trials, and legal investigations, and regardless of the appropriateness of such attention, this has heightened the public's exposure to the workings of the justice system. When Americans watch the pervasive coverage of tabloid justice cases—especially live images emanating from courtrooms, or attorney press conferences—they are given a firsthand glimpse of the behavior of lawyers, judges, defendants, and the police. The presentation of evidence and courtroom testimony are now common media topics, and a significant portion of the public may potentially have gained a working familiarity with the basic aspects of the judicial process.

Recent polls also show that the public has gained an increased awareness of the judicial process through such coverage. Thus, the media have performed their "agenda-setting" function by suggesting to the public what it should be thinking about justice and the legal system. However, we would assert that the agenda being set by the media is one that increasingly encourages Americans to think about trivial details from particular high-profile cases, such as what John Mark Karr ate on his plane trip from Thailand to the United States, whether Martha Stewart is a harsh and controlling business leader, and if it was actually Pepsi or wine that Michael Jackson served to his underage guests on private airplane trips.[21]

In addition to setting the agenda for the nation's legal and political discourse, there exists an agenda-setting function within the media system as well. When ABC News or the *New York Times* covers a story, that story gains instant legitimacy for media outlets across the nation.[22] Such coverage thus cues local news broadcasts and local newspapers to a story's importance and appropriateness for their attention.

As we consider how the media have increased their coverage of trials and legal investigations, and the manner in which they have given such stories a more tabloid-like slant, it is important to distinguish tabloid cases from what we might deem more socially important legal proceedings—those that possess broad legal, social, or public policy implications. Clearly, some legal stories do have national significance. Nearly all of the rulings of the US Supreme Court could be characterized this way. Further, many trials effectively demonstrate the functioning of the legal system and raise political or legal questions that transcend the experiences and interests of the individual participants in them. For instance, the murder trial of Sirhan Sirhan for the assassination of US senator and presidential candidate Robert Kennedy in 1968 and the trial of John Hinckley for the assassination attempt on President Ronald Reagan in 1981 were of great public importance. All US citizens share a legitimate interest in the protection of political leaders and in the stability of the regime. Similarly, the trial of Timothy McVeigh, who was convicted for the bombing of a federal government building in Oklahoma City, falls into this category, though some critics of the media's obsession with trials as entertainment have included McVeigh in their analyses.[23] And the public has a legitimate interest in proceedings that involve emerging civil liberties issues, such as the trials of Jack Kevorkian, the Michigan doctor who waged a one-person crusade for the legalization of assisted suicide. However, some have argued that the television newsmagazine *60 Minutes* went too far when it aired footage of Kevorkian actually administering a lethal injection to a patient.[24]

Whereas the aforementioned cases might have warranted national media attention, others fall almost entirely into the realm of legal entertainment. The cases involving William Kennedy Smith, Lorena Bobbitt, Susan Smith, Louise Woodward, JonBenet Ramsey, Marv Albert, O.J. Simpson, Andrea Yates, Winona Ryder, Scott Peterson, Elizabeth Smart, Natalee Holloway, Martha Stewart, and Michael Jackson had few (if any) broad societal implications.[25] The trials involving Rodney King, the impeachment of President Bill Clinton, and the Terri Schiavo affair, however, arguably raised questions of national importance, but the sensationalistic style of coverage devoted to them makes it difficult to distinguish them from the more clearly tabloid cases. The media now simply shift the "machinery" of tabloid coverage from one legal/ political story to another, without apparent regard for different history, context, and nuance. What we wish to emphasize here is that while there is no clear and firm line separating socially relevant from socially trivial legal stories, our book presents evidence suggesting that the contemporary media have over-whelmingly abandoned virtually any sense that some of these stories may be more important to the nation than others.

We next examine two prominent hard news sources, as well as the jour-nalistic ethics standards that supposedly govern the behavior of reporters in this arena. Cable news-talk channels, such as CNN, MSNBC, Headline News, and Fox News, which we also consider to be hard news outlets, are included in our later discussion of "new" media in Chapter 3.

Daily Newspapers and Weekly Newsmagazines

According to most observers, the foundation of serious journalism in the United States remains the top-rated daily newspapers.[26] These papers include the *New York Times,* the *Washington Post,* the *Wall Street Journal,* the *Los Angeles Times,* and the flagship papers in most major US cities. Newspaper coverage is crucial because the dailies set the tone for the subjects that appear on network and cable news programs later in a given day. Although newspapers lack the ability to present late-breaking stories (although this is changing as newspapers aggressively increase their presence on the Internet), they possess a level of credibility missing from much of modern journalism. Newspapers have the ca-pacity to cover trials and investigations in a manner that is impossible to dupli-cate in the typical thirty-minute television newscast.[27]

Weekly newsmagazines round out the top tier of the print medium. *Newsweek, Time,* and *US News and World Report* are generally considered the core of the hard news weeklies.[28] Although the publication cycle of weekly magazines does not allow them to compete with other news outlets in terms of reporting on breaking news, they have the opportunity to offer more in-depth stories and include more extensive analysis and contextual detail.[29] Ironically, this ability to provide relatively deeper coverage has recently contributed to the tendency of moving the newsmagazines in the direction of the tabloid exposé.

Network Television News Organizations

The three major television networks—ABC, NBC, and CBS—devote consid-erable resources to news coverage.[30] Each of these organizations presents nightly national news broadcasts with a highly credible image based on its sig-nificant role in the history of modern news. These nightly broadcasts have a tradition of legendary journalism behind them, with such figures as Edward R. Murrow, Walter Cronkite, Chet Huntley, David Brinkley, Dan Rather, Tom Brokaw, and Peter Jennings having occupied the anchor's chair. This presen-tation of the nation's most important stories of the day, however, takes place within the confines of a thirty-minute timeframe, and at least a quarter of that time is used for commercial breaks. The typical broadcast begins with what is deemed to be the most important story of the day, usually followed by coverage of an additional eight to ten stories. Thus, these newscasts are rarely able to spend more than two to three minutes on any one story.[31] This formula has changed little since the early 1970s. Beginning in 1979 ABC News offered an additional nightly news broadcast, *Nightline,* which ran after the prime-time entertainment schedule. Anchored by Ted Koppel until 2005, *Nightline* usually focused on a single topic for most of its thirty minutes, providing only brief updates on a few other important stories of the day.

In addition to the nightly news broadcasts, the "big three" networks have several other venues in which to present hard news. The morning shows—NBC's *Today,* ABC's *Good Morning America,* and CBS's *The Early Show*—offer a combination of news, features, interviews, friendly chatter, and consumer advice. Importantly, these programs also devote considerable attention to serious stories. Also, the Sunday morning talk shows—CBS's *Face the Nation,* NBC's *Meet the Press,* and ABC's *This Week*—have long been considered forums for prominent journalists to ask questions of national figures and politicians. The Sunday morning programs have often been criticized as dull viewing fare, as they tend to heavily emphasize "inside the beltway" Washington politics. Finally, television news magazines, such as ABC's *20/20,* NBC's *Dateline,* and CBS's *48 Hours* and *60 Minutes,* are very popular outlets for the networks to provide more in-depth coverage than the nightly newscasts allow. This has long been true of *60 Minutes,* which first aired in 1968, but the number of these programs increased tremendously in the 1990s, though their popularity has diminished since 2000. The fact that these shows, which air between 7:00 PM and 11:00 PM, compete for viewers with sitcoms, dramas, reality shows, and TV movies has no doubt encouraged them to move in the direction of news-entertainment. Prime-time viewers now often have a choice between entertaining news and just plain entertainment.[32] In sum, the television newsmagazines have played an integral role in fueling the news media's transition toward a stronger entertainment focus.[33]

The Ethics of Hard News Organizations

Taken together, the print and television news organizations, as well as some cable news outlets, are the sources of the "mainstream" news that the public has historically relied on for learning about important public events. Tradition and a perceived legacy of journalistic integrity distinguish these organizations from other news outlets. Reporters working for these organizations have ostensibly been bound by a self-proclaimed code of ethics, such as that promulgated by the national Society of Professional Journalists (SPJ).[34] This code presents a wide-ranging list of standards of conduct meant to assure both ethical and competent journalism. The SPJ's full code includes more than thirty topics, such as those pertaining to privacy, "sourcing" guidelines, and the maintenance of objectivity. Following is a list of seven such standards of behavior that are particularly relevant to our focus on legal coverage:

1. Only an overriding public need can justify intrusion into anyone's privacy.
2. Show good taste. Avoid pandering to lurid curiosity.
3. Make certain that headlines, news teases, promotional material, photos, video, audio, graphics, sound bites, and quotations do not misrepresent. They should not oversimplify or highlight incidents out of context.
4. Be sensitive when seeking or using interviews or photographs of those affected by tragedy or grief.
5. Recognize that gathering and reporting information may cause harm or discomfort. Pursuit of the news is not a license for arrogance.
6. Be judicious about naming criminal suspects before the formal filing of charges.
7. Balance a criminal suspect's fair trial rights with the public's right to be informed.[35]

It is debatable to what degree the mainstream press ever fully upheld these standards. That is an important question for historians of the news media. However, what can be said with great confidence is that in the era of tabloid justice these principles have been discarded on a regular basis. In fact, they may have simply been abandoned altogether. Frankly, contemporary news reporting and journalism bears little resemblance to the rarified standards listed above.

Changes in the News Business Since the 1970s

Although the mainstream news providers still exist in their historic institutional forms, there have been some significant changes in the news business since the 1970s, and particularly since about 1990. Perhaps most significant is that newspaper readership has declined dramatically since the 1960s. As newspaper readership dropped, the prominence of television news grew substantially from about 1970 onward. Today, more than three quarters of Americans identify television as their number-one source of news.[36] The big three network news organizations' audience share, however, has actually fallen since the 1990s. This decline has been accompanied by the expansion of the cable television industry. Currently, four cable channels are devoted almost entirely to news, with the rising popularity of Fox News being the most significant development. Further, the Internet now plays a substantial role in the presentation and dissemination of news and information, with 24 percent of citizens in 2005 saying it is one of their most important news sources.[37] Table 2.1 displays several of the trends under discussion here.

Because of these important changes in how people access news, mainstream news organizations have experienced a consistently shrinking audience. To maintain ratings and attract viewers, they have implemented structural, substantive, and especially stylistic changes. All of the news organizations, both print and television, for example, have gone online with sophisticated, interactive websites. NBC has aggressively moved into the cable television arena with two new channels, CNBC and MSNBC. And beyond these structural changes, the traditional hard news outlets appear to have changed their practices, too, now focusing more heavily on sensational, tabloid-style, human interest and consumer-oriented stories.

The Tabloid Conversion of the Mainstream Press

The mainstream media may have clearly left behind the journalistic principles that purportedly guided them since the 1950s. Whether in print or television settings, news organizations have redefined what constitutes "appropriate" coverage. They now spend considerable time covering tabloid-type stories, not all of which involve crime and trials (for instance, extensive attention is paid to the activities of celebrities). So, why do these trials and investigations receive such

Table 2.1   Changes in News and Information Dissemination Since 1970

Year	% of People Who Read a Newspaper Daily[a]	% of Households Viewing Network News Broadcasts on Any Given Evening[b]	Number of Internet Hosts[c]	Number of Cable Television Channels Devoted to News[d]
1970	75	75	n/a	0
1980	61	72	n/a	1
1990	53	59	313,000	3
1992	n/a	55	1,136,000	3
1994	50	57	3,864,000	3
1996	42	50	16,729,000	5
1998	43	49	36,739,000	5
2000	37	44	93,047,785	5
2002	41	41	162,128,493	5
2004	40	38	285,139,107	5
2005	n/a	37	353,284,187	5

Notes: "n/a" means data not available for that year.

    a. Data are from the General Social Survey, Roper Center, University of Connecticut. Survey conducted biennially starting in 1994.

    b. Data are from journalism.org's annual "State of the Media" survey.

    c. Data from Internet Services Consortium Domain Survey, www.isc.org.

    d. Includes CNN, CNN Headline News, MSNBC, CNBC, and Fox News.

attention? The answer may lie in the fact that these events, unlike most other types of news stories, present an opportunity for the press to provide prolonged, detailed, and relatively inexpensive coverage. On the one hand, stories about hurricanes, earthquakes, floods, fires, and other natural disasters (historically "favorites" of the media), for instance, can be sustained only for a few days. There might be a series of short reports on predisaster anxiety and preparations, several pictures and descriptions of the actual event itself, and a culmination with postdisaster victim reaction and cleanup efforts. Stories about trials and investigations, on the other hand, can be sustained for weeks, months, or even years. In fact, the sheer length of legal proceedings actually allows for suspense and interest to grow over time. Further, the relatively slow-moving nature of the justice system allows sufficient time for these cases to become national melodramas embedded in the social fabric of the culture.

Clearly, the length of trials and investigations is part of what makes them such ideal stories for news organizations. Networks can dispatch correspondents to a trial and leave them there for the duration of the proceedings. Table 2.2 shows the length of the formal legal portion of the primary tabloid justice cases we focus on in this book. It lists the time from the initial crime or charge through the legal proceedings; keep in mind, however, that national conversation about these cases often continues long after the formal legal proceedings conclude. This was certainly true in the cases of William Kennedy Smith, Rodney King, O.J. Simpson, and Scott Peterson.

Perhaps somewhat curiously, the public often claims to have little direct interest in these trials. Rather, people regularly assert that they consider these cases to be merely boring sagas and believe that the media spend too much time covering them. In a series of Times Mirror polls, 90 percent of respondents believed that the media gave too much attention to the Simpson case, 71 percent felt the same about the William Kennedy Smith trial, and 51 percent voiced this opinion about the trial of Lorena Bobbitt.[38] More recently, a Fox News national poll found that 66 percent of respondents felt that the media coverage of the Michael Jackson trial was excessive.[39] In contrast, news organizations point to increased ratings as justification for their programming choices, and polling evidence also suggests that the public does pay considerable attention to these stories, despite its claim to be uninterested in these stories (see Table 4.1). It appears plausible that citizens sometimes misrepresent their own viewing habits in surveys.[40]

It is difficult to be certain if the coverage of these trials is merely the media's response to public demand, for this demand is, in effect, denied by the citizenry in polls. Alternatively, there may be a set of internal media imperatives driving the coverage of these cases, such as the need to promote ratings or maintain a competitive edge over other media outlets. In any event, the vastly increased level of viewer exposure to the inner workings of the legal system in recent years cannot be divorced from the attention paid to tabloid justice cases.

Table 2.2   Number of Months Each Tabloid Justice Case Continued in the
Legal System

	Duration of Legal Proceedings (months)
First period	
Menendez brothers murder trial	70
(crime occurred August 21, 1989; final sentence handed down July 2, 1996)	
Rodney King beating trial	25
(videotaped beating of King first aired March 3, 1991; second trial of officers concluded April 17, 1993)	
William Kennedy Smith rape trial	8
(crime reported April 3, 1991; trial concluded December 11, 1991)	
O.J. Simpson murder trials	33
(crime occurred June 12, 1994; civil trial concluded February 10, 1997)	
JonBenet Ramsey murder investigation[a]	36
(crime occurred December 26, 1996; investigation continues; months counted through 1999)	
Louise Woodward trial	9
(murder charges filed February 9, 1997; judge overturned jury's verdict November 9, 1997)	
Second period	
Terri Schiavo legal proceedings[b]	83
(Michael Schiavo files a petition to remove Terri's feeding tube May 1998; Terry dies March 31, 2005)	
Martha Stewart financial misconduct trial	25
(first talks to FBI February 4, 2002; sentenced March 5, 2004)	
Scott Peterson murder trial	24
(Laci Peterson reported missing December 24, 2002; Scott Peterson sentenced to death December 13, 2004)	
Michael Jackson molestation trial	21
(police raid Jackson's house November 18, 2003; found not guilty on all counts June 13, 2005)	

Notes: Cases are listed chronologically from the time of initial news reports. Number of months is rounded up.

a. JonBenet Ramsey coverage reemerged briefly in 2006 with the arrest of John Mark Karr as a suspect in the case, though the bulk of coverage occurred in the three years following the murder.

b. Terri Schiavo did not gain national media attention until 2003.

Newspapers and Magazines: From Hard News to Scandal Sheets

Although television has clearly become the prominent news medium, print journalism remains important in understanding the growth of tabloid-style legal coverage. There is evidence that people rely more heavily on television news, and that they believe, perhaps surprisingly, that TV news is more credible than print news.[41] This distinction is somewhat meaningless, though, as print journalists actually conduct much of the investigative work that eventually gets reported on television and in radio broadcasts.[42] Within the journalism profession itself, the reporting of major daily newspapers carries a very high level of credibility.

Table 2.3 provides an illustration of the sheer volume of tabloid justice stories presented in major newspapers and newsmagazines. We include as major newspapers the top daily papers in the United States and the world, as determined by Lexis-Nexis, an archival and Internet search engine. Our analysis of newsmagazines relies on *Time, Newsweek,* and *US News and World Report.*[43] Table 2.3 reveals that the hard news print media have devoted considerable attention to tabloid justice stories. In fact, many of these stories have received front-page or cover story status, which places them in a category of considerable importance.

The increased volume of coverage of tabloid justice stories is not the only way the hard news print media have shifted their focus. Newspaper headlines from around the country are now often written in a decidedly "tabloidized" style as well. Importantly, the headlines assume that their readers already possess a substantial familiarity with each case; these stories are part of our national consciousness. A brief glance at several headlines from a variety of tabloid justice stories illustrates these trends:[44]

Table 2.3   Volume of Coverage and Front-Page Articles on Tabloid Justice Stories in Major Newspapers and Newsmagazines, 1989–2005

	Major Newspapers		News-magazines	
	Total Articles	Front Page	Total Articles	Cover Stories
First period				
Menendez brothers murder trial (1989–1996)	1,131	36	37	0
William Kennedy Smith rape trial (1991)	1,958	71	46	0
Rodney King beating trial (1991–1993)	6,847	447	104	6
Lorena Bobbitt mutilation trial (1993–1994)	1,562	49	12	0
O.J. Simpson murder trials (1994–1997)	22,610	1,471	173	10
JonBenet Ramsey murder investigation (1996–1998)	2,090	79	47	1
Louise Woodward trial (1997)	1,823	62	16	1
Second period				
Scott Peterson trial (2002–2004)	1,072	9	18	0
Michael Jackson trial (2003–2005)	2,738	84	48	0
Terri Schiavo (2000–2005)	2,034	267	58	3
Martha Stewart trial (2002–2004)	4,122	138	152	2

Notes: Number of articles for each story is based on a Lexis-Nexis search. The Lexis-Nexis definition of "major newspapers" in 1998, when the first-period searches were conducted, included the sixty-five domestic and international newspapers with the highest circulations. In the second-period searches, conducted in 2005, Lexis-Nexis only counted forty-three newspapers in this category. Newsmagazines considered were *Newsweek, Time,* and *US News and World Report.* For search instructions, see Appendix A.

"British Nanny Sobs After Guilty Verdict: 'Why Did They Do This to Me?'" *Orlando Sentinal*

"Foreign Faction Threatened to Kill JonBenet in Ransom Note," *Buffalo News*

"No Semen Found at Ramsey Slay Scene," *Denver Post*

"Bizarre Hypotheses Surface in Laci Peterson Case," *Houston Chronicle*

"Culkin Shared Jackson's Bed But Says He Wasn't Molested," *Washington Post*

"Ranch Manager Says Jackson Owned Erotica," *New York Times*

"Jackson's Prints Identified on Sex Magazines," *New York Times*

"Finding Hope Even in Schiavo's Barbaric Death," *Chicago Sun-Times*

"Can Martha Find Happiness Behind Bars?" *San Francisco Chronicle*

"Kidnapped Teenager Smart Possibly Held by Mind Control," *Columbus Dispatch*

"Aruba Cops Think X May Mark the Spot," *Daily News* (New York)

"Wilbanks Told Lurid Tale of Abduction, Sex Acts," *Atlanta Journal-Constitution*

These headlines discuss the various tabloid justice cases as if every American reflexively knows who the specific participants are. Tabloid-style article headlines covering the Ramsey investigation, the Marv Albert trial, the Menendez brothers trial, the Elizabeth Smart kidnapping, and the Peterson, Stewart, and Michael Jackson stories can also be found in each of the three major newsmagazines. A sampling:[45]

"The Strange World of JonBenet," *Newsweek*

"JonBenet: Taking the Hunt into His Own Hands," *Time*

"A Body in the Basement [JonBenet]," *Newsweek*

"Marv Goes to the Showers," *Newsweek*

"He's Out of the Game [Marv]," *US News and World Report*

"Murder 90210: Crime Styles of the Young, Rich, and Impatient [Menendez]," *Newsweek*

"How the Kidnappers Controlled Elizabeth," *Newsweek*

"Invasion of the Body Snatchers [Elizabeth Smart and others]," *Time*

"Jacko's Hokey-Pokey," *US News and World Report*

"From Moonwalk to Perpwalk," *Newsweek*

"Jacko's Bad Day in Court," *Time*

"Martha: Is She in Deep Doo Doo?" *Newsweek*

These headlines are similar in tone to those presented in the three top-selling supermarket tabloids: *National Enquirer, Star,* and *Globe*. For instance, headlines taken from articles appearing in the *National Enquirer* include "JonBenet Arrest Drama," "Menendez Brother Weds Wealthy Widow Behind Bars,"

"Scott Peterson's New Best Friend Is Gay Serial Killer," and "Elizabeth Smart: I Forgive My Captors."[46] It becomes clear that distinguishing the subject matter and style of presentation between the tabloids and the ostensibly more serious newsmagazines can be difficult.

The falling sales of the tabloids themselves since the 1980s may provide further evidence of the major daily newspapers and newsmagazines' shift toward tabloid justice topics. More than twenty years ago, the tabloid papers were alone in covering what today has become the agenda for virtually all news organizations. Table 2.4 illustrates the shrinking market for the tabloids. Although newsmagazines have also struggled, they have largely managed to maintain their readership over the years. The *National Enquirer,* traditionally the leader of the tabloids, and its closest competitor, the *Star,* have experienced a virtual sales free fall since the early 1980s; their total readership has dropped by roughly 70 percent. As *Newsweek* writer Richard Turner asks, "With dollops of sleaze on your doorstep and your TV everyday, who needs the tabs?"[47]

Unquestionably, the print media have moved away from the principles of journalism espoused, though certainly not always adhered to, by the old beat writers of the 1950s, 1960s, and 1970s.[48] The detailed coverage of the Simpson trial, the Ramsey case, and the Michael Jackson trial demonstrated a clear violation of many of the standards articulated in the journalistic code of ethics listed previously. Coverage of many of these cases involved significant invasions of privacy, rarely accompanied by any overriding public need. In many instances, reporters also blatantly pandered to the most lurid aspects of the public's curiosity. Indeed, in many of the cases, that factor seems to be the only reason the story was covered at all. Several of the headlines listed previously do not involve details or issues that the public had any objective "need" to know.

Table 2.4   Average Weekly Circulation of Newsmagazines and Tabloids Since 1970 (in millions)

Year	Newsweek	Time	National Enquirer	Star
1970	2.6	4.3	2.0	n/a
1980	3.0	4.6	5.0	3.4
1990	3.2	4.1	4.0	3.5
1992	3.2	4.2	3.4	2.9
1994	3.2	4.1	3.1	2.7
1996	3.2	4.1	2.5	2.3
1998	3.2	4.1	2.2	1.9
2000	3.1	4.1	2.1	1.7
2002	3.2	4.1	1.8	1.4
2004	3.1	4.0	1.5	1.2
2005	3.2	4.0	1.2	1.4

Source: Audit Bureau of Circulation, 2005.
Note: "n/a" means data not available for that year.

The Transformation of Television News

The considerable evidence of a tabloid shift in the print media pales in comparison to the "tabloidization" of television news. This is hardly surprising, given TV's disproportionate impact on American culture.[49] Political scientists and media scholars have long pointed to events such as the first Nixon-Kennedy debate in 1960 and the coverage of the Vietnam War in the 1960s and 1970s as evidence of the power of visual images to influence the public's response to political and social issues. A number of media and politics scholars have concluded that TV images of a striking and youthful John F. Kennedy in a presidential debate propelled him to victory over Richard Nixon in the 1960 presidential election, and that the shocking war pictures coming out of Vietnam and broadcast on the evening news turned public opinion against the war and played a major role in ending the conflict. It is thus no surprise that the presidential administration of George W. Bush has steadfastly refused to allow any filming of the returning American war dead from Iraq.[50]

More recent tabloid justice coverage includes similarly striking images. Most Americans have seen the videotaped beating of Rodney King, the footage of six-year-old JonBenet Ramsey performing in beauty pageants, the police pursuit of O.J. Simpson's white Ford Bronco on a Los Angeles freeway, or the rather strange scene of Michael Jackson entering the Santa Maria courtroom in his pajamas. In fact, without the presence of such memorable video images, these cases may not have risen to such elevated levels of media frenzy. For instance, media scholar Doris Graber contends that the 1992 trial of convicted serial killer and cannibal Jeffrey Dahmer did not receive extensive media attention because no striking visual images were associated with the crime.[51] Clearly, images are crucial to the success of a television story.

A careful analysis of television news coverage shows that there has been a dramatic shift in the style of coverage since the late 1960s. To examine this change, we sought to quantify the volume of trial and other legal coverage that the networks have presented in their newscasts. Table 2.5 identifies the number of trial-related news stories presented by the three nightly network newscasts since 1968, the first year such broadcasts were archived. Utilizing the Television News Archives at Vanderbilt University, we used the key word "trial" to identify the number of segments that featured this type of coverage on the ABC, CBS, and NBC national news broadcasts.[52] Thus, our analysis in Table 2.5 includes literally any type of trial, from simple murder cases to those involving war crimes. This general measure of trial-related segments is important, because trial coverage of any type potentially exposes the public to information about the judicial process.

The data in Table 2.5 are divided into pre–tabloid justice and tabloid justice eras. In turn, we have broken the tabloid justice era into the two periods that we have discussed previously. The earliest years of the pre–tabloid justice

Table 2.5 Coverage of Trials and Major Legal Investigations on Network News Broadcasts, 1968–2005

Year	Number of News Segments Focusing on Any Trial	Top Cases
Pre–tabloid justice era		
1968	57	Sirhan Sirhan, Huey Newton
1969	470	Sirhan Sirhan, Chicago 7, James Earl Ray
1970	438	Chicago 7, Black Panthers, My Lai Massacre
1971	437	Charles Manson, Vietnam war crimes
1972	280	Daniel Ellsberg, Angela Davis, Harrisburg 7
1973	257	Pentagon Papers, Watergate break-in
1974	725	Kent State shooting, Watergate
1975	331	Joan Little, Patty Hearst, John Connelly
1976	352	Patty Hearst
1977	238	No marquee legal stories
1978	281	No marquee legal stories
1979	285	No marquee legal stories
1980	290	ABSCAM, Burt Lance, Ford Corporation
1981	226	ABSCAM
1982	371	John Hinckley, Claus von Bulow, Wayne Williams
1983	138	John DeLorean
1984	195	John DeLorean
1985	269	Papal assassination, Claus von Bulow
1986	214	No marquee legal stories
1987	257	Bernard Goetz
1988	213	No marquee legal stories
1989	363	Iran/Contra, Lyn Nofzinger, Jim Bakker
1990	277	Iran-Contra, Marion Barry
Tabloid justice era: first period		
1991	168	Manuel Noriega, William Kennedy Smith
1992	277	Jeffrey Dahmer, Mike Tyson, Amy Fisher
1993	343	Menendez brothers
1994	679	O.J. Simpson
1995	882	O.J. Simpson
1996	318	No marquee legal stories
1997	676	O.J. Simpson, Timothy McVeigh, JonBenet Ramsey
1998	632	Paula Jones, Monica Lewinsky
1999	320	Clinton impeachment
2000	102	No marquee legal stories
Tabloid justice era: second period		
2001	163	McVeigh execution, Chandra Levy
2002	251	Elizabeth Smart
2003	201	Michael Jackson, Kobe Bryant
2004	148	Martha Stewart, Scott Peterson, Kobe Bryant
2005	170	Michael Jackson, Saddam Hussein

Source: Television News Archives, Vanderbilt University.

Notes: Entries indicate total number of news segments on the *CBS Evening News, NBC Nightly News,* and *ABC World News Tonight* that reference any trial. "Top cases" are listings of the most covered or most famous cases of that year. For search instructions, see Appendix A.

era, between 1968 and 1974, comprised one of the most tumultuous times in US history. To begin with, this six-year span included trials concerning the assassinations of three major American political figures. In 1968, Clay Shaw was charged with conspiracy to assassinate John F. Kennedy.[53] That same year, Sirhan Sirhan was tried for the murder of Robert Kennedy,[54] and James Earl Ray was successfully prosecuted for the assassination of Martin Luther King Jr.[55] This extraordinary period also included the various criminal investigations and trials of the Weathermen Underground, the Black Panther Party, the Symbionese Liberation Army, and the Chicago Seven.[56] The infamous Pentagon Papers case arose during this time as well. All of these cases clearly meet the previously identified baseline standard of containing broad social and political importance, as their significance transcended the individual participants in each case.

From 1975 through 1989, however, no clear pattern of trial coverage emerges. A number of nationally important stories, including the ABSCAM and Iran-Contra affairs, received considerable coverage, but they did not dominate the news as heavily as did important trials and investigations in the years from 1968–1974. Yet during the late 1970s and the 1980s, we see the media turning toward more "individualized," personality-centered types of cases. Examples include the trials of Claus von Bulow, John Wayne Gacy, and Wayne Williams, all of which were stories of individuals who were accused of murder. The latter two cases did involve serial killers, however, whose crimes were rather extraordinary.

The tabloid justice era, which began in the 1990s, started off rather slowly in terms of the number of trials and investigations covered by the media, but such stories were soon to proliferate. In fact, four of the five years in which trials received the greatest attention occurred between 1994 and 1998. The only exception is 1974, the height of the Watergate scandal and President Richard Nixon's resignation from office, when many in the Nixon administration were prosecuted for their involvement in that affair. And yet, with the exception of Panamanian dictator Manuel Noriega's case, none of the marquee trials of the early part of the 1990s involved political leaders or particularly serious political or public policy questions. Aside from the Clinton-Lewinsky matter, legal coverage since 1990 has been almost entirely concerned with crimes between individuals (husbands killing their wives, children missing or murdered, rape, and so forth). Without question, these cases involve severe individual tragedy and pain, but individually they have little broader significance or societal implications.

Although the number of law-related stories has fluctuated over the years, Table 2.5 shows that total coverage increased dramatically in the 1990s. More specifically, the data presented in Table 2.5 make clear that a sea change in the media's coverage of tabloid justice cases occurred with the 1994 criminal trial of O.J. Simpson. The mean number of trial stories per year between 1968 and 1974 was 381. This number drops off considerably from 1975 through 1990, with the mean number of trial-related news stories falling to 270. Turning to the first era of tabloid justice, 1991–2001, there was an average of almost 440 trial stories per year. Not only does this period contain the highest number of trials of any era, it was also characterized by legal stories with little or no broad public importance. In the second era of tabloid justice, late 2001–2006, there was a dramatic drop, with an average of 187 trial stories per year. This was to be expected, as nightly national news broadcasts shifted their attention to the "war on terror" and military action in Afghanistan and Iraq.

It is also important to consider the different forms of media that are present in each cycle. Traditional, mainstream news sources—newspapers, newsmagazines, network television, and wire services—dominated in the period from 1968–1974. The years between 1975 and 1990 witnessed an increasingly rapid movement of communication and delivery of the news via cable TV, computers, satellites, and fax machines. It was in the 1990s, however, that the speed with which information could be transmitted increased exponentially. Thus, the increase in media coverage of trials and legal investigations is closely correlated with technological developments. The emergence of cable and satellite television and the Internet, for example, have greatly expanded the number of forums where discussion and coverage continue long after the traditional media have abandoned a given legal story.

Comparing Trial Coverage: Charles Manson, Claus von Bulow, O.J. Simpson, and Martha Stewart

One way to illustrate the changes in media coverage over the past four decades is to compare the media's treatment of four notorious legal cases that were the most covered of their respective time periods. From the late 1960s and early 1970s we selected the trial of Charles Manson. The leader of a cult called "The Family," Manson was accused of orchestrating the brutal and grotesque murders of actress Sharon Tate, wife of film director Roman Polanski, and six other Los Angeles residents. The bizarre motive for the killing spree, according to Manson, was to bring about an inevitable war between blacks and whites in the United States. He believed that blacks would ultimately win this war and turn to him for guidance on how to govern a new society. Nearly four decades later, Manson still languishes in a California prison.[57]

We illustrate the 1980s with the trial of Claus von Bulow, a member of the wealthy elite of Rhode Island. Around Christmas of 1980, von Bulow's wife, Sunny, slipped into a coma, in which she apparently remains today (there have been no published reports of her death). The prosecutor in the case charged her husband with attempted murder and accused him of injecting his wife with near fatal doses of insulin. The prosecutor argued that with a $14 million inheritance and a beautiful young mistress at his side, von Bulow had a power-ful motive for murdering his wife.[58] The story was retold in the critically ac-claimed 1990 film *Reversal of Fortune.*

The trial we selected to represent the first period of the tabloid justice era is the 1995 double-murder trial of O.J. Simpson (see Chapter 1 for a descrip-tion of the facts of this case). And finally, more recently, the Martha Stewart financial misconduct trial represents the second period of the tabloid justice era (this case also is summarized in Chapter 1).

Although the comparisons among these cases are certainly imperfect, they share several characteristics. All four involve some degree of celebrity, as well as substantial wealth by some trial participants. An important difference is that the first three trials involve murder charges, whereas the fourth involves crim-inal financial activity. Nevertheless, they all received vast amounts of media coverage. Table 2.6 shows the number of story segments on the three major network news broadcasts that featured each of these stories. Most striking about the data presented in Table 2.6 is the staggering number of national news segments devoted to the Simpson trial. This case received roughly eight times the coverage of the Manson and Stewart trials and more than ten times the cov-erage given to the von Bulow trial. In 1994, before the trial had even begun, the Simpson case had led the news twenty-two times on NBC, twenty-three times on CBS, and twelve times on ABC.[59] The placing of a story at the top of a national newscast has historically signified that it is the most important one of the day. In contrast, the Manson and von Bulow stories never led the na-tional news broadcasts, and the Stewart story led a total of ten times.

The comparison of these four cases helps to highlight the media transfor-mation we are suggesting. The Simpson trial did not receive so much more at-tention simply because it was more "newsworthy"; it garnered more attention because it transpired in the era of tabloid justice. In fact, the Manson case was, arguably, far more intriguing than the Simpson case. The saga of a murderous doomsday cult igniting a race war with the goal of achieving political power seems far more intrinsically interesting than the relatively common story of an abusive husband allegedly murdering his ex-wife, and certainly than von Bulow's allegedly bungled attempt to kill his rich wife. Granted, the racial dy-namics of the Simpson case added an important element, as did Simpson's fame and celebrity.[60] As we discuss in Chapter 5, however, "racialized" cov-erage of the case may actually have fueled the racial overtones of the Simpson proceedings. And finally, the Martha Stewart story can only be understood as a function of her celebrity status in our culture. One looks in vain for any hint of real public importance in her case.

In terms of the legal issues at stake, the von Bulow and Manson cases were perhaps more interesting than either the Simpson or Stewart trials, which were often dominated by lawyerly wrangling. Manson, for example, was not even present for the killings with which he was charged. In the von Bulow

Table 2.6   Number of Network Television News Segments Covering Cases Involving Charles Manson, Claus von Bulow, O.J. Simpson, and Martha Stewart

Case	CBS Evening News	NBC Nightly News	ABC World News	Total
Charles Manson				
1969 (crime occurred August 9)	9	8	8	25
1970 (trial began June 15)	32	34	23	89
1971 (verdict March 29)	8	12	9	29
Total				143
Claus von Bulow				
1980 (crime occurred December 21)	0	0	1	1
1982 (trial began January 11)	14	26	23	63
1983–1984 (case on appeal)	3	2	3	8
1985 (second trial ended April 25)	13	11	9	33
Total				105
O.J. Simpson				
1994 (crime occurred June 12)	132	116	105	353
1995 (trial began January 24 and ended October 3)	241	242	195	678
1996 (civil trial began October 22)	34	36	34	104
1997 (civil trial verdict February 10)	32	28	30	90
Total				1,225
Martha Stewart				
2002 (ImClone founder Waksal arrested June 12)	17	14	16	47
2003 (indicted June 4)	9	5	7	21
2004 (trial began January 27, found guilty March 5)	31	33	28	92
Total				160

Source: Television News Archives, Vanderbilt University.

case, renowned criminal defense attorney and Harvard law school professor Alan Dershowitz convinced the Rhode Island Supreme Court to overturn the attempted murder conviction and order a new trial. In the second trial, von Bulow was acquitted.

Today's Tabloid News Coverage

Nightly Network Newscasts

We now turn to a broader examination of the prominence of tabloid coverage within national news broadcasts. The three network nightly news broadcasts now regularly report on trials and investigations that they believe will pique the nation's interest. To illustrate the prominent role of tabloid cases in mainstream media fare, Table 2.7 presents the programming schedules for the nightly news on important days during the Menendez, Simpson, Woodward, Schiavo, Stewart, and Jackson cases. We present the broadcast schedule for two editions of the evening news for each network. Table 2.7 shows how the networks, in each of the two tabloid justice periods, emphasize tabloid trials and deemphasize more politically and socially meaningful topics. For each of these specific broadcasts, the tabloid justice story received more coverage than any other topic. In ABC's broadcast, coverage of the Menendez trial matched only the duration of the news feature "Person of the Week," which is a profile of a "worthy citizen." In this same broadcast, however, additional coverage was devoted to the equally tabloid-like story concerning figure skaters Tonya Harding and Nancy Kerrigan. CBS's trial coverage of Louise Woodward and NBC's coverage of O.J. Simpson exceeded by three times any other story covered that day. Similarly, in the second period the coverage of Schiavo, Stewart, and Jackson far outweighed the attention paid even to the Iraq war.

In his study of the CBS and NBC newsrooms, Herbert Gans identified some very specific norms, procedures, and imperatives that drove network news organizations' choices. Gans found that most lead news stories received two to three minutes of attention. He noted, however, that "when events that journalists deem to be world-shaking take place . . . the normal daily format may be set aside, with 8 to 10 minutes or more given to one story."[61] This norm, which has been followed by the national news broadcasts since they went to the half-hour format in the late 1950s, was clearly discarded in the 1990s.

What else could explain the levels of media attention given to the trial of Louise Woodward illustrated in Table 2.7? Woodward, an unknown nineteen-year-old woman, came to the United States from Great Britain to work as an *au pair*. The toddler she was accused of shaking to death was not a well-known figure in the United States, and neither were his parents. The trial raised few issues of broad public concern.[62] Yet the story of Louise Woodward received substantially more airtime than did stories with potentially important domestic and foreign policy implications, such as the visit of Chinese premier Jiang Jemin to the United States, the congressional debate on campaign finance reform, and a violent attack on environmentalists who were attempting to stop development in a California redwood forest.

To provide a more complete look at the prevalent network news media coverage, we compared coverage of tabloid justice stories with the top domestic public policy issues in 1997 and 2003, fairly representative years from both the first and second tabloid justice periods. Table 2.8 shows the aggregate number of network news segments devoted to these stories. The news segments are generally anywhere from ten seconds to three or four minutes. We also broke down our analysis by the number of segments on each particular television network.

Table 2.7 Programming Schedules for Three Nightly Network News Broadcasts When Tabloid Justice Stories Were Covered

ABC World News Tonight January 28, 1994		*NBC Nightly News* July 7, 1994		*CBS Evening News* October 31, 1997	
Story	Time	Story	Time	Story	Time
Clinton crime bill	2:10	*Simpson murder case*	9:10	*Au pair murder trial*	8:50
Menendez murder trial	4:30	Colorado wildfires	2:00	Campaign fundraising	:30
Kerrigan/Harding		Floods in the South	1:50	US-China relations	:10
investigation	2:00	Clinton's Haiti policy	2:20	Stock market report	1:20
Deadbeat dad case	2:10	Russian coup trial	:20	Beef plant shutdown	:30
Earthquake relief	:20	New York police		Pepper spray attack on	
Cleveland flood	:10	corruption	2:10	environmentalists	2:00
Race and drug laws	2:20	Abortion protests in		El Niño/weather	:20
Stock market report	:20	Arkansas	:20	Saccharin and cancer	:30
Silent film star dies	:20	Medical cost of		Halloween in France	:10
Bosnia civil war	:20	smoking	:20	Travel in New Orleans	2:30
Economy and politics		Stock market report	:20		
in Russia	1:30	Dinosaur research	1:30		
Person of the week	4:30				

General totals	ABC	NBC	CBS
Introduction/previews/commercials	9:20	9:30	11:00
Total news time	20:40	20:30	19:00
Tabloid crime coverage	6:30	9:10	8:50

Tabloid crime story as a percent of total news

31	45	46

ABC World News Tonight March 31, 2005		*NBC Nightly News* March 5, 2004		*CBS Evening News* June 13, 2005	
Story	Time	Story	Time	Story	Time
Pope health	2:20	*Stewart verdict*	6:30	*Jackson verdict*	7:50
Schiavo death	7:00	Economy/employment	2:50	Iraq/Bush/Guantanamo	2:20
Iraq intelligence		Iraq/constitution	2:10	Fallen hero profile	:40
failures	3:10	Outsourcing of jobs	2:40	*Killen trial*	:30
Iraq attack	:30	Ashcroft hospitalized	:20	Taser investigation	3:00
Sandy Berger plea	:20	Gay marriage debate	2:10	AIDS	:30
Courthouse shooting	:20	Changes in airline		California earthquake	2:20
Auto black boxes	2:00	industry	2:10	Mercedes concept car	2:10
Stock market report	:20				
Koppel leaving					
Nightline	:20				
Prince Charles					
versus the press	2:00				

General totals	ABC	NBC	CBS
Introduction/previews/commercials	10:00	9:30	9:00
Total news time	18:00	19:10	19:20
Tabloid crime coverage	7:00	6:30	8:20

Tabloid crime story as a percent of total news

39	34	39

Source: Television News Archives, Vanderbilt University.
Notes: Numbers represent minutes and seconds. Tabloid justice stories appear in italics.

Table 2.8   Number of Nightly National News Segments Devoted to Tabloid
Justice Stories and Public Policy, Comparing 1997 and 2003

1997 Stories	CBS Evening News	NBC Nightly News	ABC World News	Total
Tabloid justice				
O.J. Simpson civil trial	32	28	30	90
JonBenet Ramsey investigation	37	22	27	86
Gianni Versace murder investigation	22	19	15	56
Paula Jones sexual harassment suit	22	15	11	48
Louise Woodward trial	20	13	14	47
Ennis Cosby murder trial	22	11	13	46
Marv Albert sexual assault trial	2	6	4	12
Domestic public policy				
Medicare	17	24	17	58
Abortion	22	11	18	51
Affirmative action	17	13	13	43
Welfare policy	14	13	13	40
Health care	12	10	13	35
Social security	8	6	10	24
Campaign finance reform	3	8	8	19
Federal budget	9	5	0	14

2003 Stories	CBS Evening News	NBC Nightly News	ABC World News	Total
Tabloid justice				
Martha Stewart investigation	17	14	16	47
Kobe Bryant investigation	14	15	15	44
Michael Jackson investigation	10	6	12	28
Rush Limbaugh drug problems	7	10	9	26
Elizabeth Smart kidnapping	6	6	6	18
Scott Peterson investigation	4	3	3	10
Domestic public policy				
Unemployment/jobs	37	33	42	112
Medicare	25	34	18	77
Abortion	17	13	13	43
Health insurance	9	12	12	33
Tax cuts	10	22	11	33
Gas/oil prices	11	10	9	30
Affirmative action	9	9	11	29

Source: Television News Archives, Vanderbilt University.
Note: For search instructions, see Appendix A.

The most-covered tabloid justice story of 1997 was the civil trial of O.J.
Simpson. The JonBenet Ramsey investigation and the murder of fashion designer Gianni Versace also exceeded or rivaled the coverage given to any public policy or social issue that year. Other topics that received considerable attention included the debate over reforming Medicare, affirmative action
controversies, and welfare reform policies. However, few public policy questions rose to the level of media coverage garnered by the previously mentioned

tabloid justice stories, as well as the trials involving Paula Jones, Louise Wood-ward, and the murder of Ennis Cosby (son of popular entertainer Bill Cosby). Alarmingly, most of the tabloid stories received significantly more media atten-tion than did public policy topics. Many recent critics of journalism in the United States would find this reality troubling, but probably not surprising.[63]

Although not quite as pronounced, coverage from 2003 gives rise to simi-lar conclusions. Unemployment and jobs were the most-covered subjects dur-ing that year. And while here we see no stories comparable to the dominance of the O.J. Simpson and JonBenet Ramsey coverage, attention to tabloid-type law stories reached levels similar to ostensibly more important stories about abor-tion, health care, tax cuts, gas prices, and so on. These numbers are from the time period when the invasion of Iraq was just beginning, and if we had in-cluded "war" or "foreign policy" categories in our searches, they would show that the war pushed much (but certainly not all) tabloid coverage off of the nightly newscasts for a time.

Based on our analysis of nightly network news broadcasts, we can draw two conclusions. First, the networks have increasingly come to spend more time covering human-interest trials that would formerly have been the domain of the tabloid press. The William Kennedy Smith case in 1991 seems to have triggered this coverage, but it became a frenzy with O.J. Simpson's criminal trial in 1995. Second, this analysis lays the groundwork for our contention that at no time in history have the media so frequently and thoroughly inundated the public with portrayals of the workings of the US judicial system. In Chap-ters 4 and 5 we will turn to the question of the impact of this coverage on pub-lic knowledge and attitudes.

Television Newsmagazines: Hard News or Entertainment?

Accompanying the network news broadcasts' embrace of tabloid justice stories was a tremendous growth of prime-time television newsmagazines during the 1990s. These shows became an important component in creating the media frenzy that surrounded, in particular, numerous criminal investigations and tri-als during that decade. Table 2.9 illustrates the presence of such programs since 1993. Even though the number of these programs has recently decreased, they still constitute a significant presence on prime-time television. And although some media scholars consider these programs to occupy the distant periphery of serious news, we believe that they should be considered alongside the flag-ship news broadcasts.[64] The basis for this contention is that the same journal-ists now appear on both types of programs. For instance, Dan Rather, longtime anchor of the *CBS Evening News,* also hosted the newsmagazine *48 Hours.* Tom Brokaw, the former legendary anchor of the *NBC Nightly News,* was a fre-quent contributor to *Dateline.* Similarly, for the program *20/20,* ABC uses its topflight reporters, including noted interviewer Barbara Walters, White House

Table 2.9   Growth in the Number of Prime-Time Newsmagazines on the Major
Networks (number of editions of each program shown every week)

Network	Program	1993	1999	2006
NBC	*Dateline*	1	5	2
ABC	*20/20*	1	3	1
ABC	*Primetime*	0	0	1
CBS	*60 Minutes*	1	2	1
CBS	*48 Hours*	1	1	1
Total		4	11	6

Source: Prime-time television listing, www.ultimatetv.com.

correspondent Sam Donaldson, and prominent journalist Diane Sawyer. The next generation of news anchors, including Charles Gibson, Brian Williams, and Katie Couric, have all been contributors to the TV newsmagazines.

The television newsmagazines play a crucial role in the era of tabloid justice. First, they air on the major networks during prime time, and they enjoy some of the largest audience shares of any type of regular news programming. Second, the format allows for much more detailed analysis of trials and investigations. An hour in length, the newsmagazines are usually divided into two or three fifteen-minute segments, with the rest of the hour devoted to commercials and shorter stories and updates. Often, these programs devote the entire hour to a single legal story. CBS's *48 Hours* is based on this format, whereas NBC's *Dateline* has done this on numerous occasions. These newsmagazines' segments are often structured as mystery stories, with twists and turns in a plot that remains unresolved until the very end of the program. Below are some examples of titles from the segments included in episodes aired through both periods in the tabloid justice era:[65]

"Fortunate Son?" (why John du Pont killed Dave Schultz), *Dateline,* NBC, January 30, 1996

"Murder for Hire" (trial of David Lusskin, accused of trying to hire a man to kill his pregnant girlfriend), *Dateline,* NBC, February 9, 1996

"Haunting Vision" (after twenty-seven years of secrecy, a young woman accuses her father of her mother's murder), *Dateline,* NBC, March 15, 1996

"While She Was Sleeping" (murder trial of small-town banker and mayor), *Dateline,* NBC, May 20, 1997

"The Husband and the Hitman: Man Hires Hitman to Kill His Wife," *20/20,* ABC, April 5, 2000

"The Good Son? Arlene and Seymour Tankleff Are Murdered, Their Son Marty Is Accused of Their Murder," *48 Hours,* CBS, April 4, 2004

"Sex and Lies on Grapevine Lake: The Murder of David Nixon," *48 Hours,* CBS, October 22, 2005

"Sex, Lies, and the Doctor's Wife: The Murder of Karen Tipton," *48 Hours,* CBS, November 12, 2005

"A Dancer's Secret Life and Savage Murder," *Dateline,* NBC, January 5, 2006

As their titles indicate, these programs present true crime stories as dramatic entertainment. Rarely is there an attempt to place them into the context of the real workings of the legal system, the findings of scholars, or general trends in US society. The crime presentations of newsmagazines vividly illustrate what we referred to in Chapter 1 as commodification—"the packaging and marketing of crime (and other law-related) information for popular consumption."[66]

Tabloid Justice Coverage and the Morning News Shows

The evidence presented here suggests that network nightly news broadcasts have reduced their tabloid legal coverage since September 11, 2001. Further, prime-time newsmagazines have lost some of their popularity, as the trends in Table 2.9 clearly reveal. These trends have probably been precipitated by the advent and phenomenal popularity of "reality-based" and contest-type programs, as well as the increase in purely fictional law and criminal justice programs (such as *Law & Order* and *CSI*). However, the previous intensity of tabloid justice coverage during the evening news programs appears simply to have shifted over to the morning news programs. And although there has been no increase in the absolute number of morning news shows, the attention they pay to crime and law stories has expanded dramatically, especially when compared with the coverage of either the prime-time newsmagazines or the network evening newscasts.

Table 2.10 illustrates this trend by comparing coverage of the three most prominent tabloid cases in the five years preceding and following September 11 by the morning shows and the evening newscasts. This table makes clear several important points. First, the morning news shows devoted significant resources to tabloid justice stories in both periods of the tabloid justice era. In the five years prior to September 11, the morning shows presented about 3.3 times more segments on these stories than did the nightly newscasts. However, after the World Trade Center and Pentagon bombings, the morning shows dramatically increased both their absolute number of tabloid justice stories and the ratio of such coverage to that of the evening newscasts. This may have been caused by the "war on terrorism" and the Iraq and Afghanistan invasions pushing the tabloid justice stories off of the thirty-minute evening news agenda. The morning shows, of course, typically have two hours or more to insert updates and vignettes about tabloid legal cases.

Table 2.10 Comparing Coverage of Top Tabloid Justice Cases on Morning and Evening News Programs in the Five Years Preceding and Following September 11, 2001 (number of segments on each story)

	Pre-9/11 (September 11, 1996, through September 11, 2001)				Post-9/11 (September 12, 2001, through September 11, 2006)			
	JonBenet Ramsey Murder	Louise Woodward Trial	O.J. Simpson Civil Trial	Total	Scott Peterson Trial	Michael Jackson Trial	Martha Stewart Trial	Total
Morning news								
Early Show[a]	80	81	328	489	549	560	355	1,464
Today Show	252	108	237	597	434	475	343	1,252
Good Morning America	107	61	99	267	254	308	217	779
Total				1,353				3,495
Evening news								
CBS Evening News	44	26	79	149	14	32	57	103
NBC Nightly News	28	17	75	120	12	29	52	93
ABC World News Tonight	36	18	82	136	13	32	51	96
Total				405				292
Ratio of morning news/evening news				3.3/1				12.0/1

Notes: Entries indicate total number of segments on each program focusing on that specific case. Morning news segments were tabulated using Lexis-Nexis. Nightly news segments were tabulated using Vanderbilt Television Archives.

a. *The Early Show* was known as *This Morning* until 1999.

Thus, we found that the morning shows in the second period of the tabloid justice era presented twelve times more segments on tabloid legal coverage than the evening news programs. A further illustration of this growth can be seen in the fact that *The Early Show* presented nearly twice as many stories on the 2005 Michael Jackson trial than on the 1996–1997 O.J. Simpson civil trial, and even covered the Martha Stewart story more than it had the Simpson case. By any measure the Simpson trials are the quintessential tabloid justice story; it is striking that the morning shows now devote greater resources to stories that are, if anything, even less publicly significant than the Simpson case was. One strong conclusion that we can draw is that, even in the "new world" of the post–September 11 period, tabloid justice coverage has not so much decreased as it has simply been "moved around" to different venues, from the mainstream newscasts and prime-time newsmagazines to the morning newscasts and to fictional law dramas (which we discuss in our next chapter).

Thus, the evening television newsmagazines, in conjunction with the national news broadcasts and morning news shows, have worked together to promote the media frenzy that surrounds tabloid cases. An interested viewer can often watch the latest legal developments on the nightly news, tune in for more in-depth reporting on one of the prime-time newsmagazines, and then awaken to the morning shows and receive updates on each case. News presented so obsessively and constantly begins to crowd out other news. The public becomes very knowledgeable about irregular legal proceedings, and particularly about the personalities involved, but learns little about broader issues and trends in the legal system.

A Note on Television Ratings

The pursuit of viewers has often been cited as the primary reason behind the mainstream media's increasingly more sensational styles and formats. In some instances, particularly on cable television, it is indisputable that tabloid stories have helped to boost ratings.[67] Evidence from the mainstream media, however, is not as clear. Some media outlets appear to have benefited from covering these events whereas others have not.[68] For instance, the evening network newscasts may actually have suffered from their constant coverage of the Simpson case. In the 1994–1995 television season, when the networks covered the Simpson case in epic proportions (see Table 2.6), the ratings share for the nightly news programs dropped to its lowest level in years. The *CBS Evening News* and the *NBC Nightly News* recorded their lowest shares of viewers since before 1970. *ABC World News Tonight* scored its lowest rating since 1978.[69] And since 1995 there has been a slow but steady decline in viewers for all three nightly network news broadcasts (see Table 2.1). Although the decline in viewers for the nightly newscasts certainly relates to broader trends, at the very least we can conclude that the networks' decisions to cover these cases did not inhibit their descent.

However, the ratings of other mainstream news programs, such as ABC's *Nightline* and the television newsmagazines, thrived during the first period of the tabloid justice era. Almost seventy *Nightline* programs focused on the Simpson criminal case.[70] Significantly, the average rating for these programs was 11 percent higher than programs focusing on other subjects.[71] Various accounts of news editors and producers reveal that they were often torn between continuing to cover the Simpson case and moving on to topics that might be deemed more important. The lure of ratings made this a very difficult decision. Importantly, the ratings for television newsmagazines have fallen since around 2000, and several programs such as *60 Minutes II* and some versions of *Dateline* have been cancelled. Finally, the one network news outlet that has not suffered a serious ratings decline since 2000 is the morning programs. For all three networks, ratings for the morning news programs remained relatively stable between 2000 and 2005.[72] For our purposes, this is important because these programs have become the most regular purveyor of tabloid justice stories. In any event, the importance of ratings as a factor in determining a broadcast's focus becomes even more striking in our later consideration of the cable television outlets.

Conclusion

When *Newsweek* writer Jonathan Alter wrote an article at the end of 1994 asserting that nothing could match the string of tabloid stories that paraded across our television screens that year, he probably did not expect to write a similar article in 1997.[73] With the Jackson and Schiavo stories becoming so big, he certainly could have written a similar story in 2005. In 1994 we saw extended coverage of Lorena Bobbitt, Tonya Harding, Paula Jones, O.J. Simpson, and Susan Smith. In 1997 Kelly Flynn (a female fighter pilot forced to resign from the air force over charges of sexual misconduct), Marv Albert, Kathy Lee Gifford (the popular talk show host whose famous husband was caught on camera in a sexually compromising position), JonBenet Ramsey, Louise Woodward, and O.J. Simpson (again) made the headlines. In describing the news environment in 1997, Alter lamented, "No wars? No news? No problem. The news media can just entertain us into a stupor." Further, Alter claimed that as a result of the media's blurring of scandal and hard news, much of the public could no longer differentiate between important public events and mere entertainment.[74] Perhaps most significant, we have found that even in an era of wars, natural disasters, and critical elections (such as we witnessed since 2001), the entire mass media system continues to devote extraordinary levels of attention to tabloid legal stories.

Two basic conclusions emerge from the data presented in this chapter. First, it is important to recognize the role of the mainstream media as the foundation of the news more generally. As the flagship media outlets in the United States have turned aggressively toward the coverage of criminal justice dramas and legal stories, they have in effect given a green light to the rest of the mass media at all levels to follow suit. The competition in the news business compels ever-greater degrees of sensationalism. The news media sources we discuss in the following chapter have seized upon the mainstream media's validation of these cases, thereby immersing US society and culture in tabloid-style law and crime coverage.

Second, we reiterate the point that beginning with the William Kennedy Smith trial in 1991 Americans have been exposed to an unprecedented amount of detailed information about the legal system.[75] The Smith trial, for instance, showed the public firsthand the treatment of a woman bringing a charge of rape. The Simpson trial treated the public to lengthy explanations of evidence and legal rules. The Paula Jones sexual harassment case exposed the public to extensive, technical discussions of the legal definitions of perjury and obstruction of justice. The Terri Schiavo case offered substantial opportunities for public understanding of the US Constitution, the right to privacy, trial versus appellate courts, and judicial federalism. Thus, these cases and the coverage of them provided potential opportunities for the public to learn about the judicial process. Unfortunately, this opportunity for civic education, and perhaps for an increase in public confidence, has been squandered by the style in which the media have chosen to present this information.

As the media environment rapidly evolves, the hard news outlets discussed in this chapter constitute only the more traditional sources of what David Shenk has called the "data smog" that pollutes everyone's "personal orbit."[76] The tabloidization of the media becomes substantially more apparent when we consider the new forms and variations of media that have cranked up both the amount and volume of tabloid justice coverage. We turn to the role of these new media outlets in our next chapter.

Notes

1. Howard Kurtz, *Hot Air* (New York: Basic, 1995), 138. In the end, *Nightline* aired more than seventy shows on Simpson's legal battles.

2. Scot Lehigh, "This Is TV News," *Boston Globe,* August 26, 2006, p. A15.

3. For an early analysis of the prevalence of "crime entertainment" on television, see Joseph Dominick, "Crime and Law Enforcement in Mass Media," in Charles Winick, ed., *Deviance and Mass Media* (Thousand Oaks, CA: Sage, 1978), 105–128. More recently, see Barbara Wilson et al., *National Television Violence Study,* vol. 1 (Thousand Oaks, CA: Sage, 1997); and Elayne Rapping, *Law and Justice as Seen on TV* (New York: New York University Press, 2003).

4. Andrew Kohut, "TV Trials Captivate Public," *Times Mirror Center for the People and the Press,* February 4, 1994, 12.

5. Joseph Carroll, "Public Divided on Charges Against JonBenet's Alledged Killer," *The Gallup Poll,* Gallup News Service, August 22, 2006. For earlier polls on public attitudes about the case, see Charlie Brennan, "Poll: 40% 'Know' Who Killed JonBenet, 25% Contend Mother Killed Beauty Queen," *Rocky Mountain News,* July 8, 1999, p. 5A.

6. For a collection of earlier high-profile cases, see Lloyd Chiasson Jr., ed., *The Press on Trial* (Westport, CT: Praeger, 1997); and Lloyd Chiasson Jr., *Illusive Shadows: Justice, Media, and Socially Significant American Trials* (Westport, CT: Greenwood, 2003).

7. For a brief description of these and other famous cases of the twentieth century, see Edward Knappman, ed., *American Trials of the 20th Century* (Detroit: Visible Ink, 1995). Also see Ronald Goldfarb, *TV or Not TV: Television, Justice, and the Courts* (New York: New York University Press, 1998), 4–5.

8. Identifying the one true trial of the century has become an amusing debate topic for a number of scholars and journalists. See Goldfarb, *TV or Not TV,* chap. 1; and "What Was the 'Trial of the Century'?" *Newsweek,* August 24, 1998, p. 9.

9. Theo Wilson, *Headline Justice* (New York: Thunder's Mouth, 1997), 4.

10. For example, St. Martin's Press publishes a true crime series that often presents the story behind a given crime long before the case ever goes to trial.

11. See Linda Acorn, "Crime in Prime Time: New Shows Capture Audiences," *Corrections Today,* February 1989, 44–46, 54.

12. Peter Johnson and Gary Levin, "Rivera Holds His Tongue on the Eve of 'Upfront,'" *USA Today,* August 24, 1998, p. 3D.

13. Neal Gabler, *Life: The Movie* (New York: Knopf, 1998), 3–10.

14. Derived from analysis of network news broadcasts available through the Vanderbilt Television News Archive. See also Table 2.8.

15. Michael Janofsky, "Marv Albert Pleads Guilty and Is Dismissed by NBC," *New York Times,* September 26, 1997, p. A1.

16. Duff Wilson and Jonathan D. Glater, "Files from Duke Rape Case Give Details but No Answers," *New York Times,* August 25, 2006, p. 1.

17. For further evidence of this transformation, see Richard Davis and Diana Owen, *New Media and American Politics* (New York: Oxford University Press, 1998), 94–107. Although these authors do not address media coverage of the legal system and judicial process per se, they effectively present an account of how the new media culture interacts with the broader political system.

18. Most recent texts on the mass media and politics suggest that, while the media environment is rapidly shifting, the mass media still serve as a gatekeeper to inform the public of important events. See W. Lance Bennett, *News: The Illusion of Politics,* 7th ed. (New York: Longman, 2006); and Hoyt Purvis, *Media, Politics, and Government* (Ft. Worth, TX: Harcourt, 2001).

19. Richard Davis, *The Press and American Politics,* 2d ed. (Upper Saddle River, NJ: Prentice-Hall, 1996), 108–109.

20. For a discussion about how national wire services play a significant role in establishing news for *all* types of news organizations, see David L. Paletz, *The Media in American Politics* (New York: Longman, 1999), 62–63; and David Morgan, *The Capitol Press Corps: Newsmen and the Governing of New York State* (Westport, CT: Greenwood, 1978), 134.

21. For a discussion of how the media set the agenda for policy debates in the criminal justice system, see Ray Surette, *Media, Crime, and Criminal Justice: Images and Realities,* 3d ed. (Belmont, CA: Wadsworth, 2007), 213–217.

22. Davis, *The Press and American Politics,* chap. 8.

23. Gabler, *Life,* 181–184.

24. For a recounting of the *60 Minutes* decision to run the videotape, see Ira Byock, "Snuff Film," *Washington Post,* December 6, 1998, p. C7.

25. Many would argue that these cases, particularly the criminal trial of O.J. Simpson, did raise important national issues. We would argue that the Simpson case only came to symbolize larger issues, such as race or gender relations, as a result of the enormous levels of media coverage involved in the case.

26. Doris Graber, *Crime News and the Public* (Westport, CT: Praeger, 1980), 44. See also Jeremy Harris, Harris Lipschultz, and Michael L. Hilt, *Crime and Local Television News: Dramatic, Breaking, and Live from the Scene* (Mahwah, NJ: Lawrence Erlbaum, 2002).

27. For a description of how newspaper writers have covered trials in the past, see Wilson, *Headline Justice,* 3–11.

28. Stephen Ansolabehere, Roy Behr, and Shanto Iyengar, *The Media Game* (New York: Macmillan, 1993), 40.

29. Herbert Gans, *Deciding What's News: A Study of CBS Evening News, NBC Nightly News, Newsweek, and Time* (New York: Vintage, 1979), 4.

30. Certainly CNN could be considered in this category, as it is a widely and highly regarded television news network. We have chosen to address CNN in Chapter 3 in our discussion of cable news outlets.

31. Gans, *Deciding What's News,* 3–5.

32. The difference between crime news and crime shows can become blurred, as Surette points out in *Media, Crime, and Criminal Justice.* See also Paletz, *The Media in American Politics,* 299.

33. Teresa Ortega, "Dateline Dominates," www.utlimatetv.com.

34. The Society of Professional Journalists revised its code of ethics in 1996 and posted it on the Internet at http://www.spj.org/ethics/index.htm.

35. Ibid.

36. "Project of Excellence in Journalism Survey," Pew Research Center for the People and the Press, June 2005.

37. Ibid. See Joe Abernathy, "Casting the Internet: A New Tool for Electronic News Gathering," *Columbia Journalism Review,* January/February 1993, 56.

38. "Simpson Story Loses Audience: Democratic Congressional Prospects Worsen," *Times Mirror Center of the People and Press,* October 13. 1994, 4.

39. Fox News Opinion Dynamics Poll, December 5, 2003.

40. For a discussion of audience interest levels and the marketing of the Simpson case, see George Lipsitz, "The Greatest Story Ever Sold: Marketing and the O.J. Simpson Trial," in Toni Morrison and Claudia Brodsky Lacour, eds., *Birth of a Nation'hood: Gaze, Script, and Spectacle in the O.J. Simpson Case* (New York: Pantheon, 1997), 3–29.

41. Ansolabehere, Behr, and Iyengar, *The Media Game,* 42–45; and Mathew Robert Kerbel, *Remote and Controlled* (Boulder, CO: Westview, 1995), 12.

42. See Bill Kovach and Tom Rosenstiel, *Warp Speed: America in the Age of Mixed Media* (New York: Century Foundation, 1999).

43. It is common to rely on these three newsmagazines. See Martin P. Wattenberg, *The Decline of American Political Parties: 1952–1988* (Cambridge, MA: Harvard University Press, 1990), 92–98.

44. "British Nanny Sobs After Guilty Verdict, 'Why Did They Do This to Me?'" *Orlando Sentinel,* October 31, 1997, p. A1; "Foreign Faction Threatened to Kill JonBenet in Ransom Note," *Buffalo News,* September 3, 1997, p. A1; Marilyn Robinson, "No Semen Found at Ramsey Slay Scene," *Denver Post,* March 15, 1997, p. A1.; Julia Prodis Sulek, "Bizarre Hypotheses Surface in Laci Peterson Case," *Houston Chronicle,* October 12, 2003, p. 7; Tamara Jones, "Culkin Shared Jackson's Bed but Says He Wasn't Molested," *Washington Post,* May 12, 2005, p. A01; Nick Madigan, "Ranch Manager Says Jackson Owned Erotica," *New York Times,* May 11, 2005, p. 14; Nick Madigan, "Jackson's Prints Identified on Sex Magazines," *New York Times,* March 26, 2005, p. 9; Cathleen Falsani, "Finding Hope Even in Schiavo's Barbaric Death," *Chicago Sun-Times,* April 1, 2005, p. 28; Bill Daley, "Can Martha Find True Happiness Behind Bars?" *San Francisco Chronicle,* February 11, 2004, p. E-1; Mark Ellis, "Kidnapped Teenager Smart Possibly Held by Mind Control," *Columbus Dispatch* (Ohio), March 23, 2003, Sunday; George Rush and Joanna Molloy, "Aruba Cops Think X May Mark the Spot," *Daily News* (New York), August 5, 2005, p. 16; and Tasgola Karla Bruner, "Wilbanks Told Lurid Tale of Abduction, Sex Acts," *Atlanta Journal-Constitution,* May 12, 2005, p. 8JJ.

45. Jerry Adler, "The Strange World of JonBenet," *Newsweek,* January 20, 1997, p. 43; Richard Woodbury, "JonBenet; Taking the Hunt into His Own Hands," *Time,* August 4, 1997, p. 12; Marc Peyser, "A Body in the Basement," *Newsweek,* January 13, 1997, p. 38; Matthew Cooper, "Marv Goes to the Showers," *Newsweek,* October 6, 1997, p. 40; Dorian Freedman, "He's Out of the Game," *US News and World Report,* October 6, 1997, p. 8; Jerry Alder, "Murder 90210: Crime Styles of the Young, Rich, and Impatient," *Newsweek,* August 2, 1993, p. 60; Elise Christianson, "How the Kidnappers Controlled Elizabeth," *Newsweek,* March 31, 2003, p. 8; Walter Kern, "Invasion of the Baby Snatchers," *Time,* August 26, 2002, p. 38; Lisa Stein, "Jacko's Hokey-Pokey," *US News and World Report,* May 10, 2004, p. 16; David J. Jefferson and Andrew Murr, "From Moonwalk to Perp Walk," *Newsweek,* December 1, 2003, p. 38; Richard Corliss, "Jacko's Bad Day in Court," *Time,* March 21, 2005, p. 56; and Mark Hosenball, "Martha Stewart: Is She in 'Deep DooDoo'?" *Newsweek,* August 19, 2002, p. 10.

46. These headlines can be found in the archives of the *National Enquirer* website: http://www.nationalenquirer.com.

47. Turner, "A Tabloid Shocker," 70.

48. Wilson, *Headline Justice,* 3–11.

49. The argument that we are now a "snapshot culture" has been put forward in a number of seminal works by scholars in different fields. For instance, see Neil Postman, *Amusing Ourselves to Death: Public Discourse in the Age of Show Business* (New York: Viking Penguin, 1986); Michael Parenti, *Inventing Reality* (New York: St. Martin's, 1986); and Arthur Asa Berger, *Manufacturing Desire* (New Brunswick, NJ: Transaction, 1996).

50. For a description of US policy regarding fallen soldiers in the Iraq War, see Gregg Zoroya, "Return of US War Dead Kept Solemn, Secret," *USA Today,* December 31, 2003, p. 4A. For an analysis of the role of media in Vietnam, see Daniel C. Hallin, *The "Uncensored War": The Media and Vietnam* (New York: Oxford University Press, 1986).

51. Doris Graber, *Mass Media and American Politics,* 5th ed. (Washington, DC: Congressional Quarterly Press, 1997), 152.

52. We included, in the totals for 1997 and 1998, segments mentioning JonBenet Ramsey and Monica Lewinsky that did not include the term *trial*.

53. For a discussion of the criminal investigation and trial proceedings, see Jim Garrison, *On the Trail of Assassins* (New York: Sheridan, 1988).

54. See John Christian and William Turner, *The Assassination of Robert Kennedy* (New York: Random House, 1978).

55. For a discussion of all three of these assassinations, see Stephen Goode, *Assassination! Kennedy, King, Kennedy* (New York: Watts, 1979).

56. For a description of many of these and other notable cases, see Knappman, *American Trials of the 20th Century.*

57. For a full account of the Manson crimes and trial as written by the lead prosecutor in the case, see Vincent Bugliosi with Curt Gentry, *Helter Skelter: The True Story of the Manson Murders* (New York: W. W. Norton, 1974). Also see Tex Watson, *Will You Die for Me?* (Old Tappan, NJ: Fleming Revell, 1978).

58. For a full account of the case, see Alan M. Dershowitz, *Reversal of Fortune* (New York: Random House, 1986); and William Wright, *The Von Bulow Affair* (New York: Delacorte, 1983).

59. These tabulations are based on an analysis of the Television News Archives, Vanderbilt University.

60. O.J. Simpson is, perhaps, the most famous person ever to be tried for murder in the United States, and this automatically dictated that there would be a substantial amount of interest in the crime.

61. Gans, *Deciding What's News,* 3.

62. Many media outlets attempted to link the circumstances of this case to broader issues of childcare. In other words, the story was of national interest because the death of a small child at the hands of a childcare worker evoked the fears of many who trust their children to babysitters or daycare facilities. But although this may explain some of the interest, this case would not appear to raise these issues any more clearly than hundreds of other cases of child neglect and endangerment that occur each year.

63. Many who study the mass media, particularly in the arena of politics, have concluded that there is very little issue coverage. See, for instance, Guido H. Stempel III and John Windhauser, *The Media and the 1984 and 1988 Elections* (Westport, CT: Greenwood, 1991).

64. See Paletz, *The Media in American Politics,* 357, for a brief but concise explanation of why newsmagazines are difficult to classify.

65. First-period examples are drawn from program descriptions of *Dateline NBC* and CBS's *48 Hours* based on the schedules maintained by Burrelles Transcript Service. Second-period examples are drawn from program title listings found on abc.com, nbc.com, and cbs.com.

66. Surette, *Media, Crime, and Criminal Justice,* 21.

67. Cynthia Littleton, "Verdict Propels Tabloid Ratings," *Broadcasting and Cable,* October 1, 1995, p. 7.

68. Joe Mandrese and Thomas Tyler, "Simpson Shakes New TV Season," *Advertising Age,* October 16, 1995, p. 8.

69. Information received directly from Nielsen Media Research, 1998.

70. Based on ABC News Program Listing guide, provided by ABC News, Livonia, Michigan.

71. Based on *Nightline's* ratings for the period of June 12, 1994, through October 10, 1995, provided by Nielsen Media Research.

72. "The State of the News Media 2006: An Annual Report on American Journalism"; information can be accessed at http://www.stateofthenewsmedia.com/2006, see section on "Network News."

73. Jonathan Alter, "America Goes Tabloid," *Newsweek,* December 26, 1994, p. 34.

74. Ibid.

75. Howard Kurtz, "TV in Court: Healthy or 'Debasing' Eye on Justice?" *Washington Post,* December 12, 1991, p. A1.

76. For a wide-ranging discussion of the role of "information" in the daily lives of citizens, see David Shenk, *Data Smog: Surviving the Information Glut* (San Francisco: Harper, 1998).

THREE

Tabloid Justice and the Evolution of New Media

I have dedicated over two years of my life to covering the Simpson case and I will see it through to the end.

> —Geraldo Rivera, host of the CNBC
> mid-1990s program *Rivera Live*[1]

The trajectory of the JonBenet case highlights a new stratification of television news. The major broadcast networks that once set the nation's agenda have settled into a less powerful evening niche offering more traditional journalistic fare while their cable rivals have matured into a kind of 24-hour tabloid broadcast. . . . As such they're more likely to focus on the sensational to keep the ratings up.

> —Alexandra Marks, *Christian Science Monitor* reporter,
> writing about the 2006 reemergence of the JonBenet Ramsey case[2]

When news oozes 24 hours a day it's not really news anymore. The TV becomes ambient noise. The newspaper becomes wallpaper. Finding the patterns of importance becomes hard. It's easier—and more profitable—just to make the consumer gape.

> —Jonathan Alter, writer for *Newsweek* magazine[3]

We live in an age where news (and every other imaginable type of information) is available at a moment's notice. Gone are the days of eagerly awaiting delivery of the morning newspaper or presentation of the evening newscast to learn what was going on in the world. Now, the *New York Times* and the *Washington Post* are rarely the first to break a big story, and even if they are, the story is likely to have been reported the night before on a cable television news outlet such as CNN or MSNBC, on the Internet (whether on various independent sites or on blogs), or in several such venues almost simultaneously. For example, in the summer of 1998, the *New York Times* received the first word that President Clinton planned to change his previous story and admit to a sexual relationship with Monica Lewinsky. Long before the article appeared in the morning paper, cable television widely broadcast the revelation. Similarly, Court TV anchor Diane Diamond broke the story of Michael Jackson's imminent arrest, which set off a journalistic frenzy on cable and network television news, as well as on the Internet.[4] John Temple, editor and publisher of the *Rocky Mountain News,* the "paper of record" for the JonBenet Ramsey murder investigation, illustrates further the rise of the Internet. Whereas that paper's Internet coverage was little more than an afterthought during the original investigation of the murder in 1997, with the arrest of John Mark Karr as a suspect in the case in 2006 the paper's website garnered almost twice as many hits as the paper's typical daily circulation. Temple notes that the public's thirst for information about the case apparently needed to be satisfied before the newspaper itself could be delivered each day.[5] Clearly, we live in an environment where we no longer wait for the news—today's news is immediate, and it permeates our lives.

In the midst of this fast-paced news environment, tabloid justice coverage has become omnipresent. Stories and news about O.J., Monica, JonBenet, Scott and Laci, Kobe, Martha, Michael, and the "Runaway Bride" flow, it seems, from every direction. Nightly newscasts contain information about these cases. Morning newspapers carry headlines about the trials and investigations. Magazine covers depict the players. And as we stand in supermarket checkout lines, tabloid headlines provide further rumors and details. Nowhere is the discussion of these cases more prominent and more enduring, however, than in the new and emerging forms of mass media, and in the changes to existing media institutions.

The primary forms of new media on which we focus in this chapter are cable television and the Internet, but we also briefly consider the importance of the new fictional law and crime dramas, and the continuing presence of talk radio. Each of these sources has provided extensive and ongoing coverage of the whole range of tabloid cases. In 1994 and 1995, for instance, several cable talk television programs, most notably *Rivera Live* and *Charles Grodin* (both of these shows have gone off the air), discussed the Simpson case almost every evening. In fact, roughly 400 *Rivera Live* programs covered the Simpson case, making it, in effect, a show entirely devoted to covering a single story.[6] Even the October 3, 1995, conclusion of the Simpson criminal trial did not end the news media's coverage. Rather, it marked the beginning of yet another new phase—the civil trial. In 1996 and 1997 the cable talk programs also devoted intense coverage to the Louise Woodward case and the JonBenet Ramsey murder investigation. In 1998, cable talk shows turned their full attention to the presidential scandal involving Monica Lewinsky, covering it just as they would any other tale of sexual misconduct and intrigue. A relentless drumbeat of talk television "analysis" surrounds these tabloid justice trials and investigations. Further, these trends have become "normalized" since 2001, such that few Americans even take notice of the fact that on "important" days in the Peterson, Kobe Bryant, Martha, or Michael stories, cable news coverage is saturated with the discussion of these cases.

Alongside cable news programs, the Internet has emerged, especially in the past ten years, as the newest and most complex form of new media. The Internet combines all previously existing sources of news and information—print journalism, visual news reporting, interactive news websites, citizen reporting and commentary, and real-time discussion. Simply typing the key words "Jon-Benet," "Laci Peterson," "Monica Lewinsky," or "Martha Stewart" yields an almost overwhelming array of news stories, games, video and audio clips, and editorials on these subjects. The increased ownership of laptop/notebook computers (especially now that there is widespread wireless capability) and the developing Internet tools available through cellular telephones and "palm pilots" now make it possible to access such information without even being physically tied to a particular place. In the modern media age, talk, news, and information are always easily available and readily accessible.

In this chapter we argue that the emergence of the new media forms and variations has substantially inundated and presented the public with information about tabloid trials and investigations. The almost-constant news and commentary about these cases keep them in the forefront of our national consciousness. Long after more traditional media outlets move on to other stories, the new media outlets continue to prod, discuss, dissect, and examine tabloid stories from every possible angle. As a result, Americans now receive previously unmatched amounts of information about the legal system. In this era of expanded coverage the public has the opportunity to view firsthand the judicial process and its actors, such as judges, prosecutors and defense lawyers, law enforcement officers, criminologists, and expert witnesses. In many instances, the viewer is able to consider the same evidence that jurors see. In particular, those under the age of thirty now learn much of what they know about the legal system through exposure to tabloid justice cases in the electronic media, including fictional television presentations of crime and the judicial process.

To explore the prevalence and impact of the new media in the era of tabloid justice, we first offer a more specific description of just what we mean by the term *new media,* and we identify the central features of the new media environment. Second, we analyze the manner in which cable news television, talk radio programs, the Internet, and fictional law dramas help to fuel the frenzy that often surrounds tabloid cases.

Defining the New Media

The creation of new technologies has always precipitated broad changes in the style, delivery, and focus of the news. Media scholars Richard Davis and Diana Owen have asserted, however, that defining the new media is a difficult task, as the role that the media play in people's lives is now so much more multifaceted.[7]

They argue that a complicated mix of "rapidly changing technology, increased public discussion, and a limitless potential to educate" distinguishes the new media from the more traditional hard news outlets.[8] Even the Pew Research Center for the People and the Press, which offers a purely "technological" definition of new media (simply, cable television and the Internet), emphasizes that the US media culture has changed dramatically since the 1990s.[9] Discussing the 1992 presidential election, media scholar Hoyt Purvis found that candidates were seeking out "new media" outlets on cable news, late-night TV, and radio, representing the first year presidential candidates received meaningful and extensive coverage beyond the mainstream media.[10]

Prior to discussing the structural factors that have converged to create the new media environment, it is important to refer to several noteworthy events in the early 1990s that provided an impetus for ushering in the new media era. Some analysts identify CNN's coverage of the Gulf War in 1991 as the event that lent credibility to the around-the-clock news concept.[11] Coverage of the first conflict in the Gulf provided viewers with continuous footage of "smart bombs," fighter plane and missile deployments, and daily military press briefings. The coverage that accompanied the war allowed Americans, for the first time, to follow the conflict closely and visually. Although there has been some serious criticism of CNN's war coverage, the increase in its ratings during the period indicated to other news organizations that 24-hour news could be successful.[12] In sum, although CNN's nonstop news format had already existed for more than a decade, the Gulf War validated the credibility and utility of this approach.

The 1991 trial of William Kennedy Smith and the 1991 Senate confirmation hearings of Supreme Court nominee Clarence Thomas were two other events central to ushering in the new media environment, albeit in different ways.[13] As previously discussed, the Kennedy Smith episode served as the first marquee trial to receive gavel-to-gavel coverage on the then-new Court TV channel. The dramatic confirmation hearings of Thomas, who faced charges of sexual harassment by former government employee Anita Hill, riveted the country for three days. Many cable and broadcast networks chose to air the hearings in their entirety. The dynamics of race (Justice Thomas was only the second African American ever nominated to the Court) and allegations of sexual misconduct riveted the nation as more than 80 percent of the public claimed to have watched at least some of the live Senate hearings.[14] These events, which included lurid and explicit language about pornography, rape, and sex, as well as strenuous accusations by Thomas that he was a victim of racism, may have helped to normalize the presentation of specific details about sexual and graphic allegations in mainstream news broadcasts.

As the 1990s unfolded, a number of structural and social factors converged to create the new media environment. Not only had technology changed, but the boundaries of acceptable subject matter appeared to be changing as well. It is important to note that most of the new media outlets on which we focus share many of the fundamental characteristics of the traditional media discussed in Chapter 2. Because many cable television news outlets and Internet sites are formally affiliated with mainstream news organizations, they acquire the same veneer of legitimacy with which the major networks and more respected print outlets are regarded. But despite the new media's similarities to the traditional outlets, at least three characteristics—*new technology, commercialism,* and *populism*—distinguish them.[15]

First, since 1990 there has been rapid growth in new technology, and especially in new uses of existing technology. In recent years the importance of cable television as a news medium has grown dramatically. And although cable is not a new outlet per se (it dates from at least the early 1970s), its widespread use as a setting for all-news channels is unprecedented. Beyond the growth of cable, the biggest change in the technological environment involves the emergence of the Internet. Never before has an information source instantaneously provided thousands of pages of information about virtually any topic from an endless array of sources. The Internet is now used by journalists and writers to research stories, and by news organizations to present information and interact with consumers.[16] Online-only "magazines" such as *Salon, Slate,* and the *Drudge Report* broke major news stories about Paula Jones and Monica Lewinsky. Gossip websites are also having their impact by breaking stories. For instance, TMZ.com, a self-described "24/7 on-demand entertainment news network on the Web," was the first to break the news of movie star Mel Gibson's drunk-driving arrest and antisemitic rant in 2006.[17]

More important, a significant portion of the public now looks to the Internet as its primary source of news, information, and entertainment.[18] The number of Americans who can access information online has increased exponentially. A 1998 survey by the Pew Research Center found that 41 percent of Americans had Internet access, and more than 50 percent of those regularly accessed news on the Net.[19] By 2006 it was estimated that about two-thirds of American citizens, or over 200 million people, had regular Internet access.[20] Although it is still too early in the evolution of this technology to comprehend its ultimate impact on the dissemination of news and information, the Internet has turned into a critically important vehicle for political, legal, social, and cultural discourse of every kind.[21]

A second important aspect of the new media environment is commercialism. Historically, numerous commentators have raised concerns about the objectivity and fairness of the news media.[22] Many have suggested that the news cannot be delivered objectively when news organizations must compete for viewers and profits.[23] Other observers have voiced concerns about the trend toward corporate consolidation of media outlets.[24] The paramount importance of attracting viewers, readers, or computer users may undermine the many idealized media roles discussed in our introductory chapter. Further, the intensified competition spurred by the new media environment may corrupt decisions about newsworthiness by allowing commercial considerations to trump the intrinsic importance of a story.

In providing coverage of tabloid justice cases, the new media outlets emphasize the characteristics of serialization and personification, which we discussed in Chapter 1. The media benefit from lengthy trials, which allow anticipation and drama to build to an often unpredictable verdict. The serialization of these proceedings is particularly important for cable television because of the high number of programs that are fully or partly devoted to covering legal proceedings. The constant tracking and regular updating of cases appears to garner large audiences (at least by cable television standards). There is a seemingly endless pool of willing attorneys and other pundits to be interviewed. To further create interest, the new media also strongly emphasize personification. Apparently, trials and legal investigations are more engaging to consumers when viewers have an intimate knowledge of the individuals involved, even at the expense of a particularly clear understanding of the legal and structural components of these dramas.

A final characteristic of the new media environment is populism. In the 1990s, news and information outlets encouraged—and in some cases, overtly relied upon—citizen input and participation. Writing in *The New Yorker,* Nicholas Lehman calls this "journalism without journalists."[25] As Richard Davis and Diana Owen explain, "The new media enhance the public's ability to become actors, rather than merely spectators."[26] Talk radio, which began to gain popularity in the late 1970s, was the first medium to incorporate citizen participation (via listener calls) into the basic format of most programs. The top talk radio hosts of the late 1990s based the format of their programs on incorporating the opinions and comments of citizen callers. Further, radio hosts like Tom Leykis, a national talk radio host who frequently discusses tabloid justice cases, often use listener e-mail to establish the subject of each program.

Beyond radio, many cable television news programs, such as CNN's *Larry King Live,* the Fox News Channel's *The O'Reilly Factor,* and MSNBC's *Scarborough Country* and *The Abrams Report* either take live phone calls or solicit e-mails from viewers. But even though talk radio and news-talk television encourage the active participation of their audiences, the Internet offers an even more accessible—and less demanding—means for citizen participation in the realm of news and commentary.[27] Most news organizations now have interactive websites and blogs, many of which ask people to reply to questions or post their opinions on timely topics, often including tabloid justice cases. Electronic chat rooms have also created opportunities for people to carry on cyber-conversations with complete strangers. In today's news environment, citizens need not merely absorb information or settle for passive entertainment. They can easily become a part of the news themselves.

One final new "vehicle" for tabloid justice–style legal information has come about through the amazing growth of fictional criminal justice and other law-related dramatic shows. This development warrants additional discussion, and we deal with this phenomenon in a later section of this chapter.

Cable Television Programming in the Tabloid Justice Era

The Rise of Cable News Channels

Cable television's 24-hour presentation of news plays an important role in creating the media frenzy surrounding high-profile legal stories. Viewers surfing through various cable channels repeatedly hear the soon-to-be-familiar names of the famous and the infamous players in each drama. CNN has been the pioneer in this around-the-clock news coverage. It first went on the air in 1980, adding a second 24-hour news channel, Headline News, in 1982. CNN's ratings languished for much of the 1980s, though, and the network did not gain full public recognition as a news leader until its 1991 coverage of the Gulf War.[28] CNN now presents a diverse schedule of programming that includes narrowly tailored shows dealing with sports, entertainment, fashion, business, travel, and politics, in addition to more straightforward newscasts. The programming schedule of Headline News is mostly composed of a continuous succession of thirty-minute national broadcasts.

Although CNN and Headline News were the only cable news channels to emerge during the first several years of the 1980s, a number of other news-related cable channels, such as CSPAN, the Discovery Channel, Lifetime, the History Channel, and ESPN, all began to develop during the mid-1980s as well. This expansion helped to promote cable television as an outlet for news and other kinds of increasingly specialized programming. By the end of the 1980s and throughout the 1990s, several additional news channels developed. CNBC, for example, concentrates heavily on business news, although for most of its history during prime time its format changed to talk television, with programming that often emphasized legal and political commentary. MSNBC and the Fox News Channel, the two newest entrants in the 24-hour news game, embrace formats that are most likely to encourage constant discussion about tabloid cases. Their programming schedules are almost entirely devoted to general news and commentary. For the purposes of our discussion, we also include Court TV, which presents 24-hour coverage of various legal proceedings (heavily skewed toward murder trials). This channel also provides news and analysis about trials and legal issues throughout the country. In 1997, Court TV began broadcasting reruns of dramatic fictional crime series (such as *Law & Order* and *NYPD Blue*) as well, further blurring the line between the real judicial process and criminal justice infotainment. The Court TV phenomenon was surely a precursor to the trend that began in about 2001, which saw an explosion of fictional legal dramas, many of which liberally adapted characteristics and plots from the actual tabloid justice cases of the day. Regardless of programmatic nuances, each of these channels has devoted extensive attention to the tabloid justice cases under consideration here. A listing of these news channels and their start-up dates are presented in Table 3.1.

Beyond the national cable news programs, an important trend has been the development of local 24-hour news stations. By 1997 there were at least twelve such ventures, some based in cities such as New York and Chicago, with others seeking to provide the news of an entire state.[29] By 2005 many smaller metropolitan areas, such as Albany, New York, and Austin, Texas, also had their own local 24-hour news channels. These broadcasts are also regular transmitters of national-level tabloid justice stories.

The Style and Substance of Cable News Programs

To provide a better sense of the formats of these 24-hour news channels, we have presented the daily programming schedule for the Fox News Channel in Table 3.2. Although one of the later entrants into the 24-hour news game, Fox News now ranks as the highest-rated cable news network. Its rapid rise since 1996 has been the subject of considerable discussion, especially given the well-documented conservative leanings of the station and its viewers. Programs on the cable news networks tend to fall into three categories: guests/pundits, straight news, and focused programs.

The guests/pundits format usually has a primary host, is organized around a topic or topics of the day, and offers a panel of "expert" commentators typically composed of lawyers and political activists, although politicians and actual trial participants often appear as well. Panels engage in lively and, at times, quite rancorous discussions of the topic du jour. *Dayside,* a mid-day program, adds a live studio audience to the mix. The straight news category includes programs with anchors and short news stories, a format similar to that of tradi-

Table 3.1   **Start-up Dates of 24-Hour News Channels**

Channel	Start-up Date
CNN	June 1, 1980
CNN's Headline News	January 1, 1982
CNBC	April 17, 1989
Court TV	July 1, 1991
MSNBC	July 15, 1996
Fox News	October 17, 1996

Source: Network offices.

Table 3.2 Programming Schedule of Fox News, July 2006

Time Slot	Program Title	Program Type	Show Description
6 a.m.–7 a.m.	Fox & Friends First	Guests/pundits	Political and news talk, with news headlines, interviews, and reports.
7 a.m.–9 a.m.	Fox & Friends	Guests/pundits	Political and news talk, with news headlines, interviews, and reports.
9 a.m.–1 p.m.	Fox News Live	Straight news	Covers top news stories of the day with commentary and discussions.
1 p.m.–2 p.m.	Dayside	Guests/pundits	Hosted by Mike Jerrick and Juliet Huffy. Covers news topics in front of a live audience.
2 p.m.–3 p.m.	Fox News Live	Straight news	Covers top news stories of the day with commentary and discussions.
3 p.m.–4 p.m.	Studio B	Straight news	Hosted by Shepherd Smith. Covers top news stories of the day.
4 p.m.–5 p.m.	Your World	Focused program	Hosted by Neil Cavuto. Covers business and stock market news.
5 p.m.–6 p.m.	The Big Story	Guests/pundits	Hosted by John Gibson. Covers the major news stories of the day with interviews and debates.
6 p.m.–7 p.m.	Special Report	Guests/pundits	Hosted by Brit Hume. Covers political news and features a roundtable discussion on the day's biggest stories.
7 p.m.–8 p.m.	Fox Report	Straight news	Hosted by Shepherd Smith. Covers major stories of the day. Modeled on network nightly news shows.
8 p.m.–9 p.m.	The O'Reilly Factor	Guests/pundits	Hosted by Bill O'Reilly. Features commentary on news items, interviews, and debates.
9 p.m.–10 p.m.	Hannity & Colmes	Guests/pundits	Hosted by Sean Hannity and Alan Colmes. Features political debates between conservatives and liberals.
10 p.m.–11 p.m.	On the Record	Focused program	Hosted by Greta Van Susteren. Focuses on legal and criminal issues. Features expert analysis and commentary.
11 p.m.–12 p.m.	The O'Reilly Factor	Guests/pundits	Replay
12 p.m.–1 a.m.	Special Report	Guests/pundits	Replay
1 a.m.–2 a.m.	Your World	Focused program	Replay
2 a.m.–3 a.m.	Hannity & Colmes	Guests/pundits	Replay
3 a.m.–4 a.m.	On the Record	Focused program	Replay
4 a.m.–5 a.m.	The O'Reilly Factor	Guests/pundits	Replay
5 a.m.–6 a.m.	Your World	Focused program	Replay

Source: Programming schedule from www.foxnews.com/fnctv/index.html as of July 15, 2006.

tional newscasts. The third category, focused programs, offers shows that cover a specific news area, such as sports, travel, fashion, or entertainment. For instance, a show such as *Your World,* hosted by Neil Cavuto, which focuses almost exclusively on business and the economy, is not really conducive to a sustained discussion of tabloid trials. In contrast, Greta Van Susteren's *On the Record,* another focused program, is designed to cover legal stories.

If a news story is deemed to merit special coverage, though, the 24-hour news stations can quickly adapt their programming accordingly. In fact, the cable news outlets are much more likely to devote significant time to these trials and legal investigations than the major networks (ABC, CBS, and NBC), which tend to stick with their normal programming schedules. Even narrowly focused cable news programs readily alter their schedules to present interesting legal investigations and trials. For instance, during O.J. Simpson's criminal trial, CNN provided extensive live coverage that preempted much of its normal schedule. In another example, in August 1998 the Fox News Channel, CNN, and MSNBC each broadcast the entire four hours of President Clinton's previously recorded grand jury testimony. And, as already mentioned, on the day of the Michael Jackson verdict each of the cable news channels interrupted their regular programming schedules to broadcast several hours of live coverage from the Santa Maria courthouse and the Neverland Ranch.

To illustrate the prevalence of tabloid justice cases in cable news programming, we examined one of the top-rated programs from each of three networks—CNN, MSNBC, and Fox News. Table 3.3 shows the presence of tabloid justice coverage on *The O'Reilly Factor* (Fox News), *Larry King Live* (CNN), and *Countdown with Keith Olberman* (MSNBC) during 2005. We sought to determine what percentage of the total number of these shows included a high-profile tabloid justice story in their nightly programming. Such a story was defined as one focusing on one of the five most dominant legal cases of 2005, which were those involving Michael Jackson, Natalee Holloway (the Alabama teen who went missing on the island of Aruba), Martha Stewart, Terri Schiavo, and Jennifer Wilbanks (the so-called Runaway Bride). This method of counting ultimately produces a low number as it does not include all of the times the programs focused on lower-profile criminal stories. One interesting finding is that *Larry King Live,* which one might consider to be the "softest" of the three programs in that it predominantly features show-business personalities in addition to political and current events figures, actually included the lowest percentage of tabloid justice stories in 2005. (However, King obviously covers a much smaller absolute number of different stories per program—while focusing on each piece more extensively than the other two shows in question.) *The O'Reilly Factor,* which fancies itself as a hard-hitting program confronting the most important issues of the day, contained about three times more tabloid justice coverage as *Larry King Live,* while Olberman's show gave about twice as much attention to these five stories as did King's.

Only one of the five cases appearing in Table 3.3 can be thought of as even remotely having serious national public policy implications—Terri Schiavo. Arguably, though her actual case involved only Schiavo and her family, the end-of-life issues raised could have potentially shed light on a set of problems confronted by thousands of Americans each year. The other four cases are, as we have already observed, largely of interest for their entertainment value rather than for what they might teach us about the legal system. That said, it is interesting to note that the most-covered story on *The O'Reilly Factor* was the case of Natalee Holloway, while on the other two shows it was Michael Jackson. In over a third of all his shows that year, O'Reilly included a segment on Natalee Holloway, and, as that case has still not been solved as of this writing, he continued to cover it throughout 2006 as well.

The pervasiveness of tabloid-style legal stories and the degree to which they are pursued on cable news channels is further illustrated in Table 3.4. This table lists all of the legal participants, family members, witnesses, journalists, and experts interviewed by Greta Van Susteren, the host of *On the Record,* in covering the Natalee Holloway story. Over the course of about a year, from June 2005, when the story first broke, to July 2006, at which point the case remained unsolved, Van Susteren covered the story almost daily, interviewing a total of more than fifty-six different people. Van Susteren herself traveled to Aruba several times to report from the crime's locale. Several individuals appeared on the show more than once, such as Holloway's mother, Beth, who was interviewed on the program forty-one times during the year. As this example illustrates, these stories are turned into melodramas where anyone with any relevant perspective or intriguing piece of information is considered to be a legitimate news source.[30]

Table 3.3   Presence of Tabloid Justice Cases in Selected Cable Programs, 2005

	The O'Reilly Factor (Fox)	Larry King Live (CNN)	Countdown with Keith Olberman (MSNBC)
Total number of programs	233	369[a]	252
Number of programs that discussed a legal or tabloid-style case, by topic			
Michael Jackson	59 (25)	49 (13)	113 (45)
Natalee Holloway	80 (34)	24 (7)	9 (4)
Martha Stewart	13 (6)	32 (9)	29 (12)
Terri Schiavo	29 (12)	17 (5)	19 (8)
Jennifer Wilbanks	15 (6)	10 (3)	19 (8)
Percentage of programs that discussed a legal or tabloid-style case	64	24	54

Sources: Show transcripts for *The O'Reilly Factor* and *Larry King Live* available through Lexis-Nexis. *Countdown with Keith Olberman* transcripts available on www.msnbc.com.

Note: a. This number includes the weekend versions and multiple daily editions.

Entries in parentheses represent the percentage of programs in 2005 that discussed the case.

Table 3.4   All Participants or Experts Interviewed for the Natalee Holloway Story by _On the Record,_ June 2005–July 2006

Individual Interviewed, Connection to Case	Number of Times Interviewed
Beth Holloway Twitty, Natalee's mother	41
Dave Holloway, Natalee's father	16
George "Jug" Twitty, Natalee's stepfather	13
Arlene Ellis Schipper, Aruban attorney	11
John Q. Kelly, Twitty family attorney	9
Dr. Michael Baden, forensic pathologist	7
Tim Miller, founder, Texas Equusearch	7
Robin Holloway, Natalee's stepmother	4
Linda Allison, Natalee's aunt	4
Chris LeJeuz, attorney for Abraham Jones, suspect	3
Ruben Trapenberg, spokesman for Aruban government	3
Lincoln Gomez, Aruban attorney	3
Nadira Ramirez, mother of suspects Deepak and Satish Kalpoe	3
David Kock, attorney for Satish Kalpoe	3
Joe Tacopina, attorney for Joran Van Der Sloot	3
Noraina Pietersz, attorney for suspect Antonius Mickey John	2
Marcia Twitty, Natalee's aunt	2
Antonious Mickey John, former suspect	2
Mariaine Croes, Aruba prosecutor's spokesperson	2
Paul Reynolds, Natalee's uncle	2
Frances Ellen Byrd, friend of Natalee Holloway	2
Anita Van Der Sloot, mother of suspect	2
Rudy Oomen, attorney for suspect Deepak Kalpoe	2
Ricardo Yarzagaray, Aruban criminal defense attorney	2
Joe Houston, Texas Equusearch	2
Richard Freer, Emory University law professor	2
Joran Van Der Sloot, main suspect	2
John Larmonie, Aruba police sergeant	1
Emily, had encounter with suspects in Aruba	1
Alvin Cornett, friend of one of the Aruba suspects	1
Dr. Werner Spitz, forensic pathologist	1
Ivin Roekimin, friend of Kalpoe brothers	1
Hubert Brete, director, Discovery Tours Aruba	1
Alana Jordan, friend of Natalee Holloway	1
Ruth Mcvay, friend of Natalee Holloway	1
Paulus Van Der Sloot, father of suspect	1
Rufo Solognier, uncle of suspect Steve Croes	1
Steve Croes, former suspect	1
Charles Croes, talked to Joran Van Der Sloot	1
Jan Van Der Straaten, Aruba police superintendent	1
Luis Ramirez, Deepak and Satish's stepfather	1
Dale Nute, forensic diver	1
Ruud Ofringa, attorney for Deepak Kalpoe	1
Elgin Zeppenfeldt, attorney for Satish Kalpoe	1
Jennifer Fornaro, tourist who found bone on Aruba beach	1
Katherine Weatherly, friend of Natalee Holloway	1
Antonio Carlo, attorney for Joran Van Der Sloot	1
"Junior," saw people dumping body in landfill	1

continues

Table 3.4   Continued

Individual Interviewed, Connection to Case	Number of Times Interviewed
Eduardo Mansur, volunteer searcher	1
Vinda de Sousa, Holloway-Twitty family attorney	1
Helen Lejuez, Beth Holloway Twitty's attorney	1
Gerald Dompig, deputy chief of Aruban police	1
Jamie Skeeters, polygraph examiner	1
Rep. Spencer Bauchus, attended meeting of Aruban officials and FBI	1
Bob Plummer, chaperone on the fated Aruba trip	1
Bo Dietl, private investigator	1

Source: Examination of show transcripts from June 1, 2005, through June 30, 2006. Transcripts available through Lexis-Nexis.

Beyond the intensive investigation of tabloid justice stories as illustrated by Table 3.4, a hallmark of the coverage of these cases is sensationalism. Cable news-talk programs regularly characterize legal investigations and criminal trials as "astounding," "incredible," or "earth-shaking" events, implying or asserting that they have wide-ranging public significance. For instance, on the day of the verdict in the O.J. Simpson criminal trial, this is how Geraldo Rivera, host of *Rivera Live,* began his program: "'Not Guilty' is our inevitable title. It's the end of an incredible saga, an incredible story, an incredible chapter of American history. The defining story of our times, certainly the defining story for the end of the twentieth century here in the United States of America."[31] Rivera characterizes the O.J. Simpson drama as, apparently, more important than the Vietnam War, the civil rights movement, Watergate, the various oil crises, the federal budget deficits, the AIDS crisis, or any presidential election. The hyperbole of this assessment again demonstrates the level of overstatement that prevails in the era of tabloid justice.

In another example, on MSNBC's *The Big Show,* Jack Ford, NBC's legal affairs correspondent, summed up the judge's reversal of the jury's verdict in the Louise Woodward trial by commenting: "I've been covering cases for about thirteen years. . . . I can't remember as dramatic a change in a serious case as this."[32] The broadcast never made clear why Ford considered this to be such an important case. After all, in 1996 almost 2,000 children were murdered in the United States, and many of these cases went to trial.[33]

In a more recent example taken from MSNBC's *Scarborough Country,* Yale Galanter, a regular MSNBC legal affairs pundit, summed up the prosecution's behavior in the Duke University lacrosse team rape story: "I have tried cases for about sixteen years, I've been covering cases for about thirteen years, and between them, I can't remember as dramatic a change in as serious a case as this."[34] Host Joe Scarborough heartily agreed with Galanter's assessment.

The broadcast never made clear why Galanter and Scarborough believed this to be such a publicly important case. After all, it is estimated that there are more than 90,000 rapes in the United States each year, many of which involve charges and legal proceedings at least as complex and troubling as those in the Duke case.[35] Because of the apparent public interest associated with the Duke case, however, the story was typically discussed in dramatic terms such as these. Ultimately, all charges were dropped and the case was dismissed.

In a final example of sensationalism, consider how the Scott Peterson murder trial was discussed on various programs on the Fox News Channel. Coverage of this story routinely included assertions by legal experts that it was one of the most dramatic trials on record. The Fox News legal editor, Stan Goldman, referred to watching Amber Frey's testimony as "one of the most dramatic mornings ever spent in a courtroom," and assistant San Francisco district attorney Jim Hammer called the testimony in the penalty phase of the Peterson trial "the most dramatic thing that ever happened . . . so intensely personal and so painful that it's a wonder, frankly, people don't just pass out under the stress."[36] In referring to the jury's deliberations, former prosecutor Dean Johnson characterized the job of the jury as "not only the most important decision of Scott Peterson's life [but] the most important decisions of their lives," and Greta Van Susteren echoed this view on her own program, saying, "This is the most important decision they will make in their lives. They can't take it back."[37]

Beyond the constant pronouncements of dire importance and the urgent tone of these programs, the quality of debate and discussion tends to emphasize conflict over analysis. In perhaps an extreme representation of what Neil Postman warned of in his classic work, *Amusing Ourselves to Death,* television is a very poor medium for thoughtful discussion and conversation. Postman notes that the imperatives of television offer little opportunity for measured thinking, because showing someone thinking does not make for interesting viewing. The consequence is that whenever discussion and analysis occur on television, the arguments or ideas presented are usually simplistic and poorly articulated.[38] Postman would undoubtedly be dismayed by the quality of commentary and discussion that dominates cable television talk shows. For instance, a 2004 broadcast of *On the Record* with Greta Van Susteren contained a typically confusing exchange regarding the Peterson trial. This extended exchange illustrates the chaotic nature of discussion on these types of shows. Van Susteren introduced the segment and began to ask each of her guests for their perspective, but the guests immediately and spontaneously begin talking and interrupting one another:

> *Van Susteren:* We're going to go to the first juror No. 5 to be dismissed from the Peterson case. Joining us from Kansas City, Missouri, is the first juror dismissed from the Peterson case, Justin Falconer. And joining us from New

York, former Westchester County judge and current Westchester County DA Jeanine Pirro. In Detroit, defense attorney Geoff Fieger. And defense attorney Jayne Weintraub joins us in Miami.

Van Susteren: All right . . .

Pirro: His parents have to deal with the fact that they may lose their son. This is a sad event.

Weintraub: I don't think they bounced jurors . . . [cut off]

Van Susteren: Geoff Fieger . . .

Weintraub: . . . until they coerced a verdict in O.J.

Pirro: Oh! You know what? This isn't about coercion. This is about the system working . . . [cut off]

Weintraub: Really?

Pirro: . . . the way it should.

Weintraub: I think that will . . . [cut off]

Pirro: The record is solid on this one, Jayne.

Falconer: You know, Greta, can I say something . . . [cut off]

Weintraub: I don't think so. I think juror misconduct is going to be the lead issue on appeal, and I think it's a very important issue.

Pirro: It'll be an issue, but it's not going to be . . . [cut off]

Weintraub: And I'll tell you what else . . . [cut off]

Falconer: Greta, can I . . .

Pirro: . . . a basis for reversal.

Falconer: Greta, can I get in here real quick?

Weintraub: . . . the judge didn't even instruct the jurors today not to listen to the news tonight or read the newspaper tomorrow morning. Come on!

Van Susteren: All right. Well, I . . . [cut off]

Pirro: There's a lot of room for reversal. What would you want to do, lock them up until the next event? I mean, what . . . [cut off]

Weintraub: No, they should have immediately . . . [cut off]

Pirro: . . . is your point, Jayne?

Weintraub: . . . gone into a death phase, like they do in most death penalty cases, Jeanine.

Pirro: Well, you know what? I . . .

Van Susteren: All right, everyone stand by . . . [cut off]

Pirro: . . . sequestered juries, and you know what?

Van Susteren: Everyone . . . [cut off]

Pirro: This jury made a decision, and right now, they get a week off to make the most awesome decision.

Van Susteren: All right, we need to . . . [cut off]

Pirro: And that is whether or not they're going to put him to death.

Van Susteren: . . . take a break, Jeanine. And we need to take a break.[39]

This style of chaotic and contentious exchange is a staple of news-talk television programs. In fact, one person who had direct involvement in the Peterson case, dismissed juror Justin Falconer, could not even get a word in over the arguing of the professional pundits. Another example, drawn from MSNBC's 1990s program *Internight,* again illustrates what constitutes "discussion" on these shows. With guests interrupting one another and speaking in increasingly belligerent tones, host John Gibson (who now hosts a program on

Fox News), a panel of attorneys, and a judge discuss the final verdict in the Louise Woodward trial:

> *Jeralyn Merritt* (criminal defense attorney): And I think judges have complete discretion in sentencing. And he considered what he considered to be the relevant factors. And in his opinion today, he stated that he thought she was frightened. . . . But he didn't think that she intended to kill this baby . . . and I think that he was correct in saying "Let's just get all this behind us." He wasn't trying to minimize . . . [cut off]
>
> *Cynthia Alksne* (former prosecutor): John, I can't believe that . . . [cut off]
>
> *Merritt:* . . . what happened to the Eappen baby, but . . . [cut off]
>
> *Mike Hanley* (criminal defense attorney and former prosecutor): But, John . . . [cut off]
>
> *Merritt:* . . . and that really wasn't his job.
>
> *John Gibson:* Cynthia.
>
> *Merritt:* His job was to take—to sentence her as—as an individual.
>
> *Gibson:* Cynthia, I heard you interrupting.
>
> *Alksne:* I mean, ge—get—get us all—get it all behind us? The Eappens can't get it all behind them; their baby is dead. This—it is outrageous to me that this baby's life is worth so little money. And I'll tell you what this is; this is an argument . . . [cut off]
>
> *Gibson:* So little time.
>
> *Alksne:* . . . for mandatory sentencing guidelines, because in . . . [cut off]
>
> *Gibson:* But there are mandatory sentencing guidelines.
>
> *Alksne:* No, that—they're not mandatory in this case. They were volun—there's some sort of guidelines that have not been adopted in Massachusetts, and that would be three and five years.
>
> *Dan Abrams* (news correspondent): And—and . . . [cut off]
>
> *Gibson:* Dan Abrams.
>
> *Alksne:* But this child's . . . [cut off]
>
> *Abrams:* And, John—John—John . . . [cut off]
>
> *Alksne:* . . . life was worth nothing. This is justice denied.[40]

And so it goes night after night on the talk television circuit. Lawyers talk over one another, attempting to be heard by making ever-bolder assertions. Geraldo Rivera used to tell his panels of guests to "fight amongst yourselves," breaking up arguments only after complete chaos had erupted.[41]

Such discussions clearly provide entertainment and diversion first, and serious legal and political discourse second. Perhaps more troubling is that the polarizing and truncated nature of the discussion provides little room to explore the more subtle aspects of a given position or interpretation, or the context within which a story takes place. Guests seem encouraged to take stark, diametrically opposed positions—in fact, they are often invited on a show specifically to advance a particular side in the "debate." There seems to be no room for any middle ground in such an environment.[42]

Before we dismiss these programs as inconsequential infotainment, however, we must recognize their high degree of credibility among political, legal, and journalistic elites. Noted criminal prosecutors, professors of law, high-level politicians, and well-known defense attorneys regularly appear on these shows. One 1998 *Larry King Live* roundtable discussion, for example, featured six US senators discussing the Clinton impeachment and fielding calls from viewers. Representative John Conyers, the top Democrat on the House Judiciary Committee, appeared on *Rivera Live* several times during the course of the impeachment hearings. During the Michael Jackson trial, Paula Zahn, host of a program entitled *Now* on CNN, regularly interviewed participants in the trial and high-ranking officials of the Bush administration in the same broadcast. As an example, in an episode in January 2004, she interviewed Bush chief of staff Andrew Card, and then abruptly transitioned to a discussion with one of Michael Jackson's lawyers. Viewers, therefore, may grant greater levels of seriousness and newsworthiness to tabloid cases for no reason other than the presence of well-known guests and experts discussing them on these shows and for their seemingly equal prominence with stories about public policy and political debates by the federal government.

Perhaps the most distressing tendency of the cable news-talk programs is the blurring of the line between more serious issues and tabloid sensationalism. This problem has already been noted in Chapter 2, which attributed this characteristic to the networks and major newspapers as well. CNBC's November 10, 1997, episode of *Hardball* (since moved to MSNBC) serves as a prime example of the cable news programs' failure to differentiate between entertainment and nationally significant news. Host Chris Matthews began the program with a report on the ruling in the Woodward case. In the second segment Matthews, Representative Sherrod Brown of Ohio, and *Time* magazine journalist Margaret Carlson discussed President Clinton's push for trade legislation in Congress. This conversation led the three to consider the Democratic Party race for the presidency in the year 2000. Following a commercial break, though, Matthews moved away from hard news and identified his "winners and losers of the week," a segment that included portions of an interview with Marv Albert, the New York sportscaster who was accused of sexual assault. After another commercial, the host and four journalists returned to the Woodward ruling and the public's reaction to it.[43] Trade legislation and the race for the presidency were presented as relatively incidental in comparison to the Woodward trial.

Airing on the same night as this *Hardball* episode, the *Charles Grodin* program (no longer airing, but on CNBC throughout the 1990s) provides another striking example of the blurred distinctions between different categories of current events. Grodin, a former comedic actor, hosted a program that discussed a major foreign policy issue and two tabloid justice criminal cases. He began by assessing the possibility of US military action against Iraq. Grodin then proceeded to present his views on the Woodward and Marv Albert cases. Linda Kenney (a criminal defense lawyer) and Victoria Toensing (a former federal prosecutor and a regular guest on the cable news-talk circuit) joined

Grodin in an extended discussion of the significance of the Woodward and Albert cases. The host then returned to foreign policy, introducing a panel of experts to discuss the military situation in Iraq. The program allotted significantly less time to US foreign policy toward Iraq than to two criminal trials having few public ramifications.[44]

Although it is common for a news program to present a variety of stories, both of the aforementioned examples illustrate the common juxtaposition of important national and international issues with extended commentary on relatively meaningless tabloid cases. Typically, cable television hosts and guests make no distinction as to the relative importance of either topic. It is common for the same panel of guests to discuss many completely disparate topics and for viewer telephone calls to prompt discussions that veer far away from the original topic. These examples also highlight the high priority that is currently extended to the judicial process in the era of tabloid justice.[45]

24-Hour Cable Channels and the Ratings Game

The actual number of viewers who watch cable news-talk channels at any given time is quite small. The ratings of individual programs like *The Abrams Report, Tucker, Scarborough Country,* or *Hardball* are usually less than one-tenth those of the network news programs like *Dateline* or *20/20.* Programs on the Fox News Channel, such as *The O'Reilly Factor* and *Hannity and Colmes* (the highest-rated cable news programs) fare better, but ratings are small compared to network news broadcasts. However, the number of people who tune into cable news channels each day, at least for a few minutes, is quite large. In 1998 the average citizen turned on CNN roughly 2.5 times per week, the Fox News Channel 1.9 times per week, and CNBC and MSNBC 1.5 and 1.3 times per week, respectively.

These "tune-in" averages are higher than those of the three network news broadcasts on CBS (1.5), NBC (1.4), and ABC (1.3).[46] While a 2006 "State of the News Media" report showed that cable news viewership was still increasing, most of that growth had leveled off by 2005, and virtually all of the increase can be attributed to the growing popularity of Fox News. Still, in an average month in 2005, the report shows that 60 to 70 million different viewers tuned into CNN, and over 50 million to Fox News, with MSNBC closer to 40 million.[47] Despite what appears to be an edge in viewers for CNN, Fox is usually regarded as the top-rated cable news station because at any given time more people are watching Fox than the other channels. The emerging success of the cable news stations should further be considered in light of the fact that a number of these channels did not even exist before the mid-1990s.

A few examples of ratings boosts will serve to confirm our suspicion that tabloid justice stories do indeed increase the audience for the cable news programs. For instance, Court TV's ratings increased 13 percent from 2002 to 2003, and a number of commentators attributed this growth directly to the presence of stories involving Martha Stewart, Kobe Bryant, Scott Peterson, Robert Blake, famed record producer Phil Spector, and Michael Jackson.[48] At one point in 2005, *Catherine Crier Live* hit the ratings jackpot. On March 16, the day Scott Peterson was formally sentenced to death, Crier's ratings reached the second-highest ever for that program. A few hours later the Robert Blake murder trial verdict was revealed. The program's ratings jumped again to a level that outranked those of every cable channel that day except for Fox News.[49] When Michael Jackson's criminal trial ended in a not-guilty verdict in July 2005, the three major cable channels experienced a significant increase in viewers. On a typical weekday, CNN, Fox News, and MSNBC combined garner about 2 million viewers. However, on the day of the Jackson verdict, these three saw their viewership jump to approximately 10 million. Fully thirteen separate cable channels preempted their regular programming to discuss the decision, and that evening *Larry King Live* and even NBC's *Dateline* and CBS's *48 Hours* were completely devoted to Michael Jackson material.[50]

During June, July, and August 2005, Greta Van Susteren's *On the Record* saw its ratings soar as much as 60 percent some days. On several occasions her program, which took the lead in covering the disappearance of Natalee Holloway, actually exceeded the number of viewers garnered by *The O'Reilly Factor,* a top-rated cable news program.[51] And finally, during the Schiavo-story period, there were several crucial days in which cable ratings rose significantly. On March 10, 2005, the day in which a judge denied the request to remove Terri Schiavo's feeding tube, both CNN and MSNBC experienced 20 percent increases in viewers. On March 22, when a different judge allowed the feeding tube to be removed, CNN, MSNBC, and Fox News had ratings increases of 20 percent, and when Schiavo finally died, there were increases of about 10 to 12 percent for several channels. During the course of the month that the Schiavo story dominated the news, cable television overall had a 14 percent increase in viewers.[52] While traffic on the Internet can be difficult to monitor, some evidence reveals increases in total hits on websites devoted to covering tabloid justice cases. During the month when John Mark Karr was arrested in Thailand and extradited to Boulder, Colorado, Yahoo! reported that "JonBenet Ramsey" was the thirtieth-most-popular search term on the entire World Wide Web.[53]

An examination of overall ratings over time for the cable stations in the 1990s shows that tabloid justice cases have been quite important to the cable networks. When a tabloid case is at the forefront of current events, ratings appear to increase dramatically. During the second half of 1998, when the Clinton-Lewinsky scandal peaked, MSNBC and Fox News Channel's ratings more than doubled.[54] In 1995, the year of the O.J. Simpson criminal trial, CNN clearly reaped dividends from its extensive trial coverage, as it enjoyed ratings that were roughly 80 percent higher than in the years preceding and succeeding the case. Table 3.5 shows the yearly average ratings for several cable news channels. Clearly, as the volume and intensity of a tabloid justice story increase, ratings increase as well. As the table shows, ratings for Court TV and CNN were noticeably higher in 1995, the year of the O.J. Simpson trial, than in succeeding years. All of the networks (except for MSNBC, for which no ratings numbers were available for 1997) also experienced a jump in ratings for 1998, the year of the intense coverage of the Clinton-Lewinsky investigation.

To further explore the importance of legal scandal and tabloid coverage to the ratings of cable news stations, we examine the overnight ratings for two tabloid stories: the criminal trial of O.J. Simpson and the presidential scandal involving Bill Clinton and Monica Lewinsky. Table 3.6 displays both the yearly ratings average for CNN, CNBC, MSNBC, and the Fox News Channel

Table 3.5   Ratings of 24-Hour News Channels, 1995–1998

Year	Court TV	CNBC	CNN	MSNBC	Fox News
1995	122	111	573	n/a	n/a
1996	17	117	331	n/a	n/a
1997	28	158	339	n/a	17
1998	33	244	360	101	45

Source: Nielsen Media Research.
Notes: "n/a" means data not available for that year. Entries indicate average number of households (in thousands) viewing each station at any given time.

Table 3.6   Ratings of 24-Hour News Channels During Time of Scandal

Scandal	CNN	CNBC	MSNBC	Fox News
O.J. Simpson criminal trial				
Average for 1995	573	111	n/a	n/a
Day of the Bronco chase (in 1994)	1,841	45	n/a	n/a
Day of opening arguments	1,248	128	n/a	n/a
Day verdict was announced	1,705	350	n/a	n/a
Clinton-Lewinsky scandal				
Average for 1998	360	244	101	45
Day Lewinsky story broke	500	297	130	50
Day of president's grand jury testimony and apology	1,297	415	314	193
Day grand jury testimony was aired	1,657	328	471	259
Day full House voted to open impeachment inquiry	385	329	163	65

Source: Nielsen Media Research.
Notes: Entries indicate the number of households (in thousands) viewing on that particular day. MSNBC and Fox News were not in operation during the Simpson criminal trial.

and the ratings for the days that major events occurred in each of these stories. The data in Table 3.6 suggest that scandal is important business for the cable television stations. Throughout the lengthy O.J. Simpson drama, major events such as the infamous "Bronco chase," the trial's opening arguments, and the day of the verdict's announcement led to a doubling or tripling of the ratings for CNN. This effect was not as clear for CNBC, whose level of attention to the case evolved more slowly during the year.

Turning to the coverage of the Clinton-Lewinsky investigation, we see that the story started out relatively slowly. A small upturn in ratings occurred on the day the media reported that President Clinton may have been sexually involved with a White House intern. As the scandal began to unfold, however, ratings for the four cable news programs soared. On the day that Clinton's grand jury testimony was televised, Fox News's ratings were five times their 1998 daily average, while CNN's were four times higher. Further, Table 3.6 illustrates that by the time of the impeachment vote in the House of Representatives, cable ratings had fallen and were only a little above the yearly average. The public had grown weary of this story, the outcome of the trial never seemed in doubt, and an overwhelming majority of Americans never believed that President Clinton would be removed from office. In essence, the drama and ensuing ability to sell the story had run their course.

Tables 3.5 and 3.6 demonstrate the importance of a good serialized scandal or trial in attracting viewers. As in any TV drama or soap opera, more compelling moments attract more interested viewers. It is quite plausible to conclude that commercial considerations drive the substantive emphasis of such programs. What else could explain a news program devoting so much time to certain stories? Indeed, if we subscribe to the notion that the media simply cover stories of interest to the public, these programs would probably be foolish not to emphasize such stories. Although this tactic may make business sense, it also clearly reveals that the commodification of tabloid events has trumped any idealized vision of the role that the news media should play in a democracy.

The Rise of Punditry

The pervasive culture of talk, argument, and gossip constitutes a critical component of the contemporary media. The new media environment, or what Jonathan Alter has called the "American wilderness of noise," is dominated by heated—and at times quite undignified—"discussion" by pundits of all types.[55] This differs greatly from both the traditional, sober reporting characteristic of Walter Cronkite and Dan Rather and that of the established Sunday morning political talk shows, such as *Face the Nation*, *This Week*, and *Meet the Press*. In the recent past, journalists who covered legal and political news events did not seek out venues in which to argue with other journalists and lawyers about the proper interpretation of legal and political events. The discussion on the news-talk programs often focuses on nothing more than how the media have covered an event, as opposed to the substance of the story. This dynamic represents a sea change in the way that reporters view themselves, and certainly in the way that they interact with the subjects of their stories. On a regular basis, reporters from all types of publications and programs argue with members of Congress and previously obscure trial attorneys about how to interpret the day's legal and political developments.

Regardless of the subject, the cable news channels regularly feature panels of political and legal experts jousting with members of the news media about various topics. Just as any issue can apparently be presented in this manner, guests are presented as authorities on any topic that happens to arise during a program. The same guests discuss everything from Marv Albert, the death of Princess Diana, the disappearance of Natalee Holloway, and Mel Gibson's alleged antisemitism to the congressional elections, the crisis in the Middle East, Hurricane Katrina, the Enron scandal, and global warming. In the episode of *Hardball* discussed previously, the same panel of experts discussed trade legislation, the 2000 presidential campaign, and the verdict in the Louise Woodward trial. And, although it is reasonable for reporters to cover a number of disparate topics, it is quite another situation when reporters are presented as experts on virtually all public issues that arise. Although *Hardball* is certainly not unique in this regard, that show has continued this trend by inviting a revolving panel of "experts" called the *Hardball* Hotshots, which consists mostly of hosts from other MSNBC talk shows, to discuss everything from the Iraq War to presidential campaign politics to the Duke lacrosse case.

A number of pundits who entered the legal-political talk show circuit, or who even became hosts of their own news-talk shows for a time, rose to prominence during the O.J. Simpson criminal trial. Many of the trial participants and commentators from that trial went on to either host programs or comment on other legal proceedings. In an important sense, these pundits, as well as many others, became public "educators" about the legal and political system. This group constituted a sort of revolving roundtable of talking heads, and these figures appeared on numerous news-talk shows, apparently willing to discuss any topic.[56] Some of these commentators, such as Dan Abrams, John Gibson, and Greta Van Susteren, remain a strong presence on cable news, while others, such as Mark Fuhrman, Dr. Michael Baden, Barry Scheck, and others appear frequently as legal experts.

The rise of punditry as an aspect of general reporting marks a significant shift that has occurred in the era of tabloid justice. This phenomenon received considerable analysis based on journalistic reporting throughout the Clinton-Lewinsky scandal. In their book *Warp Speed,* veteran journalists Bill Kovach and Tom Rosenstiel contend that in the initial days of the scandal, over 40 percent of the journalistic output on the Clinton-Lewinsky affair "was not factual reporting at all but was instead journalists offering their own analysis, opinion, speculation, or judgments—essentially, commentary and punditry."[57] After citing a litany of examples in which journalists offered opinionated and completely speculative comments on both network news and cable news outlets, Kovach and Rosenstiel concluded that the scandal showed the "degree to which the supposed information revolution is not actually about gathering information, but instead about commenting on information that others have gathered."[58] The emerging dual role of journalists as news reporters and commentators is a change that carries with it important consequences for the role of the media, and it merits further exploration both within that profession and by those who study the news business.

A Note on Talk Radio

Talk radio has also helped to propel tabloid justice cases to high levels of prominence. And even though news-talk television and the Internet have stolen much of talk radio's thunder in the past few years, radio remains an important element in the new media environment. Talk radio is still the fastest growing radio format (though some studies claim that country and western is), with the number of talk radio stations in the United States having doubled between 1992 and 1998.[59] Although talk radio cannot be considered a completely new medium, its popularity and growth in the 1990s makes it a noteworthy phenomenon. The pinnacle of talk radio's influence has often been associated with the national midterm elections of 1994. At that time, syndicated radio host Rush Limbaugh fostered a strong antigovernment and anti-Clinton sentiment among his listeners. Many analysts viewed this as a crucial factor in the Republican takeover of both houses of Congress that year, and Limbaugh himself appeared to take partial credit for the Republican victory.[60]

A number of commentators have identified talk radio as a critical component in the development of contemporary political attitudes in the United States.[61] In her book *The Angry American,* Susan Tolchin very effectively illustrates the influential role that talk radio has played in setting the political agenda.[62] For instance, scholars have demonstrated that talk radio has played an important role in motivating its listeners to contact their representatives and other public officials.[63] On issues ranging from gun control, abortion, trade policy, and the impeachment of President Clinton to the war in Iraq, talk radio fosters a sense of efficacy and activism among its listeners. Tolchin persuasively argues that talk radio fueled the general feeling of antigovernment anger and alienation during the 1990s.

In terms of high-profile legal proceedings, talk radio provides a forum conducive to constant discussion. Most radio markets offer a wide range of personalities who are willing to discuss the political and tabloid stories of the day. Nationally known talk show hosts, such as Rush Limbaugh, Sean Hannity, Don Imus, Howard Stern, G. Gordon Liddy, and Laura Schlesinger, all offer, to varying degrees, commentary on cultural, political, and tabloid stories. Many lesser-known local and regional personalities carry on these conversations, too. In the past four years, the Air America radio network has sought to create a more liberal ideological presence on talk radio, but its affiliates still do not reach most areas of the country. The topics of discussion can range from the more serious, such as "the O.J. Simpson case and race relations in the United States" or a constitutional debate on whether "Monica-gate constitutes an impeachable offense," to the more crude and bawdy, such as "Is the president a pervert?" or "Why would anyone sexually harass Paula Jones?" Nationally syndicated radio talk show host Mike Gallagher has commented that even years after his trials, "nothing gets the phones going like the mention of O.J. Simpson."[64]

In the second period of the tabloid justice era, talk radio often continued the coverage of these cases. Radio hosts spent countless hours discussing JonBenet Ramsey (with the arrest of a suspect in 2006), Scott Peterson, the "Runaway Bride," schoolteachers who seduce their male students, Martha Stewart, and, of course, Michael Jackson. Sean Hannity, who usually discusses politics, was able to take time out from national affairs to interview the fiancée of Jennifer Wilbanks, the Runaway Bride. Hannity also scored a ratings coup when he was granted the first media interview with Elizabeth Smart, the Salt Lake City girl who had been kidnapped from her home. Missing teenager Natalee Holloway was also a subject of intense discussion on some radio programs, with one host even accusing her parents of "ignorance" for letting a naïve and ill-prepared young woman go on a trip to Aruba.[65] Finally, and perhaps most prominently, the Terri Schiavo case, because of the political dimensions of the debate, dominated conservative talk radio for weeks. Radio host Glenn Beck even claimed to have raised $5 million to buy Terri's guardianship rights from Michael Schiavo.[66]

The Internet and Tabloid Justice

Although scholarly analysis of the broad impact of the Internet is just beginning to emerge, a number of studies have assessed the importance of the Internet in terms of the political process.[67] At the very least, this medium now plays an important role in covering legal and criminal justice issues and in creating and maintaining the culture of tabloid justice. It is the only venue that combines print and broadcast material, punditry, citizen input, partisanship, and the culture of celebrity, all with little regulation or restraint. Foremost, tens of thousands of news and information websites now deal with law and criminal justice, broadly defined. The Internet has even been used to fight crime, as information posted on the Web has led directly to the actual arrests of fugitives and criminal suspects.[68]

Further, in numerous high-profile cases, legal institutions have themselves used the Internet as a means of disseminating important information. When Judge Hiller Zobel overruled the jury in the Woodward trial, he first issued his ruling online. The US House of Representatives posted the infamous Starr Report on the Internet, ostensibly to make Bill Clinton's impeachment an open and accessible process. The US Supreme Court, as well as several other lower appellate courts, now posts its decisions on the Internet, providing instantaneous information to lawyers, scholars, and the interested public. The Net is now clearly regarded as a legitimate and respectable medium for the dissemination of legal news and information.

Of course, the Internet, as cyber-gossip and online magazine editor Matt Drudge has asserted, also allows any citizen the opportunity to be a reporter or publisher of news and information.[69] It is relatively easy to create an online "report" covering Monica Lewinsky, JonBenet Ramsey, the Runaway Bride, Natalee Holloway, or some other "tabloidized" figure. The Internet also gives anyone the ability to "publish" information on any topic and make that information available to a potentially worldwide audience. Top news organizations, government agencies, think tanks, and interest groups have developed home pages. Many well-known authors and scholars also have personal websites, and many of these sources of information are seen to have the same legitimacy as broadcast networks and top newspapers and newsmagazines.

At the other end of the continuum there exist many sites sponsored by highly partisan, extremely opinionated, openly conspiratorial, agenda-driven citizens and organizations. Further, online chat rooms allow users to carry on real-time conversations about almost any subject imaginable. This interactive component of the World Wide Web has fostered an essential technological populism; anyone can be a part of the discourse.

Since the Internet's explosion in popularity and accessibility in the mid-1990s, it has played a significant role in fueling the news media's focus on tabloid justice cases and fostering the public's interest in them. Many Internet home pages provide information about trials and other legal stories. Court TV's home page, for example, lists all of the "major trials" going on in the country at any given time. The Court TV site also contains an elaborate database of stories dealing with "famous trials" and a glossary of legal terms, courtroom simulations, links to government documents, and, of course, advertising.[70] This website, which exists for those very attentive to the legal issues in high-profile cases, has been praised by both the *Los Angeles Times* and the *New York Times* as an example of good journalism on the Internet.[71]

The Internet also contains a bewildering array of far less reputable information. The average user must wade through a jumbled list of relatively traditional hard news and highly subjective and factually suspect information. For instance, a search using the key words "Lance Ito" (the trial judge in the Simpson criminal case) yields a link for the Court TV home page, followed by a link for the "Lance Ito, Eat My Burrito!" site.[72] The key words "John and Lorena Bobbitt" confront the user with a suggestion to try the "Ballad of the Bobbitt Hillbillies" page.[73] "Monica Lewinsky" leads to a website that reprints the Report of the Office of the Independent Counsel, but also to a page that markets the "Gen-U-Wine, Multi-Purpose, Monica Lewinsky–approved, kneeling mouse pad."[74] A Google search for "Natalee Holloway" reveals a list of over 1.1 million hits, including the Natalee Holloway home page, hundreds of news reports, and more distasteful fare such as the "F*** Natalee" page and the "Natalee Holloway: Who Cares?" site.[75] In short, there is little organization, context, or quality control in terms of the information obtained online.

To further illustrate the wealth of information about tabloid justice cases on the Web, we conducted searches using key words associated with some of our selected cases. We also sought to compare the "Web presence" of high-profile cases from the first and second tabloid justice periods. There is of course a tremendous difference in the reach of the Internet between the first and second of our time periods. Table 3.7 reveals the number of Web pages for several of the cases that we have been considering. Because each Internet search engine classifies websites differently, we examined results from the two most prominent search engines in each time period, Netscape and Yahoo! in 1998, and Google and Yahoo! in 2006.

The disparate numbers in Table 3.7 reveal that these two search engines have different methods for identifying sources. Nevertheless, in each case,

Table 3.7   Number of Web Pages Mentioning Tabloid Justice Stories on Netscape/Google and Yahoo!

Tabloid Story	Number of Webpages	
	Netscape/Google[a]	Yahoo!
First period		
Marv Albert	217,000	141,000
Menendez brothers	83,100	57,200
Lorena and John Bobbitt	113,000	4,000
O.J. Simpson	4,530,000	82,000
Louise Woodward	76,400	50,100
JonBenet Ramsey	178,000	3,530,000
Second period		
Michael Jackson	4,430,000	3,070,000
Scott Peterson	1,610,000	1,450,000
Terri Schiavo	4,424,000	2,780,000
Martha Stewart	2,760,000	2,480,000
Natalee Holloway	1,020,000	735,000

Notes: Web browser searches conducted in November 1998 for first period, June 2006 for second period. For specific search instructions, see Appendix A.

a. In the first period, Netscape was used; in the second period, Google was used.

typing a few key words produces literally hundreds of thousands (and in some cases millions) of sites pertaining to these cases. What is most striking is the phenomenal growth of the Internet between 1998, when we conducted our first-period searches, and 2006, when we did our searches for the second part of the tabloid justice era. While O.J. Simpson dominated the Internet in the first period, in the more recent period several cases approached Simpson's numbers. It is hard to imagine a Natalee Holloway search in the first period resulting in over a million Web hits.

One aspect of the Internet that was almost nonexistent until 2000 or so, but which now has an enormous presence on the Web, is the so-called blogosphere. Blogs (short for "web logs") are online diaries, or personal chronological series of thoughts and observations, usually reflecting the personality and interests of the writer. Updated anywhere from every few days to almost continuously, blogs (which are maintained by "bloggers") have exploded in popularity in the past five or six years. One estimate sets the current number of blogs at somewhere in the range of 12 million, which would constitute about 6 percent of the overall number of Americans with Internet access.[76]

The Pew Internet and American Life Project conducted a national study that found that about 37 percent of bloggers wrote about "personal affairs and life experiences," while only 11 percent focused on politics and current affairs.[77] While this may at first glance seem like a small number, it actually means there are currently almost 1 million blogs that focus on news and politics. Further, a significant number of these sites have discussed the various tabloid justice cases. As Table 3.8 indicates, there is a large disparity between blog discussions of our first period and second period cases. The vastly increased number of blog entries dealing with tabloid justice stories since 2001 corresponds with the geometric growth in the presence of blogs since about that year.

What is somewhat striking is that the Duke lacrosse team rape case garnered more blog attention than any case in the entire tabloid justice era. The blogosphere's attention to this story dwarfs that given to Scott Peterson, Martha Stewart, Terri Schiavo, and even Michael Jackson. It is clear, however, that tabloid justice is a burgeoning enterprise on the Internet.

Fictionalized Crime and Law-Related Television Dramas

One of the most interesting developments of the tabloid justice era has been the tremendous growth in a number of crime- and law-related fictional television shows, especially since 2000. Many of these shows purport to give audiences a "behind-the-scenes" view of the criminal justice system and the judicial process, and a number of them include fairly detailed material about legal investigations and trial proceedings. This development seems to constitute a continuation of the trend of transforming the legal system into a vehicle for entertainment rather

Table 3.8   Prevalence of Tabloid Justice Cases on Internet Blogs, 2005

Tabloid Story	Number of Blog Entries
First period	
William Kennedy Smith	250
Rodney King	7,722
Menendez brothers	390
O.J. Simpson	38,904
Louise Woodward	266
JonBenet Ramsey	3,879
Second period	
Andrea Yates	14,875
Martha Stewart	26,828
Scott Peterson	20,137
Terri Schiavo	44,459
Michael Jackson	31,090
Natalee Holloway	32,012
Duke lacrosse	63,029

Source: Google blog search, conducted August 1, 2006.
Note: Entries are tracked by Google blog search from around June 2005.

than for education. Many of the plots are thinly disguised versions of actual criminal trials and investigations.

Most recent scholarly studies have found that these fictional shows present a picture of society in which violence, murder, rape, assault, and robbery occur far more than they do in real life.[78] For years, similar studies have found that television criminals are more likely to be wealthy, white, and suburban-dwelling than annual FBI statistics reveal, and that serious crimes are more likely to be "solved" by the end of the show than accords with the reality of the legal system.[79]

Table 3.9 illustrates the growth of prime-time network law programs for a selection of three years during the tabloid justice era: 1993, 1999, and 2005. It should be noted that there exist many more crime and law shows than we have listed here, and indeed it is difficult to decide just what "counts" as such a program. We have excluded shows such as *Cops,* which is a "reality" program, and *The Shield,* as well as other traditional syndicated crime shows, as they have little to do with the legal system per se. Rather, we have counted only those prime-time fictional shows that appear on the four major networks. Table 3.9 demonstrates that the number of these shows nearly doubled between 1993 and 2005. And yet, only one show that aired in 1993, *Law & Order,* remained in production by 2005. Indeed, this show and its numerous offshoots, as well as the programs associated with CBS's *CSI: Crime Scene Investigation,* now account for fully one-third of all legal dramas on either broadcast or basic national cable television.

The ubiquity of law dramas is hard to overstate or even to avoid if one chooses to watch any television at all. During a typical week in the summer of

Table 3.9 Growth of Prime-Time Network Law and Crime Dramas, 1993, 1999, and 2005

1993	1999	2005
Law & Order (NBC)	Law & Order (NBC)	Conviction (NBC)
Unsolved Mysteries (NBC)	The Practice (ABC)	Crossing Jordan (NBC)
L.A. Law (NBC)	NYPD Blue (ABC)	Heist (NBC)
Matlock (ABC)	JAG (CBS)	Law & Order (NBC)
Show Sirens (ABC)	Nash Bridges (CBS)	Law & Order: Criminal Intent (NBC)
Murder, She Wrote (ABC)	Martial Law (CBS)	Law & Order: Special Victims Unit (NBC)
The Commish (ABC)	Walker, Texas Ranger (CBS)	Boston Legal (ABC)
Bodies of Evidence (CBS)	America's Most Wanted (Fox)	The Evidence (ABC)
Picket Fences (CBS)	Ally McBeal (Fox)	inJustice (ABC)
Walker, Texas Ranger (CBS)		Close to Home (CBS)
America's Most Wanted[a] (Fox)		Cold Case (CBS)
		CSI: Crime Scene Investigation (CBS)
		CSI: Miami (CBS)
		CSI: New York (CBS)
		Criminal Minds (CBS)
		NCIS (CBS)
		NUMB3RS (CBS)
		Without a Trace (CBS)
		America's Most Wanted (Fox)
		Bones (Fox)

Source: For 1993 and 1999, shows drawn from April television listings published in the *New York Times*. The listings for 2005 are based on analysis of each network's prime-time lineup in April as found on network Web pages.

Notes: Lists include all fiction-based programs that cover some aspect of the legal system, usually focusing on lawyers, law enforcement officers, or court-rooms.

a. *America's Most Wanted* is a reality-based program but does show dramatic reenactments of real cases.

2006, one could watch the now-syndicated *Law & Order* a total of nineteen times (providing one had basic cable service). The TNT network alone aired approximately 8.5 hours of crime and law dramas per day.[80] During that same week, the USA and FX channels ran twelve and five law dramas, respectively.[81] Even Court TV, ostensibly dedicated to covering the "real" legal system, aired numerous episodes of *Law & Order* and *NYPD Blue*. During the week of August 6, 2005, TNT's *The Closer* opened its second season with the highest ratings ever for a scripted cable television show. Aside from NASCAR, it was the highest-rated show on cable in the nation for that entire week.[82] Clearly, this type of show has saturated both network and cable programming and is being enthusiastically received by the viewing public.

Not only has the number of these programs rapidly expanded, but their popularity is now very high as well.[83] Table 3.10 shows the ratings for primetime shows in fall 2005. Of the top thirty programs on evening television, fourteen are crime- and law-related. Three *Law & Order* variants and three *CSI*-related shows appear on the list.

How accurate are the depictions of the criminal investigation and judicial processes that appear in these shows? What explains the tremendous recent growth in the number of law-oriented shows? And, most important, what has been the impact of this trend on the public's knowledge of and confidence in the US legal system? As we have previously noted, these are difficult questions to answer, and, not surprisingly, little scholarly work has been done in this area. Most of the existing literature has found that these shows do a poor job of realistically presenting the objective, factual conditions and processes at work in the US legal system.[84] In our most recent national survey (reported on in Chapters 4 and 5), however, over 52 percent of respondents agreed that one can learn a lot about the legal system from shows like *CSI* and *Law & Order.*

Uncovering the effects that these shows have on the viewing public's attitudes about crime and law is a very difficult task, however. While some media effects theories posit little substantive impact on viewer attitudes, recent work has considered whether potential criminals, jurors, and witnesses have come to perceive as factual the images of law that are on display in these programs.[85] In short, the law-crime television phenomenon of recent years is unprecedented in its sweep, and it will take scholars a number of years to seriously explore whether the public is adopting viewpoints directly from these shows. At present, evidence of media effects is largely anecdotal rather than systematic and representative.

Conclusion

In this chapter, we have drawn three main conclusions. First, new media outlets have grown substantially since 1990, and especially since 2000. The 24-

Table 3.10   Television Ratings from Fall 2005 Prime-Time Schedule

Show	Ratings
1 *CSI*	**10.0**
2 *Desperate Housewives*	8.9
3 *Without a Trace*	**7.3**
4 *Lost*	6.6
5 *Grey's Anatomy*	6.6
6 *Survivor: Guatemala*	6.5
7 *CSI: Miami*	**6.4**
8 *NCIS*	**6.0**
9 *NFL Monday Night Football*	5.9
10 *Cold Case*	**5.6**
11 *Extreme Makeover: Home Edition*	5.5
12 *Law & Order: SVU*	**5.5**
13 *60 Minutes*	5.4
14 *Two and a Half Men*	5.4
15 *CSI: NY*	**5.3**
16 *Commander in Chief*	5.2
17 *E.R.*	5.1
18 *Criminal Minds*	**4.8**
19 *House*	4.7
20 *My Name Is Earl*	4.5
21 *Las Vegas*	4.4
22 *Crossing Jordan*	**4.3**
23 *Out of Practice*	4.3
24 *Law & Order*	**4.3**
25 *Law & Order: Criminal Intent*	**4.3**
26 *Medium*	**4.3**
27 *NUMB3RS*	**4.1**
28 *Boston Legal*	**4.0**
29 *Ghost Whisperer*	4.0
30 *Close to Home*	3.9

Source: Ratings compiled by AllYourTV Inc., available at http://www.allyourtv.com.

Notes: Ratings are compiled for three-month period from September 19, 2005, through December 11, 2005. Crime dramas appear in bold. A single national ratings point represents 1 percent, or 1,102,000 households with a television set.

hour cable news channels, the Internet, and talk radio became integral aspects of the mass media universe in the final years of the twentieth century, and since the year 2000 there has been a rapid growth in law-related television dramas as well.

Second, we have suggested that the new media are now important outlets for covering tabloid justice investigations and trials. Nightly cable television news-talk programs, many of which are affiliated with respected network news organizations, serve as the leading sources of information and analysis about these stories. These shows sustain the sense of importance and urgency behind tabloid cases, and they present even the casual viewer with around-the-clock information about the legal system. Lloyd Chiasson, who has written extensively about trial publicity in the United States, has commented that even though crime is big news, it quickly fades from public consciousness. The prolonged nature of many investigations and trials, however, fosters a sustained sense of interest among citizens.[86] The recent explosion of new media has dramatically enhanced the tendency for tabloid justice cases to linger in the public mind.

Finally, these new forms of media have given the public an unprecedented level of exposure to the inner workings of the legal system. In the William Kennedy Smith case, viewers not only directly watched the work of judges, prosecutors, and defense attorneys but also saw the difficulties confronted by alleged rape victims in pursuing justice in the courts. In the Bobbitt and Menendez trials, the public gained heavy exposure to issues such as domestic violence, child abuse, and the insanity defense. The Louise Woodward case furnished attentive Americans with an opportunity to examine judicial behavior and discretion, as Judge Zobel took the unusual measure of overturning the jury's verdict. In the Simpson criminal trial, viewers learned about everything from preliminary hearings to pretrial motions to attorney procedural maneuvering to expert witnesses to jury consultants to judicial discretion. In the presidential scandals involving Paula Jones and Monica Lewinsky, viewers were treated to extensive analysis of grand jury and impeachment proceedings, as well as extended debates about perjury and obstruction of justice. The Peterson and Michael Jackson trials highlighted numerous problems with the use of expert witnesses, while the Natalee Holloway case continues to raise issues of international law, ways in which the Aruban legal system differs from that of the United States, witness confidentiality, and the role of private investigators in murder cases.

The presence of the new media has greatly magnified the specific facts of each case and the perceived importance of the specific topics that are raised in each instance. In short, the public has received an unprecedented level of exposure to the legal system through the presentation of these cases. The quality and accuracy of this education remains a matter of debate, however. In addition to the central characteristics of the new media (new technology, commercialism, and populism), an underlying theme in this chapter has been that the conversation about the legal system that is carried out on the new media outlets may not adequately reflect the range of important public issues facing Americans in the twenty-first century. In our remaining chapters we examine the impact of this media inundation on actual public attitudes about justice in the United States.

Notes

1. *Rivera Live,* September 14, 1995, provided by Burrelles Transcript Service.

2. Alexandra Marks, "Why Cable News Pursues the JonBenet Ramsey Case," *Christian Science Monitor,* August 21, 2006, p. 3.

3. Jonathan Alter, "In the Time of the Tabs," *Newsweek,* June 2, 1997, p. 32.

4. Steven Winn, "Jackson Booked on Molestation Charges, Released," *San Francisco Chronicle,* November 21, 2003, p. A1.

5. John Temple, "Story Shifts from Cable to Internet," *Rocky Mountain News,* August 19, 2006, p. 2A.

6. This calculation is based on an analysis of each show's descriptions as provided by Burrelles Transcript Service.

7. Richard Davis and Diana Owen, *New Media and American Politics* (New York: Oxford University Press, 1998), 7.

8. Ibid., 7–9.

9. The Pew Research Center, "Stock Market Down, New Media Up," November 9, 1997, p. 1.

10. Hoyt Purvis, *Media, Politics, and Government* (Ft. Worth, TX: Harcourt, 2001), 58–60. For a discussion of the new media environment effects on the judicial process, see Jill Schachner Chanen, "Stay Tuned," *ABA Journal* (October 2004): 45–48, 56–58.

11. Davis and Owen, *New Media and American Politics,* 53.

12. For a good discussion of many aspects of the Gulf War coverage, see Lance W. Bennett and David L. Paletz, eds., *Taken by Storm* (Chicago: University of Chicago Press, 1994).

13. Davis and Owen, *New Media and American Politics,* 195.

14. This figure is from a CBS News/*New York Times* poll cited in David L. Paletz, *The Media in American Politics* (New York: Longman, 1999), 289.

15. In describing these three components of the new media environment, we rely heavily on the definition provided in Davis and Owen, *New Media and American Politics,* chap. 1; and Barry Brummett, "Mediating the Laws: Popular Trials and the Mass Media," in Robert Hariman, ed., *Popular Trials: Rhetoric, Mass Media, and the Law* (Tuscaloosa: University of Alabama Press, 1990), 179–193.

16. See Kathleen Hall Jamieson and Karlyn Kohrs Campbell, *The Interplay of Influence: News, Advertising, Politics in the Internet Age* (Belmont, CA: Wadsworth, 2005); and Gary Selnow, *Electronic Whistle-Stops: The Impact of the Internet on American Politics* (Westport, CT: Praeger, 1998).

17. Abigail Tucker and Dan Thanh Dang, "The Scoop on the Scoop: Online Outlets Are Making Over Realm of Celebrity Gossip," *Baltimore Sun,* August 1, 2006, p. 1A.

18. For a report on a major recent academic study of media consumption habits, see Erika D. Smith, "Media Madness," *Indianapolis Star,* September 26, 2005, p. C4.

19. "Online Newcomers More Middle Brow, Less Work-Oriented: The Internet News Audience Goes Ordinary," *Pew Survey Report,* January 14, 1999.

20. *Internet World Stats,* "Population and User Statistics," http://www.internetworldstats.com/top20.htm (accessed September 15, 2006).

21. See Selnow, *Electronic Whistle-Stops;* Sara Bentivegna, "Talking Politics on the Net," Joan Shorenstein Center on the Press, Politics, and Public Policy, 1998; Richard Davis, *The Web of Politics: The Internet's Impact on the American Political System* (New York: Oxford University Press, 1998); and Sarah Oates, Diana Owen, and Rachel Kay Gibson, *The Internet and Politics: Citizens, Voters, and Activists* (New York: Taylor and Frances, 2005).

22. See Michael Parenti, *Inventing Reality* (New York: St. Martin's, 1986), 27–34. Also see Arthur Asa Berger, *Manufacturing Desire* (New Brunswick, NJ: Transaction, 1996).

23. Russell W. Neuman, *The Future of the Mass Audience* (New York: Cambridge University Press, 1991).

24. See, for instance, the first chapter, "The Endless Chain," in Ben Bagdikian, *The Media Monopoly,* 5th ed. (Boston: Beacon, 1997), 3–26; and, more recently, Bagdikian's *The New Media Monopoly* (Boston: Beacon, 2004).

25. Nicholas Lehman, "Amateur Hour: Journalism Without Journalists," *The New Yorker,* August 7 and 14, 2006, 44–49.

26. Davis and Owen, *New Media and American Politics,* 7.

27. See Kevin Hill, *Cyberpolitics: Citizen Activism in the Age of the Internet* (Lanham, MD: Rowman and Littlefield, 1998); and Oates, Owen, and Gibson, *The Internet and Politics.*

28. Stephen Ansolabehere, Roy Behr, and Shanto Iyengar, *The Media Game* (New York: Macmillan, 1993), 46.

29. Jeffery R. Sipe, "Local News, All the Time," *News World Communications,* May 5, 1997, p. 40.

30. See Matea Gold, "Straight from Van Susteren," *Los Angeles Times,* July 20, 2005, p. E1.

31. *Rivera Live,* October 3, 1995, provided by Burrelles Transcript Service.

32. *The Big Show,* November 10, 1997, provided by Burrelles Transcript Service.

33. Cited in Lisa Levitt Ryckman, "Legacy of JonBenet: For Friends, Cops, Neighbors, Tragedy Leaves Scars," *Denver Rocky Mountain News,* December 21, 1997, p. 5A.

34. MSNBC, *Scarborough Country,* transcript, April 20, 2006.

35. "Sexual Assault Statistics," *Men Against Sexual Assault,* http://sa.rochester.edu/masa/stats.php (accessed September 15, 2006). Also see Federal Bureau of Investigation, "Forcible Rape: Crime Statistics," http://www.fbi.gov/ucr/cius_04/offenses_reported/violent_crime/forcible_rape.html (accessed September 15, 2006).

36. Goldman was quoted in a segment entitled "Frey Testifies Against Scott Peterson," *O'Reilly Factor,* transcript, Fox News Channel, August 12, 2003. Hammer was quoted from *On the Record* with Greta Van Susteren, transcript, Fox News Channel, December 8, 2004.

37. "Analysis of Latest Developments in the Scott Peterson Trial," Fox News Channel, transcript, *The Big Story Weekend Edition,* December 11, 2004. The Van Susteren quote is from "Analyis of the Scott Peterson Murder Trial Developments," Fox News Channel, transcript, *On the Record,* October 27, 2004.

38. Neil Postman, *Amusing Ourselves to Death: Public Discourse in the Age of Show Business* (New York: Penguin, 1986), chap. 1.

39. Van Susteren is quoted from her own program, October 27, 2004.

40. *Internight,* November 10, 1997, provided by Burrelles Transcript Service.

41. *Rivera Live,* October 3, 1995, provided by Burrelles Transcript Service.

42. Postman, *Amusing Ourselves to Death,* chap. 1.

43. *Hardball,* November 10, 1997, provided by Burrelles Transcript Service.

44. *Charles Grodin,* November 10, 1997, provided by Burrelles Transcript Service.

45. Ibid.

46. Frank N. Magrid Associates, cited in Michael J. Wold and Geoffrey Sands, "Fearless Predictions: The Content World, 2005," *Brill's Content,* August 1999, p. 110.

47. See "The State of the News Media, 2006" section entitled Cable News, http://www.stateofthenewsmedia.com/2006/index.asp (accessed August 1, 2006).

48. "Trials and Tribulations," National Public Radio, *On the Media,* January 2, 2004.

49. "Peterson, Blake Boost Court TV," Newswire Multichannel, Reed Business Information, March 17, 2005.

50. "Ratings Do Jackson Jump," *Broadcasting & Cable,* June 15, 2006.

51. Matea Gold, "Straight from Van Susteren," *Los Angeles Times,* July 20, 2005, p. E1.

52. Don Kaplan, "Schiavo Right to Die Case Has It All," *New York Post,* March 25, 2005, p. 109.

53. See, for instance, "Media Frenzy for JonBenet Ramsey Continues Online, with Search Activity Jumping 2,000 Percent Over Past 72 Hours," Yahoo! Financial News, September 9, 2005, http://biz.yahoo.com/prnews/060823/new034.html (accessed September 15, 2006).

54. Marjorie Williams, "Man of the Hour," *Vanity Fair,* January 1999, p. 112.

55. Jonathan Alter, "The New Powers That Be," *Newsweek,* January 18, 1999, p. 25.

56. "Titans of 'tude," *Newsweek,* January 18, 1999, pp. 32–34.

57. Bill Kovach and Tom Rosentiel, *Warp Speed: America in the Age of Mixed Media* (New York: Century Foundation, 1999), 17.

58. Ibid., 18.

59. Michael J. Wold and Geoffrey Sands, "Fearless Predictions: The *Content* World in 2005," *Brill's Content,* August 1999, p. 113.

60. Robert S. Lichter and Linda S. Lichter, "Take This Campaign, Please," *Media Monitor,* September/October 1996, p. 5.

61. Peter Laufer, *Inside Talk Radio: America's Voice or Just Hot Air?* (New York: Birch Lane, 1995). For a more academic study on the impact of talk radio, see David C. Barker, *Rushed to Judgment* (New York: Columbia University Press, 2002).

62. Susan J. Tolchin, *The Angry American* (Boulder, CO: Westview, 1995), 83–87.

63. Howard Kurtz, *Hot Air* (New York: Basic, 1995).

64. Mike Gallagher, speaking on his syndicated radio show, April 14, 1999.

65. "Holloway Case Sparks Talk Show Controversy," NBC13.com, http://www.nbc13.com/news/7266600/detail.html (accessed August 8, 2006).

66. "Glenn Beck Suggests Buying Schiavo," *Radio Ink,* http://www.radioink.com/HeadlineEntry.asp?hid=127857&pt=todaysnews (accessed August 8, 2006).

67. For a range of assessments, see Selnow, *Electronic Whistle-Stops;* Tim Jordan, *Cyberpower: The Culture and Politics of Cyberspace and the Internet* (New York: Routledge, 1999); and Davis and Owen, *New Media and American Politics,* 113–116.

68. Ray Surette, *Media, Crime, and Criminal Justice: Images and Realities,* 2d ed. (Belmont, CA: Wadsworth, 1998), 232–233.

69. Drudge made these comments at the National Press Club on June 3, 1998. See Howard Kurtz, "Internet Gossip Parries the Press," *Washington Post,* June 3, 1998, p. D1.

70. See the Court TV website at http://www.courttv.com.

71. Ronald L. Goldfarb, *TV or Not TV: Television, Justice, and the Courts* (New York: New York University Press, 1998), 149.

72. Yahoo! search using the key words "Lance Ito," conducted November 15, 1998.

73. Yahoo! search using the key words "John and Lorena Bobbitt," conducted November 15, 1998.

74. Yahoo! search using the key words "Monica Lewinsky," conducted November 15, 1998.

75. Google search using key words "Natalee Holloway," conducted June 20, 2006.

76. See Amanda Lenhart and Susannah Fox, "Bloggers: A Portrait of the Internet's New Storytellers," Pew Internet and American Life Project, July 16, 2006, http://

www.pewinternet.org/PPF/r/186/report_display.asp (accessed September 15, 2006).

77. Ibid.

78. Tom R. Tyler, "Viewing *CSI* and the Threshold of Guilt: Managing Truth and Justice in Reality and Fiction," *Yale Law Journal* (March 2006): 155 ff; Timothy O. Lenz, *Changing Images of Law in Film and Television Crime Stories* (New York: Peter Lang, 2003); and Amy Lennard Goehner, "Where *CSI* Meets Real Law and Order," *Time,* August 11, 2004, pp. 69–71.

79. See, for instance, Surette, *Media, Crime, and Reality;* and Tyler, "Viewing *CSI* and the Threshold of Guilt."

80. TNT program schedule as of August 1, 2006, available online at http://www .tnt.tv/title/?oid=333808-560.

81. USA and FX program schedules as of August 1, 2006, available online at http://www.usanetwork.com/schedules/sched.php?sdate=7/24/2006 and http://www .variety.com/article/VR1117873475?categoryid=1303&cs=1, respectively.

82. See cable ratings in "Latest TV Ratings," AllYourTV.Com, http://allyourtv .com/latestratings/weblog.php?id=C0_7_1 (accessed August 1, 2006).

83. Rick Kissell, "Nets Hope Crime Pays Off This Fall," *Variety,* August 4, 2003, pp. 17–21; John Consoli, "CBS Defends Crime Dramas," MediaWeek.com, July 19, 2005, http://www.mediaweek.com/mw/search/article_display.jsp?vnu_content_id= 1000981462 (accessed July 7, 2006); Megan Larson, "More Crime Shows at A & E," MediaWeek.com, January 7, 2004, http://www.mediaweek.com/mw/search/article_dis- play.jsp?vnu_content_id=2063499 (accessed July 7, 2006).

84. The conclusion that fictional accounts of the legal system do a poor job of ed- ucating the public about the real workings of the system has been drawn by a number of the authors we cite. For a recent example, see Kit R. Roane, "The *CSI* Effect," *US News and World Report,* April 25, 2005, pp. 48–54.

85. Richard Ericson, "Television and the Drama of Crime: Moral Tales and the Place of Crime in Public Life," *Contemporary Sociology* 22 (November 1993): 855–857; and R. Andrew Holbrook and Timothy G. Hill, "Agenda-Setting and Prim- ing in Prime Time Television: Crime Dramas as Political Cues," *Political Communica- tion* 22 (July/September 2005): 277–295.

86. Lloyd Chiasson Jr., ed., *The Press on Trial* (Westport, CT: Praeger, 1997), x.

PART TWO

The Impact of the Media Culture on Public Attitudes

FOUR

Public Opinion, Trial Coverage, and Faith in the Criminal Justice System

There's a legal system—but I'm not sure there's any justice.
>—resident of Denver, Colorado,
>responding to the Simpson verdict[1]

I guess it really pays to be a star. If he were anyone else, he would have been found guilty.
>—resident of Fenton, Missouri,
>responding to Michael Jackson's acquittal[2]

I don't believe that if one of my children got kidnapped that the FBI would step in and it would be a great, big deal.
>—resident of Salt Lake City, Utah,
>on the Elizabeth Smart case[3]

As our previous chapters have shown, the public has received a steady diet of legal coverage emanating from recent investigations and trials. At times, this coverage has been sensationalistic and filled with overly graphic details or tawdry revelations. In other instances these cases have been presented as the most important news in the nation, in that they have been given more airtime and print space than competing stories. The public's interest in these legal proceedings has been evidenced by an increase in ratings for many news programs, and in the explosion in popularity of fictional legal dramas in prime time. Americans appear to have been the willing recipients of information about tabloid legal proceedings, and these stories have come, at times, to pervade the public discourse.

In 1994 nearly two-thirds of Americans claimed to have had conversations about Lorena Bobbitt and the Menendez brothers.[4] These numbers were likely even higher for the more heavily covered Clinton impeachment, the O.J. Simpson trial, the JonBenet Ramsey murder investigation, Terri Schiavo, Michael Jackson, and others. But beyond general, casual conversations about the guilt, innocence, or moral culpability of the various participants, Americans have discussed these cases in far more specific and legalistic terms. Media stories have prompted widespread popular discussion of legal topics such as perjury, reasonable doubt, standards of evidence, proper police procedure, the place of judicial discretion, jury behavior, expert witnesses, privacy, and parental and spousal abuse. We have come to discuss formerly esoteric topics with a casual familiarity normally reserved for chats about our favorite sitcoms or dramatic television programs. But again, while public interest in formerly obscure legal issues has presented an opportunity for civic education, the tabloid-like nature of the media's presentation has for the most part meant squandering that possibility.

Beyond a fascination with tabloid cases, the public, at least in several instances, has been dismayed by the actual conclusions to some of these stories. Public opinion polls have shown that a clear majority of Americans disagreed with the verdicts in the O.J. Simpson criminal trial and the first trial of the officers who beat Rodney King. Smaller but still substantial numbers of Americans have been alarmed by the acquittals of William Kennedy Smith and Michael Jackson, the deadlocked jury in the first trial of Erik and Lyle Menendez, and the judicial reversal and release of Louise Woodward. A media machine that has greatly turned up the volume and criticism in its presentation of these cases has fueled public distaste with their resolution.

In this chapter we turn our attention to the actual effects of tabloid justice media coverage on the public's knowledge and attitudes about the legal system. Does the current media culture affect how citizens view the system? Has increased media coverage of the legal system created a more informed citizenry? More specifically, as a result of tabloid-style media coverage, do citizens have less faith that juries can do their jobs properly, that judges can adequately control their courtrooms in an objective and fair manner, that lawyers will behave ethically, or that the police will treat all Americans in a fair and lawful way? If the answer to these questions is no, then perhaps the era of tabloid justice should be seen only as an era of media excess and irresponsibility. However, if this coverage has actually influenced what people know and what they think about the judicial process, then it is clear that scholars, policymakers, and interested citizens must come to better understand the broader effects of the tabloid justice era.

We will address these and other concerns by examining the results of two national public opinion polls that we conducted in 1999 and 2005 (i.e., during both the first and second periods of the tabloid justice era).[5] Ultimately, we will argue that the media's tabloid-style focus on these cases has done little to increase public knowledge about the legal system and has to some significant degree undermined faith in the US judicial process for a substantial number of citizens.

Media Coverage, Public Opinion, and the Legal System

Considering that the typical American is by far most likely to encounter "the law" at the level of local trial court proceedings and that so much of local news is concerned with crime coverage, it is rather surprising that relatively little academic research has been directed at examining citizen opinion about the justice system.[6] The limited information that does exist must normally be culled from polls that have focused on broader measures of public opinion. For instance, a 1994 poll conducted by the Times Mirror Center for the People and the Press sought to ascertain citizen opinion about the US court system. About 43 percent of the respondents held a generally favorable view of the system, while about 53 percent harbored a generally negative view about the courts.[7] By 2006, 46 percent viewed the courts positively, while 43 percent viewed them negatively. In both surveys, however, nearly three-quarters of Americans viewed the US Supreme Court positively.[8] Even so, this level of generality tells us little about how citizens perceive the more specific components of the legal system and nothing about how they might have formed those perceptions, but it does indicate that confidence in the system is at best a mixed bag.

Since 1993 the most consistent survey tool for measuring general public attitudes toward the justice system has been an annual poll conducted by the Gallup Organization. In the poll Americans are asked to assess their general confidence in a host of political, professional, and social institutions in the United States. In 1994, the year in which the O.J. Simpson criminal proceeding began, the number of people expressing confidence in the criminal justice system fell to a record low of 15 percent.[9] This statistic ranked the legal system lower in public esteem than other frequently vilified and distrusted institutions such as the public schools, organized labor, big business, and the US Congress.[10] Confidence in the legal system was already very low. So, for many who viewed the system negatively during the era of tabloid justice, the increased exposure to the courts provided an opportunity to reevaluate or perhaps reinforce previously existing attitudes.

Beyond the relatively few polls that address attitudes about crime and the justice system, there is a small body of work that focuses on public views of the US Supreme Court. Several of these studies have claimed that mass media coverage of the Court has influenced the attitudes of citizens. Public reaction to the Court seems to be largely based on the general political popularity of its decisions, rather than on any substantive knowledge about its work or its role in the broader constitutional order.[11] Simply put, politically popular decisions lead to positive public assessments of the Court, and politically unpopular decisions lead to negative assessments.[12] Although public approval levels for the Court are consistently higher than for Congress, this may be based on nothing more than the public's general lack of awareness of just what it is that the Supreme Court does. The more that poll questions address narrower, specific aspects of the Court's work, the more "don't know" and negative responses dominate.[13] These studies do show a correlation between coverage of the Supreme Court's decisions and public reactions to the institution. Of most relevance to our study, they indicate that public agreement with a decision in particular cases—and, more important, the way that the issues are presented by the media—often serves as a compelling factor in how citizens assess the overall body of the Supreme Court. In general, the manner in which the Court is presented fosters the legitimacy of that institution in the public mind.[14] Thus, one can plausibly conclude that the type of coverage in a given case does impact public opinion.

In thinking more specifically about whether coverage of high-profile legal proceedings has influenced public opinion, a number of writers have linked the public's negative attitudes toward the legal system with the mass media's increasingly negative tone in its reporting about the US judicial process.[15] In exploring the potential influences of recent crime coverage in the media, there are a number of possible consequences of this coverage. First, given that news organizations possess a limited amount of resources to expend, extensive tabloid justice coverage may reduce the attention paid to arguably more important issues of public concern. The mass public's lack of interest in, and meager knowledge of, important political and social events and issues have been well chronicled. Since the early 1960s voter turnout is generally down, citizens have far less trust in the institutions of government, and public apathy about politics and government has become a constant feature of politics in the United States.[16] The causes of such high levels of disinterest and low levels of knowledge lie far beyond the scope of this book. Nevertheless, it is worth noting that this thirty-five–year decline in political efficacy in the United States closely coincides with changes in the news business during that same period, which we have chronicled in Chapters 2 and 3.[17]

In the contemporary journalistic environment, it is common for news outlets to neglect important legal and political issues in the process of "chasing sleaze and celebrities."[18] Journalist Richard Krajicek and others have noted that this is particularly true of the media's coverage of crime and justice issues, as the pursuit of flashy crime dramas has led to a neglect of ostensibly more important events involving foreign policy, governmental corruption, welfare policy, campaign finance reform, the environment, and so on. Americans know and discuss the intimate details of JonBenet's final days, Monica Lewinsky's sexual proclivities, or Michael Jackson's pornography collection even as they are unable to find Iraq or Afghanistan on a map or name the chief justice of the US Supreme Court. And although the public's lack of basic knowledge about national or current events is nothing new, the explicit coverage of tabloid events may be further eroding public awareness of important domestic or international developments. At the very least, media coverage has trivialized or marginalized other important news events by prioritizing tabloid legal cases.

A second potential consequence of the tabloid justice style of media coverage is that many Americans may routinely be misled about the operation of the legal system. This possibility stands in contrast to the traditional view that increased public awareness of the courts will result in a more informed citizenry. It is interesting to note the number of scholars and journalists who have said that the O.J. Simpson and other legal dramas served as "grand civics lessons" for all Americans.[19] But while citizens have been exposed to the intimate workings of the justice system during these dramas, the processes and behavior on display were at times so unusual that the long-term educational value in conveying the reality of the legal system is questionable.

For instance, legal scholar Angelique Paul undertook a study of this tendency toward misinforming and attempted to test a number of hypotheses about how television trial coverage miseducates the public.[20] Paul surveyed people who had watched a significant portion of the Simpson criminal trial. She found that the respondents believed that a high percentage of criminal cases are resolved through jury trials; they thought that they knew significantly more about criminal rather than civil procedure (even though civil procedures are far more common); and they believed that violent crime was far more widespread than it actually is.[21] In essence, those who had followed the Simpson trial closely were much more likely to draw highly inaccurate conclusions about the realities of the legal system. Similarly, David Harris has persuasively argued that the media's focus on murder trials leads the public to believe that all defendants receive a "generous serving of due process" protection, when in reality most cases are quickly and routinely resolved through "mumbled questions and incantations in a crowded courtroom, before a judge taking plea after plea."[22]

A final possible consequence, and the primary focus of this chapter, involves the possibility that tabloid-style coverage of the judicial process has resulted in increasingly negative assessments of the justice system on the part of US citizens. Obviously, this concern is related to the second, that the public has been misinformed about the real operation of the system. But here we are concerned specifically with a loss of public trust, rather than with the question of what factual knowledge citizens have about the legal system. The view of the system that is on display during these tabloid-style cases is distinctly negative in tone. The cases selected for sustained media coverage tend to be highly anomalous; for the most part they exaggerate the inefficiencies and shortcomings of American law and involve proceedings that are not reflective of the everyday functioning of the system.

For instance, the prosecution of the Menendez brothers lasted almost seven years, which is far longer than a typical murder prosecution. This conveys the sense that the system is very ineffective. Similarly, when Judge Hiller Zobel overruled the jury's verdict in the trial of Louise Woodward, the decision was dissected on the cable news talk shows, which suggested this might be a frequent occurrence, when in fact it is quite rare for judges to overturn jury decisions that are consistent with the judge's original instructions. In another example, John Mark Karr, the man who confessed to JonBenet Ramsey's murder in 2006, was extradited from Colorado to California on misdemeanor child pornography charges, implying that this is a routine process, when in fact it is almost unheard of for such an extradition to take place for a misdemeanor charge.

Inaccurate images of the judicial process were, perhaps, most pervasive during the Simpson criminal trial. Coverage of the Simpson trial might have given the public the impression that defense attorneys routinely give press conferences at the end of each day's trial proceedings. Not surprisingly, when Christopher Darden, one of the key prosecutors in the Simpson criminal trial, was asked what US college students could learn about the criminal justice system from that case, his answer was "absolutely nothing." According to Darden, the Simpson case was so bizarre, unusual, and celebrity-driven that it was impossible to understand the daily workings of the system by watching that trial on television.[23] To cite just one example, it is well documented that about 80 percent of all criminal defendants in the United States are indigent, and in California 93 percent of all criminal cases are settled through the process of plea bargaining.[24] However, the Simpson case might lead one to conclude that defense lawyers regularly wreak havoc in courtrooms, when in reality that occurs in only a small percentage of cases.

Law professor Peter Arenella, a frequent media commentator on the Simpson case, cautioned that the media messages emanating from that trial might lead the public to demand some hasty, unnecessary, and even dangerous changes to the system. Accordingly, in the wake of the Simpson criminal trial, there were calls in California to ban cameras from courtrooms and to do away with the unanimous jury requirement in criminal trials.[25] Neither of these proposals was adopted, but both were debated in the California legislature.[26]

Based on the preceding discussion, both here and in Chapters 2 and 3, we have developed four hypotheses that will guide the analysis in this chapter. The foundation for each is our central concern with how tabloid-style coverage affects citizen attitudes and knowledge about the legal system. The hypotheses are as follows:

1. *Public knowledge of and familiarity with the high-profile tabloid trials are extensive.* For the tabloid cases and coverage of those cases to matter, there must be public retention of some of the facts and emotions emanating from these cases.
2. *Public knowledge and understanding of the legal system will not be greatly increased as a result of all the increased legal coverage in the tabloid justice era.* Though coverage of the legal system has increased in this time period, the excessive coverage of unusual and often

celebrity-focused legal proceedings has not led to greater public understanding of the system.

3. *Public exposure to tabloid cases has diminished public confidence in the legal system.* This hypothesis is a primary focus of this chapter and is supported by evidence that citizens have been distressed by the outcomes in several of the tabloid cases that we consider.

4. *Individual levels of news consumption and viewership of legal dramas will be correlated to a citizen's level of confidence in the legal system.* If exposure through the media causes negative perceptions of the legal system as speculated in the preceding hypothesis, then it would logically follow that even higher levels of media exposure would result in even more negative assessments.

The remainder of this chapter is devoted to assessing these hypotheses.

The Public's Knowledge of High-Profile Legal Investigations and Trials

As previously mentioned, only a handful of studies explore public attitudes about courts and the specific actors and components of the judicial process. Nevertheless, previous polling has shown that Americans believe they know a great deal about the specific cases that we focus on in this book. The Pew Research Center conducts regular polls that ask citizens about the issues in the news that they have followed most closely. Their results are relevant to our study, as their 1997 summary of surveys showed that 92 percent of Americans followed the first Rodney King trial, 77 percent followed the O.J. Simpson criminal trial, 66 percent followed the William Kennedy Smith trial, and 40 percent paid attention to the Menendez trial. In contrast, public awareness of, and interest in, stories such as the war in Bosnia (27 percent), Social Security reform (23 percent), and the Medicare debate (20 percent) lagged far behind.[27]

In the second era of tabloid justice, a national poll found that 85 percent of US citizens had been following the Terri Schiavo case either "very closely" or "fairly closely."[28] In another survey following Schiavo's death, respondents were asked to identify the one or two stories they had been following with the greatest interest in that particular news cycle, and 47 percent of respondents cited the Schiavo case, which was significantly higher than for other important stories at that time, such as gas prices (28 percent), Social Security reform (27 percent), the Pope's death (26 percent), or developments in the Iraq war (23 percent).[29] For the other tabloid cases we examine, pollsters found high degrees of interest, with roughly 62 percent following the Scott Peterson case, 56 percent the Michael Jackson trial, and 49 percent the Martha Stewart trial.[30]

However, 99 percent were aware of the verdict in the Jackson trial, and 49 percent said they listened or personally watched as the verdict was being read.[31]

Our own national polls focused directly on the tabloid justice cases that we described in Chapter 1. Conducted in spring 1999 and again in fall 2005, the polls revealed high levels of familiarity with these cases, even when they had occurred several years earlier. In addition to familiarity, in both surveys roughly 50 percent of the sample asserted that they believed that their knowledge of the legal system had increased based on what they knew about the tabloid cases.[32] Table 4.1 shows the public's level of familiarity with the cases that we have focused on in our analysis from both periods of the tabloid justice era. Because of the prominence of the Simpson case, we asked about it in both of our polls. We also asked about familiarity with the disappearance of Natalee Holloway, a story that was receiving a great deal of attention while we were fielding our second survey.

Not surprisingly, the highest levels of awareness were associated with the Simpson trial, but almost as recognizable to the respondents was the JonBenet Ramsey case (our poll was conducted before the August 2006 arrest of a suspect in the case, which again propelled the story into the national media spotlight). The Simpson case, even ten years after the conclusion of the criminal trial, remains an important cultural reference point for many Americans, with roughly 86 percent of citizens saying they are familiar with the facts of the case. Simpson himself remains a figure who is regularly covered by the press even today. Numerous stories continue to be aired and published that focus on his whereabouts, the selling and auctioning of his possessions to pay the dam-

Table 4.1   Public Familiarity with Facts Surrounding Tabloid Justice Cases

	Percentage Familiar
First period	
Criminal trial of O.J. Simpson	97
Investigation into the death of JonBenet Ramsey	86
Trial of the officers who beat Rodney King	74
Trial of Louise Woodward	65
Trials of the Menendez brothers	64
Trial of William Kennedy Smith	51
Second period	
Criminal trial of O.J. Simpson	86
Trial of Michael Jackson	79
Trial of Scott Peterson	74
Terri Schiavo case	69
Trial of Martha Stewart	69
Natalee Holloway investigation	44

Notes: First-period survey conducted in 1999, N = 1,003. Second-period survey conducted in 2005, N = 1,024. Entries are combined responses of those saying they are "very familiar" and "somewhat familiar."

ages awarded in his civil trial, and ongoing rumors about the status of his personal life and "business" endeavors. Most recently, a media storm was generated in November 2006, when the Fox News Channel announced that it would air a two-hour interview with Simpson, scheduled to coincide with the planned release of his new book, *If I Did It*. The show and the book were cancelled after a public outcry condemning the events.[33] Further, some of the central (as well as peripheral) players from the Simpson trial have gone on to enjoy successful careers in the media, and several are still called upon to discuss their involvement in the trial whenever Simpson is in the news.

In retrospect, the media precedent established in covering the Simpson trial paved the way for the press's approach to covering every subsequent tabloid justice legal story. The Simpson criminal trial coincided with the advent of the Internet and the ascendance of cable news, and these institutions were firmly in place by the time of the JonBenet murder on Christmas Eve 1996. Fully 86 percent of our first poll respondents voiced familiarity with the Ramsey case. There can be little doubt that if and when this case ever reaches a courtroom, it will be dubbed the latest trial of the century. In the ten years since JonBenet's murder, there have already been at least a dozen books written about the case.[34] And again, with the arrest of a suspect in August 2006, the case was catapulted back into the media spotlight. Greta Van Susteren of Fox News asserted that the JonBenet case had "haunted the entire world for the past ten years."[35] Such obvious exaggerations only served to fuel the drama about a case that really had no national significance.

Perhaps a bit more surprisingly, several cases from the early 1990s, including those involving William Kennedy Smith (1991), the Menendez brothers (who murdered their parents in 1989), and the officers who beat Rodney King (1992), remain highly familiar to a majority of our respondents. In addition to the cases on which we polled, the Pew Research Center has detected high levels of public familiarity with the trials involving Oklahoma City bombing suspect Timothy McVeigh, fallen televangelist Jim Bakker, boxing champ Mike Tyson, and Lorena Bobbitt.[36]

For the second tabloid justice period, the four cases we focused on showed slightly lower, but still substantial, levels of public awareness. As Table 4.1 shows, between 69 percent and 79 percent of Americans claimed to have a high degree of familiarity with the stories involving Michael Jackson, Scott Peterson, Terri Schiavo, and Martha Stewart. In our 2005 survey we found that 44 percent of respondents were familiar with the disappearance of Natalee Holloway in Aruba.

We sought to place these levels of public familiarity into context by comparing citizen knowledge about a few major political figures and social issues with knowledge about the tabloid justice cases. We were limited in this comparison by the types of factual questions asked by the Pew Research Center. Table

Table 4.2   Comparison of the Public's Knowledge of Selected Tabloid and
            Nontabloid Topics

	Percentage Answering Correctly
Tabloid topics	
Knew verdict of Martha Stewart trial	79
Aware Mike Tyson bit ear of boxing opponent	79
Amount awarded in Simpson civil trial	75
Identity of William Kennedy Smith	75
Identity of JonBenet Ramsey	70
Identity of Simpson trial judge Lance Ito	64
Nontabloid topics	
Identity of perpetrators of September 11 attacks	71
Identity of US vice president Al Gore	70
The political party that has a majority in the US House of Representatives	49
Aware that Britain returned Hong Kong to China	40
Identity of Russian president Vladimir Putin	37
Identity of US Senate majority leader Trent Lott	15
Identity of Chief Justice William Rehnquist	12
Identity of British prime minister Tony Blair	10

Source: Pew Research Center, 1991–2004.

4.2 offers a comparison of public knowledge regarding some specific legal story facts with knowledge about important political figures and events. The data suggest that factual knowledge about our selected trials and investigations regularly exceeds familiarity with ostensibly more important topics and events.

Citizens have a far greater awareness of the tabloid justice landscape than they do with the identities of some major American politicians and policy issues. In 1997 Americans were able to identify JonBenet Ramsey at the same levels as Al Gore, the vice president of the United States. Nearly seven times more Americans can estimate the dollar amount of the jury verdict in the Simpson civil trial as can recognize William Rehnquist, who served as chief justice of the United States for thirty-one years, or who know the identity of British prime minister Tony Blair, a frequent presence on US television news and the nation's chief ally in the war on terror. Less than half of respondents knew which political party currently controls the House of Representatives.

The information presented in Tables 4.1 and 4.2 lead us to several conclusions. First, the basic notion that the public has received and digested heavy doses of tabloid justice information seems unassailable. If we combine the levels of familiarity with the more specific factual knowledge depicted, we can conclude that the memory of these cases extends well beyond the time that the particular trial or investigation took place. This finding provides strong support for our first hypothesis. Moreover, we would reiterate that the prominent cases with which we are concerned have become a part of the fabric of US popular culture.

Coverage of High-Profile Legal Proceedings and Public Knowledge of the Legal System

A critical question in assessing the impact of the increase in legal coverage is whether or not the public's knowledge of the legal system has been altered. As we mentioned in our introductory chapter, a number of scholars and commentators have argued that increased exposure to the legal system should lead to improved understanding of how the system operates. In the era of tabloid justice, particularly the first era, the public has been able to closely view judges, lawyers, and law enforcement officials carrying out their roles. But has this new media focus actually led to more knowledge and a better understanding of the system?

In early 2000, nearing the end of what we regard as the first period in the tabloid justice era, the Roper Center at the University of Connecticut conducted a survey on the law and the media. The survey asked a number of questions gauging respondents' factual knowledge about the legal system. In our 2005 poll we further explored whether the massive recent increase in legal coverage and fictional legal entertainment has resulted in a more informed citizenry. Table 4.3 presents the results for five questions from the Roper poll, and Table 4.4 presents the results of eight basic factual questions that we asked in our 2005 survey. We believe that the answers to these questions provide us with an idea of how much factual knowledge the public possesses about the judicial process in the United States. In our poll, a majority of respondents provided generally accurate answers to only two out of eight questions. A majority of respondents correctly knew that the United States houses a greater percentage of its citizens in prisons than any other democratic country, and over 50 percent also knew that the prosecutor determines the actual charges in a

Table 4.3   Public Knowledge of the Legal System, Roper Center Poll, 2000

	Percentage of Respondents with Correct Answer
Roughly what percentage of criminal defendants have their cases decided by a jury trial?	28
On average, what is the length of time it takes from arrest to sentence?	28
What percentage of the nation's police officers do you think are a racial or ethnic minority?	28
What percentage of the nation's lawyers do you think are a racial or ethnic minority?	48
What percentage of the nation's judges do you think are a racial or ethnic minority?	58

Notes: The Roper Poll provided respondents with a range of possible answers. See Roper Center, Public Opinion Online, www.ropercenter.uconn.edu, for exact question wording.

Table 4.4   Public Knowledge of the Criminal Justice and Legal System

	Percentage of Respondents with Correct Answer
Know whether violent crime is increasing or decreasing	13
On average, how many cases does the US Supreme Court hear in a year?	13
Roughly what percentage of criminal defendants plead guilty?	15
Roughly what percentage of criminal defendants have their cases decided by a jury trial?	19
Roughly what percentage of defendants are acquitted in jury trials?	19
Roughly what percentage of criminal defendants are able to hire their own lawyers?	37
Know that the United States has a greater percentage of citizens in prison than other democratic countries	59
Know who decides what charges will be brought against criminal defendants (prosecutor)	64

Source: 2005 Tabloid Justice Survey, N = 1,014.

Notes: Calculations of correct answers allowed for significant leeway so that respondents offering reasonable answers were counted as providing a correct answer. See Appendix A for source information on correct answers.

normal criminal investigation, though this is a very basic fact routinely illustrated in many of the most popular television legal dramas.

Beyond these two questions from the 2005 poll, respondents demonstrated little factual awareness of the judicial process. They did not have any clear knowledge of phenomena such as the frequency of plea bargaining, the frequency of jury trials, defendant indigence, the activities of the Supreme Court, or even whether violent crime is increasing or decreasing in the country. And the Roper poll further reveals that US citizens are very poorly informed about the length of time it takes one to travel through the criminal justice system, as well as the racial and ethnic makeup of various legal system participants.

These wildly incorrect responses are central to our arguments. If Americans have been exposed to a large increase in the coverage of trials and investigations, if they now have a close familiarity with the participants and verdicts involved in these "major" cases, and if their knowledge about these stories and people exceeds their awareness of other political issues and figures, then we might expect them to have actually acquired some specific knowledge about the way US courts function. On the contrary, perhaps because the tabloid justice cases are so unusual, so unrepresentative of the normal everyday functioning of the law, citizens have actually become less informed about the system. While a more definitive assessment of how the tabloid justice period has affected public knowledge about the legal system would require gauges of citizen knowledge before the era of tabloid justice—measures that do not exist—

our findings certainly suggest that the increased degree of legal coverage since the early 1990s has not led to a more informed public. This finding runs counter to the arguments and hopes of a number of scholars that greater transparency in the legal system will result in greater citizen knowledge.

At a minimum, we feel the evidence in support of our second hypothesis is quite convincing. But does public familiarity with these cases have any broader ramifications? It is to this question and our next two hypotheses that we now turn.

Tabloid Justice and Public Confidence in the US Legal System

As we begin to assess public confidence in the justice system, it is important to recall that previous studies have revealed a generally declining trust in most government institutions since the 1970s.[37] That being said, it is not surprising that our study generally revealed low levels of confidence in the justice system. Table 4.5 shows the specific results for both of our national surveys. In general, we found that the public holds dismally low opinions of both the system generally and the various individual components/participants in it. Our findings are consistent with previous national survey data in this regard.[38] Across the two surveys, our results did reveal a slight upward trend in confidence in the criminal justice system in general and many of the parts of the legal system.

The question of central concern for our analysis is whether the coverage of the tabloid justice cases has affected public perceptions of the legal system. In our introductory chapter we noted that there are numerous difficulties involved in attempting to measure the effects of the mass media on public attitudes.[39] Cause and effect are hard to establish, for many factors can influence

Table 4.5 Confidence in the Criminal Justice System, 1999 and 2005

	Percentage Expressing Confidence	
	1999	2005
Criminal justice system in general	20	28
Police	31	36
Judges	27	33
Juries	29	32
Defense attorneys	19	18
Prosecuting attorneys	20	23
Sample size	1,003	1,030

Note: Entries are the percentage of respondents who had "complete" or "a great deal" of confidence in the criminal justice system and the listed aspects of the system.

one's perceptions of, in this case, the criminal justice system. Recognizing these difficulties, we used a number of methods in attempting to measure the influence of the coverage that we have been describing. First, in each of the national polls we conducted we randomly divided our survey sample in half. We asked one group of respondents for their level of confidence in the system as a whole and in several specific criminal justice participants prior to mentioning any of the individual cases.

For the other group of respondents, we asked numerous questions about the tabloid justice cases themselves before inquiring about the person's overall level of confidence.[40] Our intent was to determine whether first cueing respondents with the names of the cases would influence their responses. Such question ordering, or priming experiment, is a common means of attempting to measure how particular events affect a person's general attitudes.[41] In *The Nature and Origins of Mass Opinion,* John Zaller argues that public opinion measures are often the result of an individual respondent "averaging" conflicting feelings or providing an answer based on the considerations that come most quickly to mind. Zaller urges survey researchers not to view responses based on question-order effects as "methodological artifacts" but to use them to gain insight regarding what factors help to influence public opinion on a given subject.[42] He further notes that important factors shaping public attitudes can be missed in typical survey research because the respondents simply do not recall some of the elements that influence their opinions in the few moments they have in which to answer the questions posed to them.[43]

Along these lines, our research revealed that question ordering, at least in our 1999 poll, had an important impact on how respondents viewed the system. Those respondents who had first been reminded about the high-profile cases demonstrated significantly *lower* levels of confidence in the criminal justice system, the police, judges, juries, and prosecuting attorneys. And although the differences were not extraordinarily large, they reveal a clear and important pattern in which recollection of the tabloid justice trials triggered more negative responses regarding the criminal justice system. When we replicated this experiment in 2005, the experiment did not produce any statistically significant differences. The most plausible explanation for this distinction is that the first survey was conducted closer to the time of the O.J. Simpson case, and anger and dismay about that case and its outcome were much fresher.

To further explore the relationship between media coverage and public attitudes toward criminal justice in the United States, we directly queried our sample about whether media coverage of these cases had affected their confidence in the system. We inquired as to whether respondents had come to have more, less, or the same amount of trust in the system as a result of their exposure to these high-profile trials and investigations. Table 4.6 reveals the results of these questions.

Table 4.6   Influence of Tabloid Trials on Citizen Confidence in the Criminal
Justice System (percentages)

	Less Confident	More Confident	No Change	Don't Know
Change in confidence in the criminal justice system as a result of exposure to the following cases				
First period				
Criminal trial of O.J. Simpson	75	3	19	3
Investigation into the death of JonBenet Ramsey	70	2	17	11
Trial of the officers who beat Rodney King	49	5	22	24
Trial of William Kennedy Smith	36	2	16	46
Trial of Louise Woodward	25	6	34	35
Trials of the Menendez brothers	14	25	28	33
Second period				
Trial of Michael Jackson	57	8	31	4
Trial of Martha Stewart	39	38	18	5
Terri Schiavo case	37	33	21	8
Trial of Scott Peterson	13	45	38	4

Notes: N = 1,003 for Simpson, King, Ramsey, Smith, Woodward, and Menendez. N = 1,043 for Jackson, Stewart, Peterson, and Schiavo.

For the first tabloid justice period, nearly three-quarters of citizens had less confidence in the system as a result of what they saw in the O.J. Simpson and JonBenet Ramsey cases, and about half had diminished levels of faith after watching the Rodney King legal events and their violent aftermath. Very few respondents had increased levels of confidence after following these cases, and only small minorities of Americans had either "no change" or did not have opinions. For the second tabloid justice period, a strong majority of respondents lost confidence in the system after the Michael Jackson trial, while over a third had similar reactions to the Martha Stewart and Terri Schiavo cases. The only case in which almost half of those polled had an increased level of confidence was that involving Scott Peterson, who was of course convicted on all charges. In sum, it is clear that when asked directly about tabloid justice cases the public views them in a negative light, and that they have a significantly negative impact on citizen confidence in the legal system as well.

Our final method of examining the link between these cases and public trust in the legal system involved the use of *Pearson correlation coefficients*. We measured the relationship between an individual's general confidence in the system and his or her assessment of how the system operated in each of the cases. That is, if a particular person held a negative view of the performance of the justice system in the JonBenet Ramsey case, for instance, did that person also tend to hold a negative view of the system as a whole? Although Pearson coefficients do not allow us to determine causation, they do allow us to determine if there is a significant relationship between the cases and trust in the overall legal system. The entries in Table 4.7 indicate the direction and the strength of the relationship between general trust levels and the impact of the individual cases.

The data in Table 4.7 reveal a clear pattern. Although the coefficients are small, they show that almost all of the cases are related to an individual's overall assessment of the justice system. Plainly stated, negative reactions to each of the cases are correlated with lower levels of confidence in the system as a whole. Every case except for the trial of the Menendez brothers and the Terri Schiavo story revealed such a statistically significant relationship.

Based on the combined evidence presented in Tables 4.5 and 4.6, there are strong indications that the media's presentation of these cases has influenced the way that most citizens view the overall legal system. Each of the measures we have used—a question wording experiment, direct questioning, and case-specific correlations with general attitudes—points toward the conclusion that media attention to high-profile trials has worked to diminish many citizens' overall confidence in the quality of justice in the United States. This finding, which we elaborate on later, provides tangible evidence that there have been real consequences to this style of legal coverage. Additionally, this finding offers support for our third hypothesis: that tabloid-style coverage leads to more negative assessments of the legal system. We now turn to public attitudes about specific participants within the justice system.

Table 4.7   Correlation Coefficients Between General Confidence in the Criminal Justice System and the Tabloid Justice Cases

	Correlation Coefficient
General confidence in the criminal justice system correlated with confidence in the criminal justice system in the following cases	
First period	
Trial of Louise Woodward (639)	.14**
Criminal trial of O.J. Simpson (958)	.13**
Trial of the officers who beat Rodney King (751)	.13**
Trial of William Kennedy Smith (532)	.13**
Investigation into the death of JonBenet Ramsey (876)	.09**
Trials of the Menendez brothers (661)	.07
Second period	
Trial of Michael Jackson (867)	.16**
Trial of Martha Stewart (799)	.15**
Trial of Scott Peterson (801)	.12**
Terri Schiavo case (720)	.07

Notes: Sample size is shown in parentheses and includes only those familiar with the case. General confidence in the legal system was coded 1 to 5, with 1 representing the most confidence and 5 representing the least confidence. Individual cases were coded 1 to 3, with 1 representing the most confidence and 3 representing the least confidence. Entries are Pearson correlation coefficients with a two-tailed significance test, ** $p < .01$ and * $p < .05$.

Juries, Judges, the Police, and Prosecutors

Moving beyond general assessments, we asked our respondents whether these cases affected their assessment of the performance of particular figures involved in the legal process. Each of the cases we studied tended to highlight the behavior of particular aspects and participants within the system. Accordingly, in this section we examine the public's reaction to the performance of juries, judges, the police, and prosecutors, all of which have come under intense scrutiny in the media's analysis of these cases.

Juries

The institution of the jury has been characterized variously as "the most fascinating and most controversial aspect" and as one of "the most romanticized and most vilified factors" in the US judicial process.[44] Debates about the role of juries have undoubtedly been heightened by several of the high-profile criminal trials in the tabloid justice era. Controversial jury verdicts in the trials of Lorena Bobbitt, the Menendez brothers, Louise Woodward, the LAPD officers who beat Rodney King, and the O.J. Simpson and Michael Jackson cases left many wondering if the jury still serves a useful purpose in the modern justice system.[45] Discussion and debate about the role of juries have increased recently, despite overall decreases in the percentage of trials actually decided by juries. In fact, today fewer than 5 percent of all cases that enter the judicial process are ever placed before a jury.[46] Yet despite a chorus of recent criticism, most Americans continue to strongly support the fundamental ideal that any citizen accused of a serious crime (or involved in a significant civil lawsuit) is entitled to a verdict rendered by a jury drawn from the community in which the incident occurred.[47] The jury, then, remains a powerful symbol of democracy and justice, but perhaps less so as our chosen means of processing cases in the justice system.

We employed two separate means of examining how our respondents' assessments of the jury system may have been affected by intense media exposure to our chosen cases. First, we simply asked people whether the outcome of a particular tabloid justice case had affected their overall confidence in the jury system. Next, we correlated citizens' reactions to jury performance in several cases with their overall assessment of the US system of jury trials (essentially employing the same type of analysis seen in Table 4.6). We focused only on the seven cases in which there was significant public discussion about jury performance: those involving Simpson, Rodney King, Michael Jackson, Louise Woodward, William Kennedy Smith, Scott Peterson, and the Menendez brothers. As we have previously mentioned, polls show that a majority of the public believes that the juries in the Simpson criminal trial and in the first trial of the LAPD officers reached the wrong conclusions, and the same appears to be true of the 2005 Michael Jackson trial.

Table 4.8 reveals the results of the direct-assessment question, while Table 4.9 shows the correlation coefficients. Table 4.8 indicates that in three of the cases (Simpson, Jackson, and King) over a third of respondents lost significant confidence in juries. For the Simpson and Michael Jackson cases, these numbers were 62 and 50 percent, respectively. In only two cases did a significant number of people have an increased level of confidence (the Menendez brothers and Scott Peterson). Not surprisingly, these were the two cases from our list that involved murder trials that ended in fairly unambiguous guilty verdicts.

Table 4.8   Influence of Tabloid Trials on Citizen Confidence in Juries, Judges, Police, Prosecutors, and the Media (percentages)

	Less Confident	More Confident	No Change
Change in confidence in the jury system as a result of exposure to the following cases			
Criminal trial of O.J. Simpson	62	5	30
Trial of Michael Jackson	50	9	36
Trial of the officers who beat Rodney King	38	5	31
Trial of William Kennedy Smith	29	2	21
Trial of Louise Woodward	17	7	40
Trials of the Menendez brothers	11	23	33
Trial of Scott Peterson	10	44	41
Change in confidence in judges as a result of exposure to the following cases			
Criminal trial of O.J. Simpson	57	4	35
Terri Schiavo case	34	20	38
Trial of the officers who beat Rodney King	31	5	39
Trial of Martha Stewart	27	18	48
Trial of William Kennedy Smith	26	2	24
Trial of Louise Woodward	23	6	35
Trials of the Menendez brothers	10	21	35
Change in confidence in the police as a result of exposure to the following cases			
Investigation into the death of JonBenet Ramsey	67	3	19
Criminal trial of O.J. Simpson	57	6	34
Trial of the officers who beat Rodney King	52	3	20
Trial of Michael Jackson	35	11	47
Trial of Scott Peterson	12	42	42
Trials of the Menendez brothers	10	21	43
Change in confidence in prosecutors as a result of exposure to the following cases			
Trial of Michael Jackson	45	10	39
Trial of Martha Stewart	32	18	43
Change in confidence in media coverage of the legal system as result of exposure to the following cases			
Trial of Scott Peterson	35	19	41
Terri Schiavo case	44	14	34

Note: N = 1,003 for Simpson, King, Ramsey, Smith, Woodward, and Menendez. N = 1,035 for Jackson, Stewart, Peterson, and Schiavo. Rows do not total 100 because "don't know" responses are not included.

Table 4.9   Correlation Coefficients Between General Confidence in Juries, Judges, Police, and Prosecutors, and the Tabloid Justice Cases

	Correlation Coefficient
General confidence in the jury system correlated with the confidence in the jury system in the following cases	
Trial of William Kennedy Smith (521)	.24**
Trial of Michael Jackson (860)	.19**
Criminal trial of O.J. Simpson (960)	.17**
Trial of the officers who beat Rodney King (745)	.17**
Trial of Scott Peterson (795)	.16**
Trial of Louise Woodward (642)	.15**
Trials of the Menendez brothers (662)	.08*
General confidence in judges correlated with the confidence in judges in the following cases	
Trial of the officers who beat Rodney King (741)	.24**
Trial of William Kennedy Smith (519)	.24**
Trial of Louise Woodward (634)	.23**
Trial of Martha Stewart (779)	.21**
Criminal trial of O.J. Simpson (961)	.20**
Terri Schiavo case (711)	.16**
Trials of the Menendez brothers (660)	.12**
General confidence in the police correlated with confidence in the police in the following cases	
Trial of the officers who beat Rodney King (755)	.20**
Trial of Michael Jackson (839)	.20**
Criminal trial of O.J. Simpson (964)	.18**
Trial of Scott Peterson (802)	.11**
Investigation into the death of JonBenet Ramsey (881)	.08*
Trials of the Menendez brothers (656)	.08*
General confidence in the prosecutors correlated with the confidence in prosecutors in the following areas	
Trial of Michael Jackson (827)	.26**
Trial of Martha Stewart (772)	.20**

Notes: Sample size is shown in parentheses and includes only those familiar with the case. General confidence in the legal system was coded 1 to 5, with 1 representing the most confidence and 5 representing the least confidence. Individual cases were coded 1 to 3, with 1 representing the most confidence and 3 representing the least confidence. Entries are Pearson correlation coefficients with a two-tailed significance test, ** $p < .01$ and * $p < .05$.

Table 4.9 reveals that citizens who reacted negatively to jury behavior in a given case were significantly more likely to possess a generally low level of confidence in the jury system as a whole. Such correlations were statistically significant for all of the cases, and these low levels of confidence were particularly pronounced for the William Kennedy Smith, Simpson, Michael Jackson, and Rodney King (LAPD officers) trials.

Judges

Trial judges possess a great deal of power and discretion in the US legal system. From the point of arrest, or perhaps even earlier if search warrants are issued, to the final disposition of a case, judges preside over every step in the justice process. Interestingly, they often exert much of their power and discretion in negotiations and meetings with lawyers outside the courtroom.[48] Not surprisingly, this wide latitude allows trial judges to perform their duties in a variety of different styles.[49] Some judges run highly regimented courtrooms, in which they work closely with their staff, prosecutors, and defense attorneys, whereas other judges take a more hands-off approach, letting the opposing attorneys dominate trial procedures. Hence, the complex reality of the judge's role confounds the typical public notion that a judge's job consists mainly of presiding over live courtroom trials.[50]

Turning to the judges who have been at the center of our tabloid justice trials, we can see many of the advantages and possible shortcomings of judicial discretion. Arguably, in our selected cases, only three judges truly became public figures. These were Lance Ito in the Simpson criminal trial, Hiller Zobel in the Louise Woodward case, and Rodney Melville in Michael Jackson's trial. Virtually every media commentator has been highly critical of the manner in which Ito presided over the Simpson trial. Many in the legal profession believe that he did not maintain adequate control of the courtroom, adequately restrict the grandstanding of the various lawyers, or move the case along in a timely manner. In fact, in some legal circles, Ito's name is now almost synonymous with incompetent, ill-advised, and weak judicial behavior.[51]

Zobel also commanded center stage when he threw out a jury's verdict, but his actions received a more mixed response from legal observers. To some, he was a hero for overturning an unjust jury verdict. To others, he exhibited an inexcusable misuse of judicial discretion. Massachusetts appellate court justice John Greaney, who reviewed the appeal of Judge Zobel's decision, wrote in his dissent: "Here it appears that the judge [Zobel] identified himself with Woodward's cause, compromising the public's confidence in the integrity and impartiality of our courts."[52]

In contrast, although Judge Rodney Melville became well known to the public during the lengthy Jackson trial, both citizens and commentators gave him generally high marks for his handling of the case, even when they disagreed with the trial's verdict. Melville continually reined in both legal teams and by most accounts did so with a firm hand and even a sense of humor.[53]

We asked respondents about the judicial behavior on display in these and several other cases. Our goal was to determine whether the media coverage of tabloid proceedings might turn the public against judges simply through their association with negatively viewed outcomes. We asked people to rate how the judges in the Simpson, Schiavo, King, Stewart, Kennedy Smith, Woodward, and Menendez brothers trials made them feel about the work of judges overall. The results to these questions are presented in Tables 4.8 and 4.9.

The analysis of our selected cases reveals that citizens have lost more confidence in judges than in juries during the tabloid justice era. The responses to our queries reveal a pattern suggesting that the public rates the performance of judges (as was the case with juries) as a simple correlate of their overall approval of the outcome of a given case. For instance, the performance of Judge Ito in the Simpson case greatly reduced the confidence of the public in judges, undoubtedly because the outcome of the trial was greeted with such widespread public disdain. The highly publicized reversal by Judge Zobel in the Woodward case did not meet the same level of scorn, largely because this trial outcome was not viewed as negatively as the Simpson verdict. The other cases noted in Table 4.8 follow the same pattern, with some serious reservations revealed about the work of judges in the Schiavo, King, and Stewart cases. We would speculate that for those who remember the outcomes of these cases, they generally disagreed with the outcome and have, in a sense, held the judges responsible. True to form, the work of judges was more likely to meet with public approval in the trials of the Menendez brothers and Scott Peterson.

The Police

During the 1990s the Rodney King cases (and the riots in their aftermath) gave rise to an intense public debate about police behavior. Television stations throughout the nation repeatedly broadcast the infamous videotape showing members of the LAPD savagely beating King. Since the King incident, the mass media have cast a consistently watchful eye on police conduct. Such conduct was heavily analyzed during the Simpson trials and more recently during the ongoing JonBenet Ramsey investigation and in the Martha Stewart and Michael Jackson cases.

In 1998 and 1999 two highly publicized New York City incidents also called attention to the behavior of law enforcement officers. The first of these cases involved the torture of Abner Louima, a Haitian immigrant who was arrested in a bar-room brawl. Louima later claimed that New York police officers sodomized him with a toilet plunger in a bathroom at the police station, and one officer eventually pleaded guilty to that charge. The second episode involved West African immigrant Amadou Diallo, an unarmed street vendor who died in a hail of forty-one bullets fired by four undercover New York Police Department officers.[54] At the time of these cases US attorney general Janet Reno even recognized that declining trust in the police was a national problem.[55]

In order to analyze public attitudes about the police, we followed the same approach that we used to examine judges and juries. Tables 4.8 and 4.9 reveal our sample's assessments of police performance in several of the tabloid cases. The lower portion of Table 4.8 reveals some very high levels of dismay directed at police behavior in the Ramsey, Simpson, and King cases.[56] Public criticism in the King case was largely rooted in the allegedly racist behavior of members of the LAPD (we explore these racial dynamics in more detail in Chapter 5). In the Ramsey investigation, the mass media have focused heavily on supposedly less-than-stellar police and prosecutorial work. Numerous journalistic accounts have documented the police's mistakes at the beginning of the investigation,[57] and one critic characterized law enforcement efforts in the case as "utterly inept."[58]

Regardless of the accuracy of such assessments, the public perception in these cases is that the police have failed to do their jobs competently. In the Simpson case, many assailed the LAPD as both racist and incompetent. Racial slurs uttered by officer Mark Furhman, as well as sloppy evidence collection, were frequently cited as explanations for Simpson's acquittal. In contrast, reaction to the Menendez case revealed little criticism of the police, because law enforcement behavior was not an overtly relevant or controversial issue in those proceedings. Over a third of respondents had a negative reaction to the police work in the Michael Jackson case, but this is not accompanied by any real knowledge of police behavior in that case. Rather, as we will discuss shortly, this negative response is probably a function of dissatisfaction with District Attorney Tom Sneddon and with Jackson's eventual acquittal on all charges.

Prosecutors and Overall Media Coverage

In our most recent survey we included questions about the behavior of prosecutors and about reactions to the overall media coverage itself, queries that we did not include in our 1999 poll. We limited our questioning on each of these issues to trials in which these factors were the subject of significant public discussion. We sought to ascertain changes in public confidence in prosecutors by inquiring only about the Michael Jackson and Martha Stewart cases. The effect of media coverage in specific cases was explored by asking about the Scott Peterson trial and the Schiavo legal battle.

Table 4.8 shows the results of these questions. With regard to both prosecutors and general media coverage, we uncovered similar results. Very few citizens revealed a higher confidence level after witnessing these four cases. Between 30 and 45 percent of respondents in all four cases voiced a lower level of confidence, while roughly the same number answered "no change" in their confidence in prosecutors and in media coverage. It becomes clear that in the tabloid justice era, media exposure to these legal stories is highly likely to result in either a loss in system confidence or no change in one's level of confidence. What this means, of course, is that tabloid justice coverage has rarely resulted in any increase in public confidence in the legal system.

In sum, our polling on each of these specific components of the justice system shows that public faith in the system as a whole has decreased as a result of what citizens know about these specific cases. Thus, media exposure to particular trials can have the result of highlighting, and at times discrediting, particular players within the system. Further, Tables 4.8 and 4.9 indicate that the public draws conclusions about the behavior of juries, judges, the police, and prosecutors simply by assessing the outcome of particular cases. Finally, Table 4.9 reveals that respondents who held negative views about the behavior of juries, judges, the police, and prosecutors in these particular cases also held strongly negative views about these legal actors more generally.

Overall, the results lend further support to our third hypothesis. We should emphasize again that what troubles us is not that citizens are drawing negative conclusions about the system or its particular components. In at least some of our cases, such negative responses are warranted. What concerns us is that no single legal case can illuminate any of these important issues adequately, particularly when it is covered in the now-normalized tabloid justice style.

Legal Coverage and the Loss of Legitimacy

By means of a final set of questions, we sought to understand how the public's diminished confidence in the justice system might translate into changes in individual citizens' expectations about how they themselves might be treated in a potential encounter with the system. Prior to asking these questions, we encouraged respondents to think about the trials and investigations that we had been discussing throughout the questionnaire (see Appendix B). We explicitly requested that respondents reflect on the tabloid justice cases while answering these questions. Essentially, we wanted to know whether what the citizens had learned about the cases affected their expectations about what they might personally encounter if they were to come in contact with law enforcement and/or the judicial system. We asked people in both of our national polls to assess how they would feel if they or a family member were forced to interact with judges, juries, the police, and prosecuting attorneys. The results of these questions and responses are displayed in Table 4.10.

Coverage of tabloid justice cases has contributed to a large number of citizens losing faith in how they or someone close to them would be treated in the US criminal justice system. Although this loss of confidence is slightly less pronounced in our 2005 findings, it remains quite clear that many more citizens have lost confidence because of these cases than have gained more faith in the system and its various officials within the system.

As a result of what citizens have learned through the media's coverage of these cases, roughly 40 percent of our respondents claimed that they now had less confidence that the legal system would protect their rights, that prosecutors would treat them fairly, and that the police would adequately respect their privacy and due process guarantees. Perceptions of judges and juries suffered somewhat less, with about one-fourth of our sample saying that their trust in

Table 4.10   Personal Impact of Knowledge of Tabloid Justice Cases,
1999 and 2005 (percentages)

	Less Confident	More Confident	No Change
As a result of the criminal trials and investigations we have been discussing, do you have less, more, or the same confidence that:			
the laws surrounding the criminal justice system would protect your rights?	44(44)	30(14)	23(41)
you or a family member would be treated fairly by prosecuting attorneys if arrested as a suspect in a crime?	43(38)	25(9)	28(51)
you or a family member would be treated fairly by the police if arrested as a suspect in a crime?	40(37)	27(14)	27(48)
you or a family member would be treated fairly by a judge if you had been arrested and were standing trial for a crime?	32(26)	32(13)	33(58)
you or a family member would be treated fairly by a jury if you been arrested and were standing trial for a crime?	35(23)	31(14)	30(61)

Notes: N = 1,043 for 2005 survey. Numbers in parentheses represent 1999 survey results (N = 1003). Rows do not total 100 because "don't know" responses are not indcluded.

these legal actors had been diminished by their knowledge of our selected cases. Only a handful of citizens gained confidence in how they would be treated by the various components of the system, and this assertion is made clear in both our 1999 and 2005 surveys.

It is clear that exposure to these cases has undermined the confidence of a significant number of citizens. Such increased cynicism may be the most damaging effect of tabloid-style legal coverage. This overall decrease in legitimacy, when combined with low levels of factual knowledge and dismal levels of political and civic participation, is what concerns us most of all. It is not unreasonable for citizens to be dissatisfied with the operation of the justice system, even at a fundamental level. Today, however, such criticism is driven by a sensationalistic, misleading style of legal coverage, which is transmitted to a receptive—yet undiscerning—audience.

Assessing the Effects of Increased Levels of Media Exposure

Our fourth and final hypothesis focused on whether an increase in one's level of media exposure would lead to increasingly negative attitudes toward the justice system. In attempting to determine if this was true, we asked respondents in our sample about the frequency with which they watched network national newscasts, read newspapers, used the Internet, viewed legal dramas, and watched cable news channels such as Fox News, MSNBC, CNN, and Court TV.

Our results revealed that there was little or no relationship between respondents' negative attitudes about the tabloid cases and their media consumption habits. The frequency with which one watched or consumed legal news appears to have almost no significant effect on one's attitudes about either the individual cases or the overall legal system. The only clear pattern of differences that emerged was our finding that regular viewers of cable news programs claimed to have significantly higher levels (on average by about 10 percent more) of familiarity with each of the tabloid cases in the first era. In the second era, those tuning into cable news remained more likely to be familiar with the tabloid cases. This finding is one we would have expected.

Originally, we were quite surprised when we found that there were few differences in attitudes between high- and low-volume news consumers. Upon further investigation, however, these findings began to make sense. In our first sample, 70 percent of respondents said that they watched a national news program every day, 56 percent read a daily newspaper, and 45 percent said that they tuned in to a cable news station each day. While these numbers have changed somewhat, with network news and newspapers in decline, almost all Americans follow the news in some form or another. Among the respondents, more than 90 percent said that they watched or read the news at least "several times a week." Only 8 percent of the sample said that they "rarely" or "never" paid attention to any of the news outlets that we mentioned. These findings about news habits are consistent with other recent research.[59]

Ultimately, these results offer support for our contention that there is now an almost total cultural immersion in (and societal awareness of) the tabloid justice cases. Because these events are covered in every media outlet, almost all citizens become aware of them, and consequently most citizens develop opinions about them. People who follow the news at any level are well acquainted with JonBenet Ramsey, Michael Jackson, and Martha Stewart, for example. In our first survey, even among the 8 percent who indicated that they did not follow the news, over half claimed that they were familiar with the Menendez brothers, and 41 percent with Louise Woodward. In our second survey, less than 3 percent said they did not consult the news media for coverage of legal stories. In essence, there is no escape from the coverage of these cases, and we thus conclude that news consumption habits have little bearing on one's overall assessment of the justice system. Similarly, in an atmosphere of near total media saturation, it is difficult for any citizen to avoid hearing about the basic facts and outcomes of high-profile legal cases. What this means is that our poll results do not offer support for our fourth hypothesis. An increase in one's news consumption did not lead to more negative assessments of the system. In the end, a large number of our respondents, regardless of their level of exposure to the mass media, offered negative assessments of the legal system.

Conclusion

We began this chapter by posing a general question about whether the style, volume, and intensity of tabloid-style legal coverage has influenced how people think about the justice system. We operationalized this question by advancing four hypotheses. Our first hypothesis—that citizens possess substantial knowledge of and familiarity with the tabloid cases—is supported by the findings displayed in Tables 4.1 and 4.2. This is important, because no other hypothesis about media effects would be particularly plausible if citizens did not maintain some recollection of the facts or have strong feelings about the tabloid justice cases.

Our second hypothesis involved the premise that the public's knowledge about the legal system should be greater in light of the many portrayals of the legal system in the mass media. Although our data do not allow for specific comparisons over time, Tables 4.3 and 4.4 certainly suggest that the public does not have a clear understanding of even the basic procedures and practices of the legal system.

Our third hypothesis examined whether faith in the justice system has been eroded by the media's coverage of the judicial process. This decreased public confidence can be seen in opinions about individual participants and aspects within the legal process, as well as about the system as a whole. The findings presented in this chapter support such contentions. Our conclusions are most noteworthy in the sense that our poll respondents are quite explicit about how the tabloid justice cases have affected their views of justice in the United States. Thus, there is strong evidence supporting our third hypothesis.

There turned out to be little support for our fourth hypothesis, however, that a greater level of negativity toward the system would accompany greater exposure to news coverage. On the contrary, we found that given the nearly complete saturation of the public consciousness with tabloid justice information, all groups of citizens voiced similar, rather dismal levels of confidence in the justice process as a result of their reaction to the media coverage of these events.

We conclude here by once again noting two important points. The public has become quite knowledgeable about the basic facts of these cases and has reacted to the media presentation of these dramas on the one hand with morbid fascination, and on the other by drawing increasingly negative conclusions about the general state of law in the United States. Contrary to the wider public benefits hypothesized by some, increased public exposure to the workings of the judicial system has not led to more confidence on the part of citizens.[60] Lacking both a responsible press and an engaged and civic-minded public, these cases have not provided the much-needed forum for the meaningful civic discussion of important legal issues.

Notes

1. Karen Abbott, "Verdict Is the Talk of Denver: News Brings Reactions Ranging from Sadness to Prayerful Gratitude," *Denver Rocky Mountain News,* October 4, 1995, p. 30A.

2. Daphne Duret and Joel Currier, "Responses to Trial Range from Indifference to Anger," *St. Louis Post-Dispatch,* June 14, 2005, p. A9.

3. "Media Coverage for Some Kidnappings Is Greater Than Others," ABC News, *World News Tonight Sunday,* transcript, June 16, 2002.

4. Andrew Kohut, "TV Trials Captivate Public," *Times Mirror Center for the People and the Press,* February 4, 1994.

5. See Appendix B for a copy of the survey and a description of the survey methods that were employed.

6. See C. Danielle Vinson and John S. Ertter, "Entertainment or Education: How Do Media Cover the Courts?" Paper presented at the Midwest Political Science Association in Chicago, April 15–18, 1999. There has been some work examining the impact of trial coverage in terms of its effects on the victims of crime in both trials and pretrial publicity. See Debra Gersh, "Crime Victims and the Media: Press Coverage Has a Lasting Impact on Their Lives," *Editor and Publisher* 125 (September 26, 1992): 12–14; and Dorothy J. Imrich, Charles Mullin, and Daniel Linz, "Measuring the Extent of Prejudicial Pretrial Publicity in Major American Newspapers: A Content Analysis," *Journal of Communication* 45 (Summer 1995): 94–117.

7. Kohut, "TV Trials Captivate Public," 10.

8. Pew Center for the People and the Press, 2006.

9. These responses represent the combined percentages of those who said they were "highly" and "fairly" confident about the legal system.

10. Frank Newport, "Small Business and Military Generate Most Confidence in Americans," *Gallup Poll Monthly,* August 15, 1997, pp. 3–5.

11. John M. Scheb and William Lyons, "Public Perception of the Supreme Court in the 1990s," in Eliot E. Slotnick, ed., *Judicial Politics: Readings from Judicature* (Chicago: American Judicature Society, 2000), 466–469.

12. The most comprehensive study of this subject is Richard Davis, *Decisions and Images: The Supreme Court and the Press* (Englewood Cliffs, NJ: Prentice-Hall, 1994), especially pp. 10–19 and 132. Also see Walter F. Murphy and Joseph Tanenhaus, "Public Opinion and the Supreme Court," *Law and Society Review* 2 (February 1968): 357–382; Valerie Hoekstra and Jeffrey A. Segal, "The Shepherding of Local Public Opinion: The Supreme Court and Lamb's Chapel," *Journal of Politics* 58 (1996): 1079–1102; Charles Franklin and Liane Kosacki, "Media, Knowledge, and Public Evaluations of the Supreme Court," in Lee Epstein, ed., *Contemplating Courts* (Washington, DC: Congressional Quarterly Press, 1995); Gregory Caldeira, "Neither the Purse Nor the Sword," *American Political Science Review* 80 (1986): 1209–1226; and John P. Robinson and Dennis K. Davis, "Television News and the Informed Public: An Information-Processing Approach," *Journal of Communication* 40 (1990): 106–119.

13. Scheb and Lyons, "Public Perception of the Supreme Court," 466.

14. For an analysis of how different types of reporters cover the Supreme Court, see Rorie L. Spill and Zoe M. Oxley, "Philosopher Kings or Political Actors: How the Media Portray the Supreme Court," *Judicature* 87 (July/August 2003): 22–29.

15. Joseph S. Nye Jr., "The Media and Declining Confidence in Government," *Harvard International Journal of Press and Politics* 2 (Summer 1997): 4–9.

16. See, for instance, E. J. Dionne, *Why Americans Hate Politics* (New York: Simon and Schuster, 2004); William Chaloupkia, *Everybody Knows: Cynicism in America* (Minneapolis: University of Minnesota Press, 1999); Joseph Nye, Philip Zelikow, and David C. King, *Why People Don't Trust Government* (Cambridge, MA: Harvard University Press, 1997); and Stephen Earl Bennett, *Apathy in America* (Dobbs Ferry, NY: Transnational, 1986).

17. Such trends are noted in Richard Davis and Diana Owen, *New Media and American Politics* (New York: Oxford University Press, 1998); and David L. Paletz, *The Media in American Politics* (New York: Longman, 1999).

18. Richard Krajicek, *Scooped* (New York: Columbia University Press, 1998), 60.

19. Ibid., 64.

20. Angelique Paul, "Turning the Camera on Court TV: Does Televising Trials Teach Us Anything About the Real Law?" *Ohio State Law Journal* 58 (1997): 666.

21. Ibid., 693–694.

22. David A. Harris, "The Appearance of Justice: Court TV, Conventional Television, and Public Understanding of the Criminal Justice System," *Arizona Law Review* 35 (1993): 822.

23. This question was asked by the authors at a public lecture given by Darden at Indiana University–Purdue University, Indianapolis, in March 1997.

24. David Shaw, "The Simpson Legacy," *Los Angeles Times,* October 9, 1995, p. S5.

25. Ibid.

26. Frank Macchiarola, "Finding the Truth in an American Criminal Trial: Some Observations," *Cardozo Journal of International Comparative Law* 5 (Spring 1997): 97.

27. These percentages are based on respondents who said that they followed the trial "very" or "fairly" closely. See Andrew Kohut, "The Pew Research Center News Interest Index," *Pew Research Center for the People and the Press,* June 1997, p. 4.

28. Health Poll Report, Henry J. Kaiser Family Foundation, released April 25, 2005.

29. NBC/*Wall Street Journal* Poll, released April 13, 2005.

30. Numerous polling agencies asked whether people were following the various legal proceedings. The numbers presented here reflect the high point over the duration of the proceeding. To examine the trends in polling, go to the Roper Center, Public Opinion Online, http://www.ropercenter.uconn.edu., and search by the name of the case.

31. Gallup/CNN/*USA Today* poll, released June 14, 2005.

32. More precisely, in our 1999 survey, 47 percent responded that they were more knowledgeable, 10 percent said that they were less knowledgeable, and 43 percent said that there was no change in their knowledge of the criminal justice system.

33. "O.J. Simpson Book, TV Show Cancelled," CNN.com, November 22, 2006, http://www.cnn.com/2006/SHOWBIZ/TV/11/20/oj.cancel.ap/index.html (accessed November 25, 2006).

34. For a review of four of these books, see Joyce Carol Oates, "The Mystery of JonBenet Ramsey," *New York Review of Books,* June 24, 1999, pp. 31–37.

35. "John Mark Karr Goes On the Record," Fox News online, October 17, 2006, http://www.foxnews.com/story/0,2933,221517,00.html (accessed October 25, 2006).

36. Kohut, "TV Trials Captivate Public," 4.

37. See generally Dionne, *Why Americans Hate Politics;* and Nye, Zelikow, and King, *Why People Don't Trust Government.*

38. Gallup poll annual survey questions about public confidence in the criminal justice system show a confidence level hovering around 20 percent. An archive of

Gallup poll releases showing these responses can be found online at http://www .gallup.com.

39. See, for instance, Doris Graber, *Mass Media and American Politics,* 5th ed. (Washington, DC: Congressional Quarterly Press, 1997); Thomas R. Dye, L. Harmon Zeigler, and S. Robert Lichter, *American Politics in the Media Age,* 4th ed. (Ft. Worth, TX: Harcourt Brace, 1992), 106; Maxwell McCombs, "News Influence on Our Pictures of the World," in Jennings Bryant and Dolf Zimmerman, eds., *Media Effects: Advances in Theory and Research* (Hillsdale, NJ: Lawrence Erlbaum, 1994), 1–16; and Roy Edward Lotz, *Crime and the American Press* (Westport, CT: Praeger, 1991).

40. For a complete discussion of our methods, see Appendix B.

41. See Schmuel T. Lock, Robert Y. Shapiro, and Lawrence R. Jacobs, "The Impact of Political Debate on Government Trust: Reminding the Public What the Federal Government Does," *Political Behavior* 21 (1999): 239–264.

42. John Zaller, *The Nature and Origins of Mass Opinion* (New York: Cambridge University Press, 1992), 79–80.

43. Ibid., especially chapters 4 and 5. Also see John Zaller and Stanley Feldman, "A Simple Theory of the Survey Response: Answering Questions Versus Revealing Preferences," *American Journal of Political Science* 36 (1992): 579–616.

44. See William L. Dwyer, *In the Hands of the People: The Trial Jury's Origins, Triumphs, Troubles and Future in American Democracy* (New York: St. Martin's, 2002); Henry Abraham, *The Judicial Process,* 7th ed. (New York: Oxford University Press, 1998), 109; and Eliot E. Slotnick, ed., *Judicial Politics: Readings from Judicature* (Chicago: American Judicature Society, 1992), 235.

45. The trials of the 1990s have led many in the legal community to suggest a host of reforms of the system. For a good review of such proposals, see Douglas Smith, "Structural and Functional Aspects of the Jury: Comparative Analysis and Proposals for Reform," *Alabama Law Review* 48 (Winter 1997): 441–581.

46. Barbara Boland, Paul Hahanna, and Ronald Stones, *The Prosecution of Felony Arrests* (Washington, DC: US Department of Justice, Bureau of Justice Statistics, 1992). This study shows that only three out of every 100 felony arrests go to trial, and only about a third of those are tried before a jury. A recent study of criminal courts in the seventy-five largest counties in the United States found that over 95 percent of convictions were a result of plea bargaining; see "Criminal Case Processing Statistics," Bureau of Justice Statistics, August 6, 2006, http://www.ojp.usdoj.gov/bjs/cases.htm (accessed November 10, 2006).

47. Polls conducted after the Simpson trial show that almost 60 percent of Americans view a jury trial as an essential provision of the Constitution. See the *Gallup Poll Monthly,* April 1995. In addition, polling shows that a clear majority of the electorate views jury duty as a basic duty in a democracy.

48. See, for instance, Lawrence Baum and James Boyd White, *Judges and Their Audiences* (Princeton, NJ: Princeton University Press, 2006); and John Paul Ryan, Allan Ahman, Bruce Sales, and Sandra Shane Dubow, *American Trial Judges* (New York: Free Press, 1980).

49. For an outstanding review of the literature concerning judicial roles and decisionmaking, see Gregory Sisk, Michael Heise, and Andrew P. Morriss, "Charting the Influences on the Judicial Mind: An Empirical Study of Judicial Reasoning," *New York University Law Review* 73 (November 1998): 1377–1500.

50. David W. Neubauer, *America's Courts and the Criminal Justice System,* 6th ed. (Belmont, CA: Wadsworth, 1998), 183–186.

51. Paul Jacobs, "Matt Did Not Get the Title," *Los Angeles Times,* June 19, 1996, p. A3.

52. Judge Zobel's ruling was upheld, but Justice Greaney dissented from that decision. See Jack Sullivan, "Nanny Goes Free; Dissenters Rip Zobel for Compromising System," *Boston Herald,* June 17, 1998, p. 3.

53. "Jackson Trial: Winners and Losers," BBC World News, June 13, 2005, http://www.bbc.co.uk/2/hi/entertainment/4580287.stm (accessed September 13, 2006); and "Judge Clears Leno for Jackson Jokes," CNN Law Center, March 12, 2005, http://www.cnn.com/2005/LAW/03/11/jackson.trial.leno/index.html (accessed September 13, 2006).

54. This case ultimately concluded in early 2000 with the full acquittal of all four officers in a trial in Albany, New York.

55. Kevin Johnson, "'Too Many' Believe They Can't Trust Police, Reno Says," *USA Today,* April 16, 1999, p. 8A.

56. Victoria Pope and Annik Stahl, "The All-Too-Typical JonBenet Case," *US News and World Report,* December 1, 1997, pp. 32–36.

57. For instance, see Daniel Glick, Sherry Keene-Osborn, and Andrew Murr, "The Door That Never Opened," *Newsweek,* July 13, 1998, p. 32.

58. Oates, "The Mystery of JonBenet Ramsey," 32.

59. See Stephen Ansolabehere, Roy Behr, and Shanto Iyengar, *The Media Game* (New York: Macmillan, 1993), 12–15.

60. Susanna Barber summarizes this research in *News Cameras in the Courtroom: A Free Press–Fair Trial Debate* (Norwood, NJ: Ablex, 1987), especially pp. 54 and 94. Also see Ronald L. Goldfarb, *TV or Not TV: Television, Justice, and the Courts* (New York: New York University Press, 1998), 160–166; Alan M. Dershowitz, *Reasonable Doubts: The Criminal Justice System and the O.J. Simpson Case* (New York: Simon and Schuster, 1997), 129–134, 146–148, 203–204; Anna Quindlen, "Order in the Court," *New York Times,* July 25, 1994; Eileen Libby, "Court TV: Are We Being Fed a Steady Diet of Tabloid Television?" *ABA Journal* (May 1994): 47; and Ruth Ann Strickland and Richter H. Moore Jr., "Cameras in State Courts: A Historical Perspective," *Judicature* 78 (November/December 1994): 128–135.

FIVE

Race, Gender, Class, and Tabloid Justice

The majority of women think she got a bum deal. The men sort of grin. . . .
They think it's OK for a man to lie, cheat, and steal but that Martha got her
comeuppance. . . . [Men] feel kind of smug about it.
—woman reader writing to *Home and Garden* magazine[1]

There is no humanly possible way a jury could sit there and hear the testimony and see the tape and come up with the verdict they had. Some of the
police officers that were on the scene were admitting that the officers were
wrong. In that verdict, there was no concern for Rodney King or the wrong
that was done.
—resident of Ventura, California, responding to the verdict
in the first trial of the officers who beat Rodney King[2]

A poor man would be swinging by now. . . . The race issue was a pretty big
smoke screen. It's an amazing verdict with the mountain of evidence against
him.
—resident of Seattle, Washington,
responding to the Simpson verdict[3]

In this chapter we focus on the social divisions that the press has consistently
highlighted in its coverage of the tabloid justice cases. The media's presentation of these cases has often focused on race, class, and gender differences as
a means of marketing these legal dramas.[4] When a trial is portrayed as being
symbolic of the current state of race or gender relations, or of the legal benefits that accompany wealth, the story becomes much bigger than a mere expo-
sition of the criminal conduct of the participants. A case presented as a conflict
between blacks and whites or women and men or rich and poor becomes a
story that calls for widespread public attention.

As we have argued elsewhere in this book, none of these cases, with the
possible exception of the first Rodney King beating trial and the Terri Schiavo
case, warranted the volume of media attention that they received. However,

165

once they received such high levels of coverage, citizens responded to the presentation of these cases and formed judgments accordingly. Further, with so much of the coverage (especially in the first tabloid justice era) focusing on race, gender, and class issues, many citizens have used these cases as a means of assessing the fairness and effectiveness of the legal system. In the course of incorporating important social issues in these cases, the media have had an opportunity to help educate and inform citizens about the inequities of the justice system. However, the overall tenor of the coverage has often been inflammatory rather than educational and informative in nature. For instance, in the Rodney King and O.J. Simpson cases the media heavily emphasized race, whereas in presenting the William Kennedy Smith, Terri Schiavo, and Martha Stewart dramas, the coverage frequently focused on gender issues. Unfortunately, it would appear that the opportunity for civil and thoughtful reflection about the serious social issues emanating from these cases was, more often than not, lost in a blur of tabloid-style coverage.

Our goal in this chapter is to assess whether there have been significant consequences of the extensive media coverage that has focused specifically on the aforementioned social cleavages. We are concerned here with two related questions. First, do members of distinct social and demographic groups hold different views about the justice system and the specific tabloid justice cases? Second, do blacks and whites, men and women, and affluent and less affluent groups actually develop different attitudes about the criminal justice system based at least partly on how the media covers tabloid justice cases? This second question is more difficult to answer, for the response to coverage is undoubtedly among many factors that help to shape a person's views about the legal system.

Because of the difficulty of measuring something as complex as public attitudes on questions of race, gender, and class, our goals in this chapter are modest. Primarily, we will compare how members of different demographic groups view the legal system and the tabloid cases. We will then speculate on the effect that sensationalized and tabloid media coverage has had on different groups of citizens. As we note in other places in this book, the dynamics were not the same across the two eras of tabloid justice that we identify. The sensationalizing of social divisions was much more pronounced in the 1990s than in the second era of tabloid justice.

We have divided this analysis into two parts. The first begins by briefly discussing existing opinion and legal theory regarding the role of the law in the United States. In this section we also describe numerous examples of the types of polarizing coverage that we have been referring to. The second part returns to the results of our own national surveys and examines how members of different demographic groups assess the legal system and tabloid justice cases.

Tabloid Justice Media Coverage:
Sensationalizing Differences

The claim that the legal system has serious shortcomings in terms of how minorities, women, and the poor are treated was certainly not introduced by tabloid justice media coverage. Public perceptions of the legal system have shown for years that citizens believe minorities receive harsher treatment by the system and that the wealthy receive more favorable treatment.[5] The public view of how women have been treated in the legal system has been examined less frequently, and these findings have been somewhat mixed.[6] Beyond these long-standing public perceptions about fairness, scholars and legal historians have developed a number of theoretical and philosophical critiques analyzing US law by focusing on issues of race, gender, and social class.

Many of these critiques are metatheoretical works that seek to uncover and lay bare the fundamental contradictions and inequities in the legal system. The Critical Legal Studies (CLS) movement, which began in the mid-1960s, yields most of the contemporary critiques of this nature.[7] For adherents of the CLS movement, law is believed to be structured in such a way that workers, ethnic and racial minorities, women, and the poor are placed at a distinct disadvantage. The law is seen as a tool for the wealthy and for those already in power. The CLS movement has strongly influenced the development of theoretical approaches concerned explicitly with sexual and racial inequality in the law. Feminist legal theory is one such movement, and it has been quite influential, at least in academic settings, since the late 1970s.[8] Feminist legal thinking is highly diverse but begins with the premise that women continue to occupy a subordinate place in society and that the law tends to reflect and reinforce that position.[9] Finally, drawing insights from both CLS and feminist jurisprudence, critical race theory emerged in the early 1990s as an explicitly race-based critique of US law.[10] This perspective examines legal concepts, categories, and doctrines from the point of view of people of color (not only African Americans, but Latinos and East Asian Americans as well) and, like the CLS movement and feminist jurisprudence, is concerned with questions of difference, discrimination, oppression, and inequality.[11] Most recently, the insights of legal realism and CLS have led to works of so-called queer legal theory, which adapts these approaches to study the legal aspects of sexual orientation.

The tradition of such criticism has helped to further an understanding of how the system has at many times not treated citizens of different backgrounds, races, and genders fairly. Accordingly, in this chapter we focus on how, in covering the tabloid justice cases, the media have chosen to present issues of race, gender, and class in such a way that they are oversimplified and trivialized. As we have noted previously, race, gender, and class issues are often the central elements that help a legal or criminal case reach the "national media stage." A great deal of the coverage that we discussed in earlier chapters has been focused on these social divisions. The media coverage surrounding these legal events, especially in the first era of tabloid justice, often (at least symbolically) pits blacks and whites and men and women against one another. And, although these cases have occasionally raised serious and important social issues, we would contend that the larger media spectacle of the tabloid justice era generally has not allowed for a thoughtful discussion of issues such as racism and sexism in the justice system. What would appear to occur in the media presentation of many of these issues is a way of discussing these topics that exploits differences among people in order to create more dramatic story lines and "better" entertainment. A brief overview of some of this coverage will illustrate the media atmosphere surrounding many of these cases.

In both the King and Simpson cases, the mass media seized almost every opportunity to raise the issue of race. In the wake of the riots that were triggered by the acquittals of the officers who beat Rodney King, news coverage focused heavily on the racial dynamics of the case. The coverage of the King beating began with reflective tones, as the *Los Angeles Times* ran an editorial within a few days of the Rodney King video titled "Shocking Incident Leads to Worrisome Questions About LA Police."[12] The editorial raised questions about police brutality first and possible racism second. Much of the media coverage preceding the trials of the police officers explored the current state of racial dynamics in the United States. Well-known columnists such as Anna Quindlen and Art Buchwald wrote columns lamenting the deep divide between white and black Americans.[13] ABC's late-night news program *Nightline* used a subtle approach in a post-riot program titled "Two Facets of the Los Angeles Riots." This program focused on police work during the riots and on tensions between African Americans and Korean Americans.[14] However, another *Nightline* program, which had been aired immediately after the first verdicts were announced, involved a dramatic confrontation between a white juror from the Rodney King case and black Los Angeles city councilman Mark Ridley-Thomas.[15]

Overall, though, these examples highlight a relatively more reserved tone in the media coverage of the King trials. Even so, the television media's repetitive usage of the King beating videotape often undercut any truly reasoned public discussion of the story. The imagery from the videotape, consisting of a short edit of numerous white officers beating King, was played so many times on television that many of the more complex issues in the King case were effectively pushed aside.

Mass media coverage in the Simpson case was far more exploitative of racial tensions, and it highlights the increasing tabloid fervor that emerged during the mid-1990s. From the very morning after the murders, coverage around the country pointed to the racial undercurrents of the case. Within two weeks of the crime, and long before the trial itself was under way, the New York City daily *Newsday* ran an editorial titled "O.J. Triggers a Racist Quake That's Off the Richter Scale."[16] Other headlines also predicted a racial showdown. One front-page newspaper story, which appeared within a week of Simpson's arrest, trumpeted, "O.J. Case Haunted by Racial Undertone: Black Community Faces Wrenching Test."[17] Throughout the course of the trial, there was extensive and growing coverage focusing on the racial dynamics of the case.

Outlets in both the traditional and new media focused on the racial angle throughout the trial. ABC's *Nightline* and CNBC's *Rivera Live* had devoted numerous programs specifically to this issue. By its conclusion, the trial was being discussed in the news media almost exclusively in racial terms. On the day that the trial ended, NBC's *Dateline* newsmagazine titled its program "The Verdict, in Black and White." Each of the three nightly network news programs discussed race relations at the top of their broadcasts. All three networks contrasted pictures of crowd reactions that showed jubilant black citizens and distressed white citizens. In the wake of the trial, almost all of the cable talk shows devoted much of their programming to discussing the racial implications of the Simpson trial.

Cable programs such as *Rivera Live, Cal Thomas,* and *Charles Grodin* discussed the racial fallout of the trial for weeks. Following the verdict, the weekend political programs *Face the Nation, Meet the Press,* and *This Week* all welcomed prominent guests to discuss the state of race relations in the country. Significantly, in almost all of these televised venues, black and white guests were shown disagreeing about the verdict and its impact on race relations. CBS News commentator Andy Rooney characterized the Simpson verdict as "the worst thing that's happened to race relations in 40 years."[18] Further, newspapers and magazines throughout the nation ran literally thousands of stories and editorials that addressed the racial implications of the trial. *Time* magazine's cover story, released within hours of the verdict, focused primarily on the racial dynamics of the case.[19]

In covering the Simpson trial, the media had not suddenly discovered the issue of race in the United States, nor did this coverage necessarily create the gap in public opinion between blacks and whites regarding Simpson's guilt or innocence (see Table 5.3). But with their intense coverage of the case, the mass media were undoubtedly taking their cues from the activities that had unfolded in the courtroom. Simpson's defense team relied heavily on a racial explanation for the supposed police framing of Simpson, and the media were eager to deliver this story to the nation. In fact, one lasting impact of the Simpson case would appear to be the imprint it left on how race relations are discussed in the United States. But whether any single event, particularly one that is so highly charged and sensationalized, should be presented in the news media as the defining moment of race relations is an important question. Whether it was justifiable for the media to take a double murder trial with a celebrity African American defendant and two white victims and turn it into a national referendum on race relations is another. The Simpson case was simply not *Brown v. Board of Education*. But, in an attempt to maintain ratings and create interest in the story, the case was covered as the most important development in race relations in decades. The racially focused coverage in the Simpson case demonstrates how the media's agenda-setting power can be corrupted by ratings-driven sensationalism, as well as the public's ready acceptance of the media-dictated terms of public debate.

In the second era, two cases held out the potential for raising the issue of race as a central ingredient in a trial. The first involved the charges brought against African American NBA star Kobe Bryant for allegedly raping a white hotel receptionist. As the trial proceedings were gearing up, numerous media outlets were comparing the case to the O.J. Simpson case.[20] Prior to jury selection, Kobe Bryant's lead attorney, Pamela Mackey, delineated a key line of argument for the defense: "There is lots of history out there about men, black men, being falsely accused of this crime [rape] by white women."[21] During the questioning of prospective jurors, the defense team pressed the racial aspect of the case by asking jurors their opinions on interracial dating.[22] Interest in the case and perceptions of guilt and innocence clearly developed along racial lines. A Pew Study of news interest found that 47 percent of blacks, but only 13 percent of whites, were following the Bryant case "very closely."[23] In another national survey, 58 percent of blacks believed Bryant was "probably not guilty," whereas only 25 percent of whites felt the same way.[24] Ultimately, with the case dropped the day before the trial was to begin, the country was spared what would have likely turned into another media-driven referendum on race relations.

The second case, the child molestation trial of Michael Jackson, also held out the specter of being presented as a statement on race in the United States. A few months after Jackson's arrest, Jackson's brother Jermaine said that the arrest of his brother was "nothing but a modern-day lynching."[25] Jackson's friend, the performer Rick James, echoed this sentiment by commenting that "as soon as you get famous and black, [prosecutors] go after you."[26] Race, however, never became a dominant theme in the trial and was not directly addressed by the defense team. Even though interest in the trial and the assessment of the outcome broke down rather strongly along racial lines, there was never the same level of racial tension or intensity of feeling that accompanied the Simpson verdict.[27] The assessment of a number of African American pundits was that the case didn't become a racial melodrama because Michael Jackson was not seen as someone who represented the black community.[28] In the end, race was a persistent but low-intensity aspect of the case.

As with the use of race as an important feature of the news coverage in some of the tabloid stories, gender dynamics were also a frequent focus of the reporting in the 1990s. Specifically, the news media discussed gender relations in regard to the rape trial of William Kennedy Smith, the genital mutilation trial of Lorena Bobbitt, the first verdicts in the trials of the Menendez brothers, the discussion surrounding the prosecution of Martha Stewart, and the discussion of Terri Schiavo's possible marital abuse. In the first period of tabloid justice the focus on gender was most prominent in the Bobbitt and Kennedy Smith cases. For instance, the outcome of the Kennedy Smith trial became a springboard for media speculation about the prevalence of rape and the status of gender relations. In the wake of the trial, news programs across the nation often discussed the verdict in terms of men versus women. ABC News ran a lengthy special program (hosted by top news anchor Peter Jennings) entitled "Men, Sex and Rape," which was filmed in Palm Beach County, the site of the trial. Using strong rhetoric, Jennings opened the program by stating that "the William Kennedy Smith case [and others] . . . have been at the center of a pained debate among men and women." Jennings went on to state that while "there have been no bricks or bullets exchanged on this subject yet . . . the anger and fear of some women is such that perhaps men should not be surprised when they are."[29]

Some news reports hypothesized that the Kennedy Smith not-guilty verdict would cause date rape to become more common, while others speculated that the prosecution's treatment of Patricia Bowman (the alleged rape victim) would hinder other women from coming forward in future cases.[30] Paralleling the evolution of race-based coverage, the initial use of the gender angle in the Kennedy Smith case was also more reserved and reflective than some of the coverage that would come with later cases. Regardless, the nature of the coverage clearly sought to make the Kennedy Smith case emblematic of more general relations between the sexes.

Media coverage of the genital mutilation trial of Lorena Bobbitt in 1994 much more strongly conjured up images of men and women getting ready to battle each other. A search of national media outlets revealed that almost 500 news stories used the phrase "war of the sexes" in analyzing the Bobbitt case.[31] Geraldo Rivera titled one program on the Bobbitt trial "Women Slash Back." CNN analyst William Schneider casually concluded on the air that "a war between the sexes was evident in . . . the verdict in the Bobbitt emasculation trial. More women . . . sympathized with Lorena Bobbitt, and said John deserved what he got."[32] Reporters and news programs focused on the case to turn up the heat on the idea that men and women were gravely and fundamentally at odds. Articles and news stories abounded asking if a new "war between the sexes was under way."[33] The Bobbitt case, which is not one we have focused on extensively in our analysis, is a good example of the media exploiting a lurid yet largely unimportant criminal case to create a national sensation. Columnist Ellen Goodman acerbically and sensibly commented that "a sleeping man had his penis amputated. It's not a media event. It's a criminal case."[34] Goodman went on to describe with bewilderment how this case had escalated into a referendum on sexual equality.[35]

Gender dynamics were also emphasized in the media coverage of the first Menendez trial. After the jury in the trial of Erik Menendez had deadlocked along gender lines, the press immediately seized on this story angle. The Associated Press wire service released a story using the phrase "war of sexes" to describe the jury's deliberations.[36] Other headlines characterized the jury dynamics in an only slightly less incendiary manner, including "Women Say Gender War Split Jury," and "Menendez Jurors Split Between Men, Women."[37] In a final example, ABC's newsmagazine *Primetime Live* devoted a segment to the Menendez case titled "Three Angry Men." The program included several of the male jurors from the Menendez case making derogatory comments about the performance of several of the women jurors on the panel.[38]

None of the cases we focused on in the second era raised explosive gender issues of sexual assault, rape, and domestic violence as did some of the cases from the first era. There were cases, however, where husbands were accused of murdering their wives, including Scott Peterson, Robert Blake, and even Michael Schiavo. Also, there is the case of Martha Stewart, who represented, perhaps, the first case being brought against an enormously successful female CEO. In the Schiavo case, there were frequently repeated rumors that Michael Schiavo was an abusive spouse and that there was some mystery about the circumstances under which Terri Schiavo had originally fallen into a coma. One psychiatrist, Carole Lieberman, who appeared numerous times on cable news programs and talk radio, asserted that "Michael fits the profile of an abusive husband."[39] While such allegations against Michael Schiavo had already been investigated and dismissed by the legal authorities, coverage of the case frequently cast him in the light of a scheming and abusive husband.

Gender considerations more regularly appeared in the coverage of the Martha Stewart case. A *Daily News* story about the case began, "Did Martha Stewart get the third degree because she's a rich and powerful woman?"[40] The debate over the role of gender in the prosecution of Stewart was summarized well by Robert Trigaux of the *St. Petersburg Times:* "Stewart got raked over the judicial coals over a relatively minor amount of money. She was found guilty and may face prison. Yet some male CEOs on trial at the same time for looting their companies for hundreds of millions of dollars face mistrials . . . or have not even gone to trial."[41] Feminist author Naomi Wolf offered another take on Stewart's plight: "There is a social taboo against women being too powerful, too wealthy, too successful without being attached to a man."[42] The gender divide emerged in jury selection, as more prospective male jurors expressed hostility toward Stewart. Ultimately, the gender issue was a prominent feature of the news coverage of the case. Mark Effron, vice president for live programming at MSNBC at the time, commented that the debates over Stewart's high-profile role in contemporary culture, combined with her gender, were "a very good debate for cable news."[43]

The last social division we consider is wealth and social class. In many of the cases that we have discussed in this book, the issue of wealth became an important feature of the media's coverage. More specifically, the idea that wealthy defendants are able to "buy justice" in the US legal system was widely raised in the coverage. Literally thousands of newspaper articles and editorials were written in the 1990s that associated one or more of these cases with the role of wealth in the legal system.[44] In the William Kennedy Smith trial, there was widespread speculation that high-priced lawyers and jury consultants had unfairly stacked the deck in favor of Kennedy Smith. One headline proclaimed that "Jury Consultants Buy 'Justice' for the Rich."[45] Similar analyses followed the hung jury that initially produced a mistrial in the Menendez case. In both of these cases much of the media analysis portrayed wealthy defendants as the beneficiaries of special treatment by the police, prosecutors, and judges. This analysis was nowhere more obvious than in the Simpson criminal trial, as headlines such as "Justice for Sale: High-Priced Defenses Mock the System" were common.[46]

Toward the end of the first tabloid justice period, a focus on wealth and class surfaced repeatedly in the investigation into the murder of JonBenet Ramsey. Speculation about the role played by the slain child's parents was widespread. The Ramseys, a very wealthy family, have been accused of receiving special treatment from the police and prosecutors. *Denver Post* columnist Chuck Green characterized the investigation this way: "Justice is for sale in America. . . . You get the level of justice you can afford."[47] This type of assertion has come on the heels of widespread reporting that the Ramseys spent millions on lawyers and publicists, despite the fact that they were never either formally named as suspects or charged with the crime.[48]

In the second era, the perception that "wealth buys justice" continued with defendants in the legal dramas involving Michael Jackson, Martha Stewart, Kobe Bryant, and Robert Blake. In each of these cases wealthy defendants secured high-cost defense teams, and in all but the Stewart case (and despite broad public perceptions of guilt), the defendants were either acquitted or had their cases dropped. As this parade of famous defendants suggests, the second tabloid justice era was focused more on "celebrity justice" than on other social differences. More than 400 articles in major newspapers made reference to that phrase, which was most commonly used to refer to the preferential treatment received by well-known and wealthy defendants.[49]

The message presented throughout all of these cases was that wealth buys better treatment in our criminal justice system. Numerous television programs ran segments using these trials as vehicles for exposing class bias in the legal system. Geraldo Rivera hosted a program in 1998 titled "Justice for Sale: Why the Rich Get Away with Murder." Rivera began the program by stating that "murder and mayhem done by the rich and famous is often treated differently than crimes committed by the poor. That's a fact of life. . . . Justice is for sale and . . . the rich and famous are buying it."[50]

In sum, the media have utilized issues of race, gender, and class as a means of promoting tabloid cases for entertainment purposes. Again, our point is not that these cases do not present serious or alarming developments pertaining to social cleavages, because some of the cases did raise important issues. Rather, we would maintain that when phrases such as "war of the sexes," "gender battle," "racist quake," "bullets exchanged," "worst in 40 years," or "justice for sale" are employed, they are used as a means of sensationalizing the cases and making them sustained news stories and ratings enhancers. When otherwise relatively unimportant trials become avenues for assessing social dynamics, the national agenda is being driven by tabloid journalism—something that is not conducive to the thoughtful and civil engagement of important issues.

How Members of Different Demographic Groups Assess the Legal System

General Levels of Confidence in the Criminal Justice System

Given the manner in which race and gender have played a role in recent trial coverage, it is important to understand how citizens have reacted to the emphasis placed on these issues by the media. Recall that the public's overall trust in the criminal justice system is quite low. Accordingly, Table 5.1 examines whether confidence in the criminal justice system differs based on age, education, political party identification, family income, race, and sex. Here we present the results from our 2005 national survey.

In our discussion of race, we limit our analysis to black/white dynamics, as this distinction was notably featured in several of the tabloid trials. Also, in our national poll, aside from the white respondents, the sample size of the black respondents was the only other ethnic or racial group large enough to be statistically representative.[51]

Turning first to race, Table 5.1 reveals a significant disparity between blacks and whites in terms of overall confidence in the criminal justice system. Most US citizens have a dismal view of the system in general, with just over 30 percent asserting that they have a significant degree of confidence in the system. In addition, when we examine three other specific actors within the system, we see that African Americans demonstrate significantly lower levels of trust in the police, judges, and juries. Particularly regarding assessments of the police, these findings confirm what other researchers have found in previous studies. Blacks consistently voice low levels of confidence in all of these legal actors.[52]

When we turn to the gender variable, disparities between the attitudes of men and women are much smaller than those based on race. On only the measure of general confidence in the criminal justice system is there a significant gender difference, with women demonstrating lower levels of confidence in

Table 5.1   High Level of Confidence in the Criminal Justice System, Jury System, Police, and Judges Among Demographic Groups (percentages)

	Criminal Justice System	Jury System	Police	Judges
Race				
Black	15**	32ᵗ	21**	22*
White	34	43	47	41
Sex				
Women	29*	40	44	39
Men	36	42	43	41
Age				
18–29	27ᵗ	34*	36**	38*
30–49	33	40	44	38
50–59	32	38	43	39
Over 60	33	48	48	43
Education				
Some high school	17**	38	29*	32*
High school graduate	26	43	40	35
Some college	29	42	41	39
College graduate	39	35	52	41
Some graduate school	40	44	47	47
Family income				
Less than $15,000	18ᵗ	41	28**	31*
$15,000—29,999	27	41	36	35
$30,000—49,999	30	42	40	39
$50,000—74,999	36	44	48	46
$75,000—99,999	33	33	50	42
$100,000—149,999	30	45	47	44
$150,000 and over	46	43	53	52
Party identification				
Democrat	27**	40	32**	41
Republican	42	43	59	41
Independent	33	44	48	41

Source: 2005 Tabloid Justice Survey, N = 1,024.
Notes: "High levels of confidence" include those with "complete" or "a great deal" of confidence. Chi-square test performed within each category, ** $p < .01$, * $p < .05$, and ᵗ $p < .10$.

the system than men. But even the existence of small differences draws attention to the gender gap, which continues to be the subject of considerable academic investigation and media speculation.[53]

The other demographic variables we tested produced a few additional noteworthy differences. Citizens with higher incomes tend to have higher levels of trust in the criminal justice system and in its specific components than do citizens with lower incomes. Whether such a finding relates to the fact that most of our selected cases involved wealthy protagonists who were acquitted is open to speculation. The education variable produced results in the same direction as income, with citizens possessing lower levels of education tending to have less confidence in the legal system than those with higher levels of education. The political party identification variable yielded some significant finding, in that self-described Democrats indicated significantly less confidence in the police than did Republicans. This is not particularly surprising, as the ideologies of the two major parties differ, with Democrats tending to emphasize due process and civil rights, whereas the Republicans tend to emphasize crime control. Finally, the age variable did not yield any clear patterns in assessments of either the overall system or its components, although older Americans do voice slightly more confidence in the legal system.

Going beyond general attitudes toward criminal justice in the United States, and the various actors in the system, we sought to answer the question of whether different groups of citizens had changed their views of the legal system based on what they know about the tabloid justice cases. We present six cases in Table 5.2, including those involving O.J. Simpson, JonBenet Ramsey, and the Rodney King officers from the first era; and Michael Jackson, Scott Peterson, and Martha Stewart from the second era. We compare the percentages of people in each category who said they had less confidence in the legal system as a result of what they had learned about each of these cases.

The results in Table 5.2 again reveal a wide disparity in the manner in which white and black Americans view the criminal justice system, as significant racial differences exist for three of these six cases. Consistent with previous polls, white respondents are more likely than black respondents to assert that the Simpson case undermined their faith in the system. Public reaction to both the criminal and civil trials of Simpson revealed deep racial differences in perspective. African Americans have tended to view the Simpson saga as the story about racially biased police and a corrupt criminal justice system; whites have viewed it largely as the story of a wealthy celebrity purchasing his freedom. The racial disparities in the Rodney King case are noteworthy as well, with black citizens more likely than whites to state that the King case contributed to their decreased trust in the system. Nevertheless, it is notable that large percentages of both races saw the King beating as evidence of police racism.

When we turn to gender disparities in reactions to these cases, we again see somewhat smaller differences. Women are more likely than men to have less faith in the legal system as a result of each of the cases, though the result was statistically significant only for the JonBenet Ramsey murder investigation and the Martha Stewart trial.[54]

In terms of our other variables, age was statistically important in five of the cases, with older respondents this time exhibiting greater declines in confidence as a result of these proceedings. A comparison of the 18–29-year-old category with the over-60 age group reveals a sharp contrast in four out of the six cases. The discrepancy in the age variable may be a result of young people growing up in a time when sordid or scandalous events are less shocking and more common. In the time of tabloid justice, sensational and scandalous stories are reported with such regularity that younger citizens may regard them as "normal" events.[55] In contrast, older Americans might be reacting negatively to what has been per-

Table 5.2 **Lowered Level of Confidence in the Criminal Justice System Among Demographic Groups as a Result of Exposure to Six Tabloid Justice Cases (percentages)**

	First-Era Cases			Second-Era Cases		
	First Trial of O.J. Simpson	JonBenet Ramsey Investigation	First Rodney King Trial	Trial of Michael Jackson	Trial of Scott Peterson	Trial of Martha Stewart
Race						
Black	53**	79	76*	54	26*	45
White	80	78	61	61	12	40
Sex						
Women	79	82**	66	60	14*	46**
Men	76	74	62	60	12	34
Age						
18–29	67**	65**	60	53**	14*	32**
30–49	77	76	63	57	9	32
50–59	78	80	64	58	16	48
Over 60	83	86	67	69	14	54
Education						
Some high school	73	67**	61*	57**	35*	54
High school graduate	76	81	68	62	18	42
Some college	81	80	65	66	12	41
College graduate	77	71	59	57	11	40
Some graduate school[a]				47	10	40
Family income						
Below $15,000	83	82	75	59[t]	18[t]	59[t]
$15,000–29,999	74	76	68	64	24	43
$30,000–49,999	77	79	62	57	10	39
$50,000–74,999	80	78	63	56	10	39
$75,000–99,999	81	76	61	63	13	39
$100,000–149,999[a]				54	8	38
$150,000 and over[a]				58	9	25
Party identification						
Democrat	74**	76*	69*	62	16	44
Republican	84	83	60	63	9	37
Independent	77	79	61	57	15	44

Sources: First-era cases from 1999 Tabloid Justice Survey, N = 1,003; second-era cases from 2005 Tabloid Justice Survey, N = 1,005.
Notes: Chi-square test performed within each category, ** $p < .01$, * $p < .05$, and [t] $p < .10$.
a. Not included in 1999 Tabloid Justice Survey.

ceived as a loss of dignity and civility in our national discourse. Regarding party identification, Republicans hold more negative views of the Simpson and Ramsey proceedings, while Democrats' views of the King trial are more negative.

In sum, when we assess the important social divisions that emerge in this analysis of confidence in the criminal justice system and the tabloid justice cases, we do see some important differences. Race and gender (although gender to a lesser extent) have surfaced as important divisions. We now turn to a more focused examination of how tabloid coverage might affect these groups' attitudes.

African Americans and the Criminal Justice System

The two cases that most clearly raise questions involving race are those of the Rodney King officers and O.J. Simpson. The Michael Jackson case presented the potential for incorporating a significant racial component, though Jackson's race never became an important aspect of either the media coverage or his defense team's strategy. Nevertheless, blacks and whites did respond to the trial's outcome differently, as we will discuss. The case against Kobe Bryant had the potential to follow in the footsteps of the race-centered coverage of the Simpson case, but as we have previously mentioned, the charges against Bryant were ultimately dropped.

Both the Simpson case and the trials of the Los Angeles Police Department officers, discussed in detail in Chapter 1, fueled discussions of race and the criminal justice system. But, unlike the officers' trials, in which both blacks and whites appeared to lament the excessive treatment of a black suspect, the Simpson trial produced a sharp divergence of opinion along racial lines from the very beginning. Despite the importance of the Rodney King story, the Simpson drama remains the touchstone for any discussion of race and the judicial process in the United States. Table 5.3 shows racial differences in reaction to the Simpson criminal trial over a period of ten years.

What can account for the continuing wide disparity of racial attitudes about O.J. Simpson? Any answer to this question is necessarily multifaceted. However, one possible explanation is the polarizing media coverage that surrounded the trial. For instance, as noted previously in this chapter, all of the prominent television news outlets broadcast numerous programs focusing on the role of race in the criminal justice system. A great deal of the coverage presented public opinion as blacks versus whites, often employing black and white pundits to argue opposing perspectives. Several commentators complained that this type of coverage was a caricature of the public's more com-

Table 5.3   Racial Differences in Assessing the Guilt of O.J. Simpson (percentage who believed that Simpson was guilty)

	Whites	Blacks
July 1994	68	24
August 1994	61	29
March 1995	66	24
July 1995	75	25
October 1995 (after criminal verdict)	73	25
April/May 1996	66	16
February 1997 (after civil verdict)	74	26
February 1999	79	35
June 2004 (ten-year anniversary of the case)	87	29

Sources: Gallup Poll Monthly, February 1997, 1999. The 2004 poll was conducted by NBC News.

plex attitudes and that it served merely to foment an already tense situation.[56] The style of this media coverage certainly conveyed the sense that there was widespread and mounting tension between blacks and whites. One postverdict poll found that more than 74 percent of all Americans believed that the Simpson trial had "hurt" race relations in the United States.[57] Indeed, many commentators cited the media exposure of racial tensions and racially charged public opinion as the chief legacy of the case, which arguably had no real explicitly legal ramifications.[58]

Turning again to the results of our survey, we first asked respondents in both of our polls how the O.J. Simpson case made them feel about the treatment that African Americans receive from the justice system, and we also inquired about the effect of the Rodney King case. Table 5.4 shows the results of these questions. The Rodney King trial raised the highest level of concern about the treatment of African Americans. More than 40 percent of our respondents indicated that the case gave them less confidence in the legal system's ability to treat African Americans fairly, whereas only 4 percent said it bolstered their trust in the system. Roughly the same number of people said that the Simpson case had given them less confidence. This number was essentially unchanged between 1999 and 2005. Perhaps curiously, nearly one-sixth of our respondents asserted that the Simpson ordeal had given them more confidence that the system would treat blacks fairly. More than 95 percent of those who gave this response were white, however, indicating that perhaps they believed Simpson's race garnered him the benefit of the doubt and that this might possibly be granted to other African Americans as well.

Table 5.5 illustrates the different reactions of whites and African Americans to the outcomes in both the Simpson and Jackson cases. As we have stated previously, the Jackson case did not explicitly raise racial questions, and the press did not cover the case as the criminal prosecution of a black celebrity per se. Nevertheless, different racial groups responded to Jackson's acquittal in very contrasting ways. Table 5.5 shows that whites were significantly more

Table 5.4   Influence of Tabloid Justice Cases on Citizen Beliefs That the Criminal Justice System Treats African Americans Fairly (percentages)

	Less Confident	More Confident	No Change
Change in confidence that the legal system treats African Americans fairly as a result of			
Trial of the officers who beat Rodney King	42	4	30
Criminal trial of O.J. Simpson (1999)	38	16	43
Criminal trial of O.J. Simpson (2005)	38	19	38

Sources: 1999 Tabloid Justice Survey, N = 1,003; 2005 Tabloid Justice Survey, N = 1,005.

Notes: Survey respondents were asked about the Simpson case in both national surveys. Rows do not total 100 because "don't know" responses are not included.

Table 5.5   Racial Differences in Assessing the Outcomes of Second-Era Tabloid
             Justice Cases (percentage who disagree with the outcome)

	Blacks	Whites
O.J. Simpson trial (2005)	45**	81
Michael Jacskon trial	44**	62
Sample size	78	839

Notes: Questions were asked only for cases in the second era, 2005. Chi-square test performed
within each category, ** p < .01, * p < .05.

likely than blacks to disagree with the trial's outcome. This demonstrates that,
a decade after the Simpson ordeal, racial attitudes in the perception of the judicial system remain polarized.

Returning to O.J. Simpson, in an attempt to determine whether the
media's coverage of that case had any lasting impact on attitudes, the Gallup
Organization conducted extensive public opinion polls both during and after
the Simpson criminal trial. Table 5.6 includes several questions about race
asked in Gallup polls in the years before, during, and after the trial. The first
three questions in Table 5.6 focus on general attitudes regarding the criminal
justice system. The most striking transformation of opinion appears in the
first question listed in Table 5.6. In 1993, blacks and whites were about
equally likely to say that they would be more willing to believe the testimony
of a police officer over another witness. However, when asked the same question in March 1995, after the initial testimony of Detective Mark Fuhrman
(the LAPD detective who had used racial slurs) and several other police officers was completed, African Americans' trust in the police fell by more than
half, whereas trust by whites fell only slightly. The Fuhrman testimony, discussed extensively in the news media, seems to have had particularly substantial effects on African American attitudes toward the police. Stories discussing Fuhrman's reportedly racist past dominated coverage of the trial at
several different junctures. A typical headline released by the Scripps Howard
News Service stated, "O.J. Defense Set to Pounce on Fuhrman: Calls Tapes'
Racial Slur 'Chilling.'"[59] Numerous stories put the contents of the Fuhrman
tapes on the front page of newspapers throughout the United States. The *CBS
Evening News* with Dan Rather and *NBC Nightly News* with Tom Brokaw led
their newscasts several times with the Fuhrman story.[60] By that point, the
press had turned almost completely to a racial focus in its coverage of the
trial.

The second and third questions in Table 5.6 reveal some minor changes in
outlook toward the system for both blacks and whites. The responses to these
questions show that following the Simpson criminal trial verdict, the percentage of African Americans perceiving an antiblack bias in the criminal justice
system declined by more than 10 percent. By the same token, during the trial

Table 5.6   Gallup Poll Questions on the Impact of the Simpson Verdict on Racial Attitudes (percentages)

	Blacks	Whites
If you were on a jury in a trial would you be more willing to believe the testimony of a police officer than another witness who is not a police officer?		
Yes		
February 1993	43	45
March 1995	18	37
Do you think the American justice system is biased against black people?		
Yes		
April 1993	68	33
March 1995	66	37
October 1995	54	33
Who do you think is treated more harshly in this country's criminal justice system—blacks or whites—or are they treated about the same?		
Blacks are treated more harshly		
October 1993	74	35
July 1995	77	45
In general, how do you think people in the United States feel about people of other races? Do you think only a few white people dislike blacks, many dislike blacks, or almost all white people dislike blacks?		
Many and *almost all* combined		
May 1992	32	36
October 1995	30	33
Do you think only a few black people dislike whites, many dislike whites, or almost all black people dislike whites?		
Many and *almost all* combined		
May 1992	35	48
October 1995	31	46

Source: Gallup Poll Monthly, March and October 1995.

there was a 10 percent increase in the number of whites who believed that the system treats blacks more harshly. These shifts suggest that this highly anomalous case and the previously unparalleled level of media coverage actually changed the public's views about the criminal justice system.

Finally, a major concern in the wake of the Simpson drama involved whether these events and the sensationalizing media coverage worsened tensions between black and white Americans. Although this is an extremely difficult question to answer, public opinion polling has not revealed many significant or lasting changes. The last two questions displayed in Table 5.6 asked blacks and whites to assess the general level of racism in the United States. Comparing the responses from 1992 and 1995 reveals that perceived levels of racism in society were unchanged as a result of the Simpson case. Overall, about a third of Americans consistently perceive a deep-seated racism on the part of most of their fellow citizens. Thus, despite the fact that press coverage sent the message that the United States was on the verge of a virtual race war in the wake of the Simpson trial, most direct measures have shown that public opinion regarding race was changed little as a result of that case.[61]

Women and the Criminal Justice System

In addition to the preceding racial aspects, several of our chosen cases raise questions involving gender and whether the legal system treats women fairly. The Kennedy Smith, Simpson, Peterson, Schiavo, and Stewart cases contained issues variously related to sexual assault, domestic abuse, and the opinions about powerful women. In the Kennedy Smith case, defense attorney Roy Black pursued the controversial strategy of exposing and attacking the past sexual behavior of the woman accuser. This was thought by some observers to highlight the pervasive sexism present in a system unable or unwilling to protect the rights and reputations of women who bring sexual assault and harassment charges.[62]

The Simpson criminal trial also briefly became a media vehicle for exploring gender dynamics, although the outcome of the trial did not turn on this issue. The ten-year, well-documented history of domestic violence involving O.J. and Nicole Brown Simpson, in which Simpson had never been prosecuted, raised questions about the ability of the legal system to adequately address domestic violence. Further, the television media focused on the issue by constantly displaying old photographs of the bruised and battered face of Nicole Simpson and describing the history of abuse she had undergone. These photos were another example of images that the media displayed repeatedly as a means of developing interest in the trial. In the end, the domestic violence angle was overshadowed both in the trial and in the media when Simpson's defense team began to push charges of police racism.

We asked respondents in our 2005 national poll to again assess how the Simpson case made them view the legal system's treatment of women. Table 5.7 reveals that, based on their knowledge of each of these three cases, our re-

Table 5.7   Influence of Tabloid Justice Cases on Citizen Beliefs That the Criminal Justice System Treats Women Fairly (percentages)

	Less Confident	More Confident	No Change
Change in confidence that the legal system treats women fairly as a result of:			
Criminal trial of O.J. Simpson (1999)	50	3	42
Trial of William Kennedy Smith	36	1	17
Criminal trial of O.J. Simpson (2005)	29	22	40

Sources: 1999 Tabloid Justice Survey, N = 1,003; 2005 Tabloid Justice Survey, N = 1034.

Notes: Survey respondents were asked about Simpson case in both national surveys. Rows do not total 100 because "don't know" responses are not included.

spondents expressed high levels of concern about the treatment of women. Half of our sample responded that the Simpson case gave them less confidence in the system's treatment of women, and more than a third felt the same way about the William Kennedy Smith trial.

As further evidence of a gender division in some of the tabloid cases, in our 2005 national survey we asked respondents to assess whether they disagreed with the outcome of the case. Table 5.8 compares the percentages of men and women who disagreed with the outcomes of the four cases we asked about—Simpson, Peterson, Stewart, and Schiavo. For two of the four cases significant gender gaps emerged, with women more likely than men to disagree with the outcomes of the Martha Stewart trial and the Terri Schiavo drama. In the other two cases, involving Peterson and Simpson, there was such general unanimity in assessing the trial outcomes that no gender gap emerged.

Importantly, our broader search of polling data did not reveal any evidence that general views of gender equality or gender fairness have shifted significantly in the wake of the tabloid justice cases. The decade of the 1990s did not reveal many shifts in public opinion about the role of women in the family, sex discrimination, or failure to adopt the long-proposed Equal Rights Amendment.[63] Certainly, the role that gender played in the second-era cases did not lead to any seismic shifts in the broader area of gender dynamics. Questions in these areas have been the indicators used historically by pollsters and survey researchers to assess gender issues in society. Nevertheless, a small but significant gender gap clearly exists, with more women viewing the system as generally unfair. Perhaps, as with the issue of race, tabloid justice media coverage simply reinforces people's existing views about the justice system. If the coverage of these anomalous cases has solidified women's unwillingness to come forward in cases of sexual harassment, domestic violence, and rape, however, this would be particularly unfortunate and would constitute a serious indictment of the type of coverage that has arisen with these cases.

Table 5.8   Gender Differences in Assessing the Outcomes of Second-Era Tabloid Justice Cases (percentage who disagree)

	Women	Men
O.J. Simpson case (2005)	77	75
Scott Peterson case	10	9
Martha Stewart case	48**	35
Terri Schiavo proceedings	33**	23
Sample size	595	418

Notes: Questions were only asked for cases in the second era. Chi-square test performed within each category, ** $p < .01$, * $p < .05$.

Personal Wealth, Celebrity, and the Criminal Justice System

Although the inscription above the entrance to the US Supreme Court reads "Equal Justice Under Law," most Americans seem to believe that in courts of law, as elsewhere in society, the wealthy are simply "more equal."[64] Significant discussion in the media and by the public about whether, and in what ways, wealth allows one to manipulate the system accompanied many of the tabloid justice cases.[65] With the exception of the Rodney King officers, Louise Woodward, and (at least initially) the parties in the Schiavo case, all of our selected cases featured participants who could afford high-priced legal representation. This fact alone highlights the phenomenally unrepresentative nature of these trials and investigations, since it is well known that the vast majority of criminal defendants are indigent.

The substantial wealth of the Kennedy family, the Menendez brothers, O.J. Simpson, the Ramsey family, Robert Blake, Michael Jackson, and Martha Stewart has been well documented and warrants no further discussion. Even Louise Woodward, Scott Peterson, and Terri Schiavo's husband and parents, who were not exceptionally wealthy, managed to attract some extremely high-powered legal assistance. In the case of Louise Woodard, for instance, Barry Scheck, the renowned DNA expert and former member of the O.J. Simpson legal team, assisted in her defense. Further, widespread international recognition of Woodward's plight resulted in a considerable defense fund set up to help defray her legal bills.[66] As has been discussed, the notoriety of the Peterson case attracted celebrity attorneys like Mark Geragos and Gloria Allred.

We asked our survey sample how each of our six selected cases from the first era of tabloid justice made them feel about equal treatment for rich and poor defendants in the criminal justice process. Table 5.9 illustrates perhaps the strongest and most unambiguous results in our poll. In every case, respondents claimed that the trial or investigation gave them substantially less faith in the criminal justice

Table 5.9   Influence of Tabloid Justice Cases on Citizen Beliefs That the Criminal Justice System Treats Rich and Poor Equally

	Less Confident	More Confident	No Change
Change in confidence that the legal system treats people fairly regardless of whether they are rich or poor			
Criminal trial of O.J. Simpson	76	2	19
Investigation into the death of JonBenet Ramsey	69	2	18
Trial of the officers who beat Rodney King	46	3	27
Trial of William Kennedy Smith	44	1	10
Trial of Louise Woodward	27	3	35
Trials of the Menendez brothers	23	12	32

Notes: Questions were only asked for cases in the first era. Rows do not total 100 because "don't know" responses are not included.

system's ability to treat people fairly without regard to their economic status. A particularly high percentage of citizens expressed this sentiment for the Simpson and Ramsey stories, although more than 40 percent of all respondents had the same reaction to the Kennedy Smith and Rodney King cases as well.

When we attempted to determine whether a respondent's own wealth or education had an impact on how he or she viewed the system's class fairness, we (perhaps surprisingly) found no significant differences. At least in this regard, citizens from every income and education level tended to draw the same set of conclusions about the selected tabloid cases. Large majorities believe that the wealthy fare better in the criminal justice system than do the less affluent. The vast majority of Americans has long considered the criminal justice system to favor the wealthy.

Thus, the tabloid justice coverage of the 1990s may simply have reinforced this belief. The coverage of cases in the second period of tabloid justice continued to reinforce this perception, as defendants who many thought were guilty, such as Michael Jackson and Robert Blake, were acquitted (though Martha Stewart was not able to beat the charges against her). Such coverage about the "rich buying justice" or the class bias of the system may reflect accurate and understandable observations about the basic nature of law in the United States. However, stories focusing on how "the rich get away with murder" rarely consider the fundamental contradictions in the criminal justice system or, more important, what reform measures might make the system more equitable. Rather than reporting on budget cuts to the federal Legal Services Corporation or local public defender's offices, for instance, the press is more likely to offer reporting that simply foments a visceral resentment of the entire system.

Social Cleavages and Personal Expectations About the Criminal Justice System

As in Chapter 4, we conclude the presentation of our findings by turning to the question of how people expect that they themselves would be treated by the system based on what they have observed about the tabloid justice cases. In Table 5.10 we compare the answers of blacks and whites, and men and women, concerning the overall impact of the tabloid justice cases from the 1990s and also in the second era of tabloid justice. (Again, we found no significant differences associated with income and education.) Table 5.10 confirms several of the differing attitudes of black and white Americans that we have previously described. As a result of what they have learned about the tabloid justice cases, blacks are significantly more likely than whites to believe that they would be treated unfairly by the police and by judges. Fully six in ten African Americans feel they would be mistreated by police officers based on what they have learned in the tabloid justice cases, a troubling comment on the overall legitimacy of contemporary law enforcement.

Table 5.10 Personal Impact of Knowledge of Tabloid Justice Cases by Race and Sex (percentages)

	Blacks	Whites	Men	Women
Percentage of people who, as a result of these cases, have less confidence that (first-era cases, 1999)				
the laws surrounding the criminal justice system would protect their rights	46	41	37*	45
they or a family member would be treated fairly by prosecuting attorneys if arrested as a suspect in a crime	45	39	41	38
they or a family member would be treated fairly by the police if arrested as a suspect in a crime	60**	36	36	40
they or a family member would be treated fairly by a judge if they had been arrested and were standing trial for a crime	45**	24	24†	29
they or a family member would be treated fairly by a jury if they had been arrested and were standing trial for a crime	26	23	21†	26
Sample size	86	831	440	541
Percentage of people who, as a result of these cases, are less confident that (second-era cases, 2005)				
the laws surrounding the criminal justice system would protect their rights	53*	42	39*	47
they or a family member would be treated fairly by prosecuting attorneys if arrested as a suspect in a crime	55*	41	42	43
they or a family member would be treated fairly by the police if arrested as a suspect in a crime	61**	37	37†	43
they or a family member would be treated fairly by a judge if they had been arrested and were standing trial for a crime	51**	30	32	32
they or a family member would be treated fairly by a jury if they had been arrested and were standing trial for a crime	57**	32	33	36
Sample size	77	836	418	595

Sources: First-era cases from 1999 Tabloid Justice Survey; second-era cases from 2005 Tabloid Justice Survey.
Note: Chi-square test performed comparing race and sex, ** p < .01, * p < .05, † p < .10.

A troubling change between the two surveys was that in 1999 there was a significant racial difference for only two of the five questions. By 2005 there was a notable racial disparity in all five of the measures of perceived individual-level justice. Given our extensive questioning about the tabloid justice cases, the mass media coverage of these events has served to reinforce and perhaps to even increase African Americans' distrust of the justice system.

The differences between men and women, once again, are modest. For the first period, women feel somewhat less confident in judges, juries, and the system in general. These lower levels of confidence could be related to women's greater concerns about how other women were treated and how the media exploited gender issues in the Kennedy Smith, Simpson, and Stewart cases. In the second era, there were notable gender differences in perceptions of the justice system overall and in expectations about police treatment, though the differences are small.

Conclusion

We began this chapter by presenting two related questions. The first was whether members of different social and demographic groups harbor different views of the justice system and the tabloid justice cases. The second was whether blacks and whites, men and women, and affluent and less affluent groups actually developed differing attitudes about the system based on how the media have covered tabloid justice cases. Because of the complexity in answering the second question, most of our data are directed at answering the first.

Clearly, most Americans have very low levels of trust in the criminal justice system. Our poll has provided further evidence that race is the most pronounced indicator of attitudes toward the system. Not only do blacks and whites hold significantly different views but they also react to our individual trials and investigations differently. Beyond their general assessment of the law, African Americans demonstrate lower levels of confidence in juries, judges, and the police. Racial disparities, especially in evaluating the police, pose a serious challenge for the creation of a criminal justice system that is perceived as fair and just to all Americans. However, we would yet again assert that the anomalous nature of these trials and investigations does not make them useful vehicles for any clear-eyed and reflective dialogue about the legal system or police behavior in the United States.

The views of men and women are far less disparate than those of blacks and whites. The findings we have reported point to a small but significant and consistent gender gap in how citizens assess the legal system, both generally and in response to the individual cases. Although men's and women's reactions to the cases are slightly different in the aggregate, it is not entirely clear what role tabloid justice media coverage has played in shaping these opinions.

Turning to social class, apart from the fact that the wealthiest of Americans have a somewhat higher level of confidence in the criminal justice system, we uncovered no particularly pronounced differences based on income, education, community type, or political party affiliation. All groups of Americans generally agree that those with money have an advantage in the legal system. Perhaps this is because the contemporary mass media have so uniformly saturated public consciousness that people of every station in society are now exposed to essentially the same images of current events.

In the end, we find that large portions of all subgroups believe that these tabloid justice cases have demonstrated that the criminal justice system is not capable of treating blacks, women, or the poor fairly. Despite the different reactions by different groups to different trials and investigations, the nature of the mass media presentation has caused, or at least strongly contributed to, a situation in which nearly all Americans now question the basic equity of the system. Thus, we can plausibly conclude that the tabloid-style coverage we have highlighted throughout this book may have ironically brought citizens together in recognizing the need for deep reform of justice in the United States.

Unfortunately, the media presentation of these admittedly important issues is often superficial, purposely graphic and provocative, and based on an unrepresentative selection of highly unusual cases that in no way illustrate the everyday workings of the system. In other words, although this coverage draws attention to many critical issues of race, gender, class, due process, and substantive justice, its effect is weakened by its emphasis on entertainment. Essentially, the era of tabloid justice has undermined the dispassionate and detail-oriented discussion required to develop meaningful and workable public policy solutions to the many intractable legal problems that virtually everyone agrees do exist.

Notes

1. Quoted in Mona Doyle, "Martha Stewart Verdict Sparks Anti-Business Feminism," *Home and Garden Shopper Report,* April 2004, http://www.findarticles.com/p/articles/mi_mOYQW_is2004_April/ai_n9913081 (accessed November 5, 2006).

2. "The Rodney King Verdict: Aftermath Verdicts Wrong, Most Ventura Residents Say in Poll: 68% Angry Over Acquittals," *Atlanta Journal and Constitution,* May 7, 1992, p. 14A.

3. Haya El Nasser, "Reaction Illustrates Racial Divide: Verdict Called 'A Message,'" *USA Today,* October 4, 1995, p. 6A.

4. See George Lipsitz, "The Greatest Story Ever Sold: Marketing and the O.J. Simpson Trial," in Toni Morrison and Claudia Brodsky Lacour, eds., *Birth of a Nation'hood.* (New York: Pantheon, 1997), 3–29.

5. The Gallup Organization has asked many questions about race and the criminal justice system over the years. These polls consistently reveal that the general public believes that African Americans are treated less fairly in the criminal justice system.

6. Polling on public attitudes about how women are treated in the legal system is almost nonexistent. There have been some independent polls exploring attitudes about

how particular women were treated in the legal system, but these have failed to produce any clear patterns.

7. The CLS had its intellectual origins in the tradition of legal realism, an academic movement of the 1920s and 1930s that argued against the earlier belief that law was supreme, objective, and neutral. The realists contended that because good lawyers and judges could argue either side of any given case, the outcome of legal encounters depended more on the attitudes, goals, and skills of legal professionals than on the letter of the law itself. Thus, law was in no way related to science but rather was deeply embedded in the realms of politics, economics, and culture. Legal reasoning, therefore, was not a detached or objective mode of inquiry; it was a complicated function of the biases and social context in which legal questions were answered. In sum, "the law" was indeterminate and value laden, tending to reinforce existing social relations (including existing inequalities). The major difference between the two movements is that the CLS was, in large part, explicitly leftist, tending to view law as protective of society's dominant interests. The major focus of CLS theorists was attacking existing legal categories and doctrines and, simultaneously, constructing new theories and doctrines that would be more sympathetic to, and reflective of, class, gender, and racial differences. For good overviews of legal realism and critical legal studies, see Steven Vago, *Law and Society*, 7th ed. (Upper Saddle River, NJ: Prentice-Hall, 2004); Bailey Kuklin and Jeffrey W. Stempel, *Foundations of Law: A Jurisprudential Primer* (St. Paul, MN: West, 1994); Walter E. Murphy, C. Herman Pritchett, and Lee Epstein, *Courts, Judges, and Politics*, 6th ed. (New York: McGraw-Hill, 2005); Lawrence Friedman, *A History of American Law*, 2d ed. (New York: Simon and Schuster, 1986); David Kairys, *The Politics of Law: A Progressive Critique*, 3d ed. (New York: Basic, 1998); and Denis Galligan, *Law in Modern Society* (New York: Oxford University Press, 2006).

8. The feminist approach to law is fundamentally oppositional in that it is, by definition, highly suspicious of current legal arrangements, whether they take the form of sex-based legal categories or formal gender neutrality. For instance, Suzanna Sherry and others have asserted that the US Constitution, although neutral in its explicit language, strongly embodies values that are distinctly male. Feminist approaches to the law involve three main themes: (1) the difference between men and women in life experience (for example, it is impossible to treat pregnancy in a gender-neutral manner); (2) the different voice of women's moral and legal reasoning (as when a woman judge is thought to understand the balance between rights and responsibilities necessary to decide child custody cases better than a man can); and (3) the dominance of the male legal and social hierarchy (in which the vast majority of lawyers, judges, and legislators are male, who by definition give primacy to male concerns and perspectives). For good overviews of feminist approaches to the law, see Martha Chamallas, *Introduction to Feminist Jurisprudence* (New York: Aspen Law and Business, 1999); Patricia Smith, ed., *Feminist Jurisprudence* (New York: Oxford University Press, 1994); Leslie F. Goldstein, *The Difference Debate: Feminist Jurisprudence* (Lanham, MD: Rowman and Littlefield, 1992); Katharine R. Bartlett and Rosanne Kennedy, eds., *Feminist Legal Theory: Readings in Law and Gender* (Boulder, CO: Westview, 1992); Gayle Binion, "The Nature of Feminist Jurisprudence," *Judicature* (November/December 1993): 140–143; Suzanna Sherry, "Civic Virtue and the Feminine Voice in Constitutional Adjudication," *Virginia Law Review* 72 (1986): 543–591; Cass Sunstein, "Feminism and Legal Theory," *Harvard Law Review* 101 (1988): 826–848; and Nancy Levit and Robert R.M. Varchick, *Feminist Legal Theory: A Primer* (New York: New York University Press, 2006).

9. The theoretical underpinnings of feminist legal scholars have been supported by some recent empirical examinations. For instance, to address the question of gender

bias in courtrooms, thirty-six states have created task forces to investigate the problem. Although these bodies have varied in both size and scope of responsibility, one academic review of the findings of these task forces concluded that there exists a nationwide pattern of gender bias in the areas of domestic violence, sexual assault, divorce, and behavior directed toward women in the legal profession. See Craig Hemmens, Kristin Strom, and Elicia Schlegel, "Gender Bias in the Courts: A Review" (paper presented at the Academy of Criminal Justice Sciences, Louisville, KY, 1997), cited in David W. Neubauer, *America's Courts and the Criminal Justice System,* 7th ed. (Belmont, CA: Wadsworth, 2002), 194. Similarly, various studies examining the experiences of women judges, lawyers, and law enforcement and correctional officers have generally concluded that informal, institutional sexism continues to inhibit women's professional prospects in the system, as well as the quality of justice available to women defendants and victims in criminal cases. For a discussion of the gendered atmosphere in the criminal justice system, see Joanne Belknap, "Women in Conflict: An Analysis of Women Correctional Officers," *Women and Criminal Justice* 2 (1991): 89–116; Elaine Martin, "Women on the Bench: A Different Voice?" *Judicature* 77 (1993): 126–128; Susan Ehrlich Martin and Nancy C. Jurik, *Doing Justice, Doing Gender: Women in Law and Criminal Justice Occupations* (Thousand Oaks, CA: Sage, 1996); and Clarice Feinman, *Women in the Criminal Justice System* (Westport, CT: Praeger, 1994).

10. Critical race theory aims to expose the legal domination of the white majority, whether through explicit racism on the part of legal professionals, a legally supported economic system that inhibits minority economic progress, or various less easily visible historical artifacts of slavery. The major collections in the field include Kimberle Crenshaw, ed., *Critical Race Theory: The Key Writings That Formed the Movement* (New York: New Press, 1996); Richard Delgado, ed., *Critical Race Theory: The Cutting Edge,* 2d ed. (Philadelphia: Temple University Press, 1999); and Richard Delgado and Jean Stefancic, *Critical Race Theory: An Introduction* (New York: New York University Press, 2001). Also useful is Kuklin and Stempel, *Foundations of Law,* 181–182; and Galligan, *Law in Modern Society.*

11. Theorists in this area would point to racially discriminatory practices in policing techniques and sentencing as evidence to support their claims. For instance, a report by the United Nations asserted that race remains a strong indicator in sentencing disparities of prisoners on death row in the United States, with blacks significantly more likely to be sentenced to death. In addition, a study of homicides in Philadelphia concluded that blacks were four times more likely than whites to receive capital sentences. The study also reported that 98 percent of prosecutors with death-penalty authority were white; see David Rovella, "Race Pervades the Death Penalty," *National Law Journal,* June 8, 1998, p. A200. This piece provides an update to the now-famed "Baldus Study," which found that blacks were more likely to be sentenced to death in Georgia. The evidence from the Baldus Study was of central importance in *McCleskey v. Kemp,* 481 US 279 (1987), in which the US Supreme Court ruled that defendants must demonstrate the existence of racial discrimination in their own specific cases and could not rely on general or institutional studies.

The issue of racial profiling has called the practices of law enforcement professionals into question. See Paul Zielbauer, "Racial Profiling Tops NAACP Agenda 25," *New York Times,* July 11, 1999, Sec. 1, p. 23; and Thomas J. Lueck, "Bias in State Police Protested in Atlantic City," *New York Times,* July 4, 1999, Sec. 1, p. 22. Several studies have demonstrated that race is widely used as a tool by police officers in establishing probable cause to stop motorists. Researchers at Carnegie Mellon and Temple Universities have found black motorists 4.8 times more likely than white drivers to be pulled over on the New Jersey Turnpike. See Jim Dwyer, "NJ Cops Hide Race Profiling," *Daily News,* February 21, 1999, p. 8. A more elaborate study of twenty-three states showed that law enforcement officials have explicitly targeted minority travelers ("An End to Racial Profiling," *St. Louis Post-Dispatch,* June 14, 1999, p. D14).

12. "The Investigation of a Videotaped Beating: Shocking Incident Leads to Worrisome Questions About LA Police," *Los Angeles Times,* March 7, 1991, p. B6.

13. Anna Quindlen, "Will Blacks, Whites Ever Meet Across the Divide?" *Seattle Post-Intelligencer,* May 5, 1992, p. A15; and Art Buchwald, "Solving America's Racial Puzzle: Black and White Pieces Don't Connect for Whites," *Atlanta Journal and Constitution,* May 5, 1992, p. A29.

14. "Two Facets of the Los Angeles Riots," *Nightline* transcript from May 6, 1992.

15. "Rioting Follows King Verdict," *Nightline* transcript from April 30, 1992.

16. Ben Stein, "O.J. Triggers a Racist Quake That's Off the Richter Scale," *Newsday,* June 26, 1994, p. A32.

17. Shante Morgan, "O.J. Case Haunted by Racial Undertone: Black Community Faces Wrenching Test," *San Diego Union-Tribune,* June 27, 1994, p. A1.

18. Joe Urschel, "Poll: A Nation More Divided," *USA Today,* October 9, 1995, p. 5A.

19. Richard Lacayo, "An Ugly End to It All," *Time,* October 9, 1995, cover and p. 30.

20. David Usbourne, "Basketball Star's Rape Trial Recalls O.J. Drama," *Independent on Sunday,* August 29, 2004, p. 19.

21. Charlie Brennan, "Bryant's Race Is Raised: Defense Team Brings Up Subject During Wrangling over Privacy Issues," *Rocky Mountain News,* January 24, 2004, p. 4A.

22. Corky Siemaszko, "Race Becomes Issue in Bryant Rape Case," *Daily News,* June 22, 2004, p. 14.

23. "California, Kobe, and Marriages Spark Little Public Interest," Pew Research Center for the People and the Press, survey released August 14, 2003.

24. "Differing Perceptions of the Guilt or Innocence of Michael Jackson, Kobe Bryant, and Martha Stewart," *Harris Poll,* #9, February 11, 2004.

25. Cary Darling, "Jackson's Trial Could Turn on Race," *Milwaukee Journal Sentinel,* February 26, 2004, p. 2E.

26. Ibid.

27. David W. Moore, "Instant Reaction: Plurality of Public Disagrees with Jackson Verdict; Majority of Whites Disagree, Majority of Nonwhites Agree," *Gallup Poll,* June 14, 2005.

28. Darling, "Jackson's Trial Could Turn on Race," p. 2E.

29. "ABC News Forum: Men, Sex, and Rape," ABC News program hosted by Peter Jennings, May 5, 1992.

30. For typical examples of this coverage, see Steve Wick, "Rape Experts Look to Future Trials," *Newsday,* December 12, 1991, p. 7; and Susannah Vesey, "Smith Trial May Educate on Date Rape: But Women May Be Scared into Silence," *Atlanta Journal and Constitution,* December 12, 1991, p. F1.

31. This figure is based on a Lexis-Nexis search of national news sources, conducted in summer 1999, using the key words "Bobbitt" and "war of the sexes." This search turned up 478 sources.

32. "CNN Poll Shows Gender Split on Issues of Bobbitt Trial," CNN News transcript, reported by William Schneider, January 23, 1994.

33. See, for example, Rudy Abramson, "Has the Bobbitt Case Escalated the War Between the Sexes?" *Los Angeles Times,* November 22, 1993, p. E1.

34. Ellen Goodman, "Bobbitts Represent 'Two Pathetic People,' Not Latest War Between Sexes," *Fresno Bee,* January 14, 1994, p. B5.

35. Ibid.

36. Seth Mydans, "Menendez Trials' Collapse Discourages Both Sides," *New York Times,* January 30, 1994, p. 16.

37. "Women Say Gender War Split Jury," *Courier Journal* (Louisville, KY), January 30, 1994, p. 8A; and "Menendez Jurors Split Between Men, Women," *Chicago Tribune,* January 30, 1994, p. 20C.

38. "Three Angry Men," *Primetime Live,* transcript of program that aired February 3, 1994.

39. Jim Stratton, "Open Season on Schiavo's Husband Often Ignores Facts," *Pittsburgh Post-Gazette,* March 26, 2005, p. A6.

40. Lloyd Grove, "Martha: Women's Verdict," *Daily News,* March 9, 2004, p. 21.

41. Robert Trigaux, "Cracks Show in Glass Ceiling, but It's Still There in Bay Area," *St. Petersburg Times,* April 12, 2004, p. 1D.

42. Grove, "Martha: Women's Verdict," 21.

43. David Carr, "Prosecuting Martha Stewart: The Image; For the Press, a Case That Is an Irresistible Draw," *New York Times,* June 5, 2003, p. C5.

44. A series of Internet searches using Lexis-Nexis where the names of the cases were combined with terms such as "wealth," "privilege," and "buy justice" revealed that there have been literally thousands of articles that have referred to the role of wealth in relation to the legal system.

45. Peter J. Riga, "Jury Consultants Buy 'Justice' for the Rich," *USA Today,* October 13, 1994, p. 12A.

46. For another example, see Martin Dyckman, "Justice for Sale," *St. Petersburg Times,* October 5, 1995, p. 17A.

47. Jean Sonmor, "JonBenet's Quiet City in Torment; Child Beauty Queen's Brutal Murder Cast a Dark Shadow over Her Parents," *Toronto Sun,* October 12, 1997, p. 36.

48. Charlie Brennan, "The Ramsey Team: Parents of Slain Girl Have at Least 9 Professionals Working on Case," *Denver Rocky Mountain News,* January 19, 1997, p. 20A.

49. An Internet search using Lexis-Nexis where the names of the cases were combined with the term "celebrity justice" revealed well over 400 articles, though the number is closer to 400 as many of the articles reference more than one of the cases.

50. "Justice for Sale: Why the Rich Get Away with Murder," *Rivera Live,* transcript from August 14, 1998.

51. See Appendix B for a description of the sample.

52. The Pew Research Center for the People and the Press, "Trust and Citizen Engagement in Metropolitan Philadelphia: A Case Study." The findings in this study were based on a survey of 2,517 Philadelphia residents, conducted in November and December 1996.

53. The gender gap has been the subject of extensive academic inquiry. For a brief overview, see M. Margaret Conway, Gertrude A. Steuernagel, and David W. Ahern, *Women and Political Participation* (Washington, DC: Congressional Quarterly Press, 1997), 33–34, 138–139.

54. Several studies of men and women public officials and studies of the gender gap have found that women place a higher priority on children's issues. For instance, see Sue Thomas, *How Women Legislate* (New York: Oxford University Press, 1994).

55. As mentioned in Chapter 4, William Haltom refers to a process of "dramatized normality," which might be particularly strong for younger citizens who have grown up seeing abnormal cases presented as if they were normal; *Reporting on the Courts: How the Mass Media Cover Judicial Actions* (Chicago: Nelson-Hall, 1998), 186.

56. For instance, see Michael Gartner, "O.J. Circus? Blame TV," *USA Today,* October 3, 1995, p. 11A; Alexandra Marks, "O.J. Simpson Case Puts Courtroom Cameras

on Trial," *Christian Science Monitor,* September 19, 1995, p. 10; Joanne Ostrow, "Camera Equally Beholds Circus, Serious Media Fulfill Best and Worst Expectations," *Denver Post,* October 4, 1995, p. A14; and David Shaw, "The Simpson Legacy; Obsession: Did the Media Overfeed a Starving Public?" *Los Angeles Times,* October 9, 1995, p. S4.

57. *Gallup Poll Monthly,* October 1995, p. 5.

58. A good example of this type of analysis is found in Christo Lassiter, "The O.J. Simpson Verdict: A Lesson in Black and White," *Michigan Journal of Race and Law* 1 (Winter 1996): 69.

59. "O.J. Defense Set to Pounce on Fuhrman: Calls Tapes' Racial Slur 'Chilling,'" *Arizona Republic,* August 13, 1995, p. A2.

60. See the Television News Archive, maintained by Vanderbilt University, available online at http://tvnews.vanderbilt.edu/index.html.

61. The extensive polls conducted by Gallup after the trial, beyond those questions mentioned in Table 5.6, consistently revealed that the trial did not significantly change the way blacks felt about whites or whites felt about blacks. The only attitudes that appeared to be altered in terms of race were attitudes toward the justice system itself. See *Gallup Poll Monthly,* all months during 1995.

62. For further discussion of these dynamics, see Helen Boritch, "Gender and Criminal Court Outcomes: An Historical Analysis," *Criminology* 30 (1992): 293–325; and Eve S. Buzawa, *Women as Victims* (Thousand Oaks, CA: Sage, 1996).

63. Unlike poll questions about race and the O.J. Simpson trial, no polling organization has attempted to measure whether general indicators about gender roles and gender equality have been changed as a result of the tabloid justice cases. There are questions frequently asked about support for women political candidates and the proper role of women in the family structure, but there is no evidence that any of these measures have changed as a result of the tabloid cases that involved gender issues. For a summary of some of this polling, see Nancy E. McGlen, Karen O'Connor, Laura van Assendelft, and Wendy Gunther-Canada, *Women, Politics, and American Society,* 4th ed. (New York: Longman, 2004), chap. 4.

64. Perceptions that the poor do not fare as well in the criminal justice system have been supported by compelling evidence that suggests that the public may be correct in viewing the system as favoring the elite. See Jeffrey Reiman, *The Rich Get Richer and the Poor Get Prison: Ideology, Class, and Criminal Justice* (Boston: Allyn and Bacon, 1995). For a brief review of the literature assessing treatment of defendants by economic class, see Neubauer, *America's Courts and the Criminal Justice System,* 408–409.

65. For instance, the Ramsey investigation generated a great deal of discussion about the wealth of defendants. See Karen Auge, "Boulder Readies for Grand Jury Media Scrutiny: County Panel May Be Charged with Hearing JonBenet Case," *Denver Post,* April 22, 1998, p. B1. The role of wealth in the Ramsey case itself was even deemed worthy of an editorial in the *New York Times,* "New Look at an Unsolved Murder," March 14, 1998, p. A16.

66. Woodward's defense fund has variously been reported to have reached an amount somewhere between $300,000 and $500,000. See Patricia Nealon, "Eappens, Woodward Settle Suit," *Boston Globe,* January 30, 1999, p. A1.

PART THREE
Conclusion

SIX

Is There Any Escape from Tabloid Justice?

The Simpson trial was the media's Chernobyl; we [in the media] headed over the edge of a precipice and I am not sure that there is any going back.
—Robert Kovacik, former news anchor, KCOP Channel 13, Los Angeles[1]

But [Michael Jackson's] is not the only future that will be determined by the trial. How many "experts" will build their careers on the media exposure? How many books and TV docudramas will result? There is a media multiplier effect built into [these trials]. I am sure studio chiefs are asking if it has series potential in reruns.
—journalist Danny Schecter[2]

The Simpson and Jackson cases (among many others) clearly stand as defining moments in the contemporary mass media era, at least with regard to coverage of the legal system. To extend the above metaphor, if the media indeed "headed over the edge of a precipice" with their obsession with the Simpson and Jackson stories, they were speeding out of control toward that cliff at least four years prior to even the Simpson events. Indeed, the media currently show no real signs of breaking their fall from that precipice. In fact, the Simpson case (and later the Jackson trial as well) was in some ways an inevitable extension of numerous volatile trends that had begun several years prior to the violent murders in Brentwood.

Since the early 1990s, Americans have witnessed an exponential increase in the mass media's coverage of crime, legal investigations, and trials. Stories about legal events now routinely surpass attention paid to issues such as Medicare, Social Security, welfare reform, environmental protection, public education, immigration, government surveillance, campaign finance reform, and at times even the so-called war on terror. Subsequently, citizens are now exposed to the inner workings of the justice system in a way that would have been nearly unimaginable just twenty years ago. Evidence of exposure to these proceedings abounds, as polls indicate that Americans are more familiar with JonBenet Ramsey, Monica Lewinsky, Rodney King, O.J. Simpson, Martha Stewart, and Scott Peterson than with most of the highest-ranking officials in the US government. This is particularly noteworthy given that the judicial system has historically been by far the least-covered branch of government at all levels of the political system.[3]

Many journalists and scholars have argued that there would be a number of benefits to opening the judicial system up to more scrutiny by the electronic media. Indeed, numerous contemporary commentators, such as Court TV founder Steven Brill and Harvard law professor Alan Dershowitz, have continued to assert that the increasing media coverage of the courts is highly desirable and contributes to a more democratic society.[4] One of the predicted benefits is said to be an increase in civic education, as citizens supposedly become more knowledgeable about the realities of the judicial system. This is thought, in turn, to improve the behavior of juries and to prompt citizens to participate more willingly in other public proceedings. Second, casting a more public eye on the courts is believed to make the professional actors within the system more accountable. It is widely believed that there would be fewer opportunities for due process violations of all kinds, for corruption, deal making, railroading of uneducated defendants, plea bargaining, and jury tampering. In short, it is thought by some that increased media access to the courts would force them to conform more closely to the ideals of the Bill of Rights and less to the imperatives of bureaucratic efficiency and political expediency. And finally, it has been asserted that because of the greater degree of both public knowledge and accountability that would result, public confidence in the system would increase as well. Overall, it is held that the legitimacy of the justice system would be greatly enhanced if citizens understood the system better and could see that officials exercised their power in fair, just, and efficient ways.

For years, the preceding discussion focused largely on the issue of "cameras in the courtroom." Nevertheless, it follows that these same benefits might result from a generally heightened attention to the judicial process on the part of all the mass media. In fact, much of the increased attention to criminal trial proceedings in the media is a result of courtroom cameras providing dramatic footage that can be used in newscasts. The entire era of tabloid justice was really launched because there was extensive footage of the William Kennedy Smith, O.J. Simpson, and Louise Woodward trials. In the second era of tabloid justice, judges, wary of the potential negative effects of cameras in the courtroom, banned them in almost every high-profile case since the end of the 1990s. Still, cameras in the courtroom have undoubtedly led to more exposure to the system for all citizens. Thus, we are left with the question of whether the many predicted benefits have actually come to pass.

In a sense, this is the question that led us to undertake our study. More specifically, we have sought to answer two closely related questions. First, how have high-profile legal proceedings been covered in the present media culture? That is, have the amount and style of legal news fundamentally changed since the 1990s? And second, what impact has this coverage had on the public's knowledge of and attitudes about the justice system? In other words, have the widely predicted civic benefits, which are believed to accompany an increased exposure to the system, actually been realized? In the preceding pages, we have presented a wealth of both primary and secondary data that now allow us to address these questions with some level of confidence.

The Tabloid Justice Era: A Brief Summary of Findings

It is important to again note that there have been two periods in this tabloid justice era. During the first era, from about 1991 to 2001, the main elements of the contemporary media environment fell into place. As these years saw a relative absence of major foreign conflicts, natural disasters, and economic troubles, the media moved into an almost-obsessive posture with regard to coverage of the legal system. The increasingly common availability of video cameras contributed to this shift as well. Without the presence of the privately shot Rodney King footage, for instance, public interest in that case would likely have been significantly lessened. Accompanying these trends was a dramatic increase in the public posturing of trial lawyers, who became more likely to grant daily news conferences attended by an attentive press corps, effectively transforming trials into much more public spectacles. The development of numerous specialized cable news channels offered further opportunities for coverage of these events. Thus, a number of phenomena converged to greatly expand the media's coverage of legal issues, especially criminal investigations and trials.

Then came the O.J. Simpson case. As we have already extensively discussed, this case marked a perfect convergence of all of the aforementioned developments. The Simpson drama contained everything needed for a compelling public media spectacle: a celebrity defendant, famous media-savvy lawyers, race and gender aspects, live coverage from inside the courtroom, and the violent murders of a beautiful ex-wife and her dashing male friend. The nation then witnessed nearly two years of daily media saturation in the coverage of the story. And finally, the case was a ratings bonanza for a number of the new cable news shows, and an unprecedented opportunity for pundits of all kinds to garner extensive face-time on these programs. Most important, the media saw that such stories could become popular obsessions for the public. When the Simpson ordeal ended, the media tried desperately to duplicate these elements by placing an intense focus on a number of criminal cases that followed. Even the Clinton impeachment was covered in essentially the same manner, and with basically the same army of "experts," as the Simpson case.

To some degree, the tragic events of September 11, 2001, brought the media to their senses, at least temporarily. For about a year following the terrorist attacks, the attention paid to investigations and trials dropped dramatically. The invasions of Afghanistan and Iraq dominated the news, at least initially. But as Americans came to accept the war and the new security issues facing the country, the media returned to its intense coverage of legal stories. They tried, usually in vain, to elevate the Scott Peterson trial, the Martha Stewart case, the Robert Blake murder investigation, the Terri Schiavo controversy, and the Michael Jackson trial to the levels of interest that had been achieved with the Simpson story. None of these events came to rival the public interest in that case, but the machinery of tabloid justice was clearly still in place. And although lawyers attempted to essentially try these cases in the media, none of them dominated the news in the way that the Simpson story had. What had occurred, however, is that the daily coverage of tabloid justice–type cases had become "normalized" as an essentially accepted aspect of the news. Coverage of these and other recent stories continued to be presented as sensationalistic, personalized dramas rather than as opportunities for the education of the American public. Thus, the misinformation, racial and gender polarizing, and celebrity-centered focus of legal news continued as in the first tabloid justice period. And finally, the line between fact and fiction was blurred by the explosion of dramatic law-oriented television programs, and the discussion of legal news was significantly extended by the growth of the Internet, which kept legal stories in the public mind much longer than previously.

Ultimately, five broad findings emerge in our analysis that help us to delineate the central aspects of the era of tabloid justice. First, the mass media's increased focus on trials and investigations, which we have documented in Chapters 2 and 3, has largely been motivated by commercial (rather than educational and informative) interests. As news organizations have been forced to compete ever more fiercely for an audience, legal stories (and especially trials) have become "commodified" much like dramatized television shows and feature films. The use of trials and investigations as subjects for intensive news stories appears to have changed the standards of newsworthiness that are employed by media outlets. Further, the fact that it is television that exposes most Americans to these events holds enormous importance for how citizens develop attitudes about law, crime, and politics. Television possesses its own set of imperatives, which encourage the repetitive showing of striking images and the presentation of news in very short and dramatic segments. Neither of these television-specific attributes leads to the presentation of legal proceedings in a manner that is conducive to meaningful civic education.[5]

A second crucial finding is that the mainstream media are increasingly moving in a direction formerly occupied by the tabloid press. We have termed this, as regards the coverage of trials and legal investigations, *tabloid justice* coverage. This term refers to the adoption by the mainstream press of a mode of coverage that has previously been the exclusive domain of the tabloid newspapers and magazines, and it is related to what Neal Gabler has called the pervasive culture of "celebrity journalism."[6] This change is, once again, most likely the result of a more competitive news environment (and a 24-hour news cycle) that forces the old bastions of journalism to turn to topics that they normally have ignored. The importance of this transformation is that many news outlets take their cues from the national news organizations. When the most-respected venues of both broadcast and print journalism embrace tabloid legal stories as legitimate subjects for extensive inquiry, then there is nothing that prevents complete cultural saturation by these stories.

Third, it has become clear that a critical element in promoting the environment of tabloid justice is the role played by new and emerging media sources such as cable television, the Internet, talk radio, and television law dramas. The round-the-clock drumbeat of cable news stations serves to keep tabloid justice cases in the forefront of the news environment. There are several all-news stations that relentlessly cover these stories, suggesting to the public that they are very important news events. And although the audiences for most of the cable news outlets are relatively small, they include many important public opinion makers and other journalists. Further, the wealth of information on the Internet (especially with explosion of the "blogosphere") has also influenced the mass media's behavior in the tabloid justice era. The new and emerging outlets have made the entire media universe more diverse and far more competitive, which has encouraged some of the commercially motivated decisions that are clearly degrading the quality of news coverage.

The preceding developments—an enormous growth in the media's focus on legal cases and trials, a more competitive commercial environment due to the proliferation of new and emerging media forms, and the subsequent "tabloidization" of legal coverage—have actually contributed to an unprecedented level of public exposure to the workings of the system. However, contrary to the idealized prediction that greater public exposure would bring about the range of public benefits outlined previously, we believe that citizens are simply being more misinformed. The tabloid style of contemporary coverage has actually resulted in less knowledge of other important political issues and more distrust in the legal system as a whole. In short, more coverage has translated into less democratic legitimacy. In a way, as we have stated previously, citizens may now paradoxically be both more and less informed about the law.

Accordingly, our fourth central finding is that although public knowledge of and familiarity with high-profile trial proceedings, and the legal system more generally, have increased, knowledge about the legal system has not clearly increased, and faith in the system has actually decreased. Although causation is extremely difficult to establish, the data from our national surveys repeatedly point toward negative effects caused by the current mode of mass media coverage of the justice system. These data permit us to conclude that, given the extremely high degree of public familiarity with these cases and the corresponding apathy and lack of media coverage of arguably more important political and social topics, this anticipated negative effect has, indeed, come to pass. Further, we have described the essentially misleading nature of tabloid justice–style coverage. Here again, it seems clear that when citizens are fed a steady diet of legal information emanating from highly anomalous trials and investigations, they receive a distorted picture that does not comport with the everyday realities of the justice system. As we have written previously, an important opportunity for civic education is squandered by such dynamics. Our most important finding in this regard concerns the public's loss of faith (and continuing lack of real substantive knowledge about the everyday workings of the system) in the US legal system generally, as well as in many of the specific components and participants within that system.

In addition, we found that people's attitudes about the system indicated a disconcerting lack of faith on the part of citizens as to whether they themselves would be treated fairly by the system. As a result of what citizens have learned from the coverage of these tabloid justice trials, roughly 40 percent of our respondents claimed that they had less confidence that the laws would protect their rights, that prosecutors would treat them fairly, and that police would be respectful of their rights and due process protections. Thus, we strongly believe that the evidence we provide supports the notion that tabloid-style coverage of the law does work to reduce people's faith in the system. Of course, as we have repeatedly pointed out, the public may have some legitimate reasons to distrust the system. Our point is simply that it is unfortunate that the citizenry is basing its attitudes largely on the distorted presentation of highly anomalous legal events.

Fifth, we have noted some additional important attitudinal patterns based on our respondents' race and ethnicity, gender, and social class. Americans of all stripes have very low levels of trust in the legal system, and especially in its criminal justice aspects. In fact, one of our most striking findings is the basic lack of faith that all citizens hold in the police, the first line of contact with the legal system for most people.

Still, we found that racial differences are by far the most pronounced indicators of attitudes toward the justice system. Blacks and whites not only hold significantly different views about the criminal justice system in general but also react to our selected criminal cases in different ways. African Americans have lower levels of confidence in juries, judges, and the police. Clearly, this poses serious challenges for creating a criminal justice system that is perceived as legitimate, fair, and equitable.

The disparate views of men and women are considerably less pronounced than those of blacks and whites. The findings we reported point to a small but significant and consistent gender gap in how citizens assess the legal system, both generally and in response to the tabloid justice stories. But although men's and women's reactions to the cases are slightly different in the aggregate, we are unable to conclusively state that media coverage of the cases has either caused or intensified this gender gap. Finally, we should briefly note that Americans of all economic levels strongly believe that the justice system favors the wealthy over those with fewer financial resources. Our surveys suggest that such views have increased as a result of what citizens have learned by following the tabloid justice trials.

Thus, tabloid justice–style media coverage, which often sensationalizes the sexual, racial, economic, violent, and "partisan" dynamics of legal controversies, has served to reinforce existing public attitudes about these social cleavages, rather than to break them down. Although our data do not allow us to assert that this coverage has caused such social divisions, it is clear that it has solidified preexisting attitudes, often based on the mistaken impression that the tabloid cases represent the real everyday workings of the justice system.

The preceding findings force us to conclude that the scholars who see significant social benefits accruing from greater public exposure to the judicial process have been mistaken. They have not anticipated the evolution of the media that has occurred since the early 1990s. They have failed to take into account the changed nature of legal coverage, and have thus underestimated the power of the "tabloid imperative" in the presentation of these stories. We do not condemn the increase in legal coverage itself, but we do find unfortunate the detrimental consequences of the "entertainment-ization" of that coverage.

A Time of Tabloid Justice: Some Broader Implications

Our key findings and central argument are by now quite clear, but the data we have presented raise several broader concerns as well. Most notably, this study exposes the dangerous nexus between the agenda-setting function of the media and the commodification of criminal trials and investigations. Media scholars such as Shanto Iyengar and Donald Kinder have convincingly shown that news organizations set the public agenda in important ways, thus essentially dictating "what the news is."[7] It is disingenuous for journalists to claim that their coverage of the legal system is simply driven by consumer demand, or by a simple desire to educate and inform the public. The endless drumbeat, graphic nature, and purposeful controversy of such coverage give tabloid legal cases a public prominence that most of them do not deserve. Such coverage appears to be driven by simple commercial imperatives rather than true newsworthiness, which leads to the serialization, personalization, and commodification of law stories.

As we have noted, investigations and trials readily lend themselves to *serialization,* or the presentation of news as a series of short dramatic events (involving a relatively small number of recurring characters with specific roles) over an extended period of time. Further, we have noted the *personification* of the presentation of events through a focus on the emotional, personal, and human aspects of a story, which are routinely presented at the expense of context, background, structure, and meaningful analysis. This is the manner in which the television medium presents virtually all news, but it is particularly problematic when this style of coverage is used to present images of the judicial process. After all, in theory the law should strive for objectivity, fair procedures, stability, predictability, and equality. The emotional states, biases, and personal backgrounds of the participants are not expected to influence the outcomes of investigations and trials. All of these media strategies embody attempts to draw in viewers and increase ratings shares with the hope of (sometimes rather crudely and transparently) maximizing profits. Most media organizations have abandoned their idealized roles as public watchdogs and the signalers of important events in favor of the pursuit of bottom-line commercial success. We may ultimately end up with a world of legal news in which the agenda is driven not by the presence of important issues or social phenomena but by simple marketability. Again, we are not so naïve as to believe that such imperatives are anything new. Rather, as we attempted to show in Chapters 2 and 3, the changing dynamics of the news business, including the emergence of cable television, the Internet, and fictional law-related television shows and films, have exponentially increased the ever-present pressure for a share of what is ultimately a finite audience.

Another broader concern that emerges from our study is the need to better understand the role of the mass public in encouraging the tabloid justice environment. In this analysis we have focused on the tactics of the media, and often condemned them, but certainly the public's role in driving tabloid coverage is also crucial. However, the public's interest in tabloid cases is often paradoxical. In some surveys, citizens claim that they have no interest in these trials and investigations and that they believe the press gives them far too much attention. Yet, as we have demonstrated in Chapters 2 and 3, the ratings of many newscasts have significantly increased at key points in particular tabloid justice trials and investigations. Additionally, the respondents in our surveys had a high level of familiarity with these cases, even those involving events that had occurred several years prior to our polling. This seems to undermine the notion that there is no public demand for tabloid justice information. And, of course, the media themselves point to the aforementioned ratings increases as a justification for their pursuit of an ever-increasing number of tabloid justice stories.

And yet, recalling our previous discussions of the agenda-setting function of the press, it is still possible that the internal imperatives of the media lead them to decide unilaterally to cover these stories rather than others that could plausibly be deemed more newsworthy. We seem left with an incomprehensible and vicious cycle similar to that identified by Robert Entman in his classic work *Democracy Without Citizens*. Entman asserts that we cannot expect the media to produce and market high-quality and thoughtful journalism to a citizenry that is intellectually ill-equipped to comprehend and digest it and that is not particularly interested anyway.[8] In the end, it is clear that much more scholarly inquiry is needed if we are to determine the true public role in encouraging the tabloid trends in the mass media.

An additional question raised by our findings is whether there are any benefits to be derived from the type of coverage we have described. Some observers might conclude that tabloid-style coverage, which we have deplored throughout our book, has actually brought citizens together in recognizing the need for the deep reform of law in the United States. We would respond that this is not the case, as the presentation of many potentially important social issues contained in at least a few of these stories tends to be superficial and based on a selection of highly anomalous cases that do not represent the everyday workings of the system. In other words, while this coverage does sometimes draw attention to many critical issues of race, sex, class, due process, and substantive justice, its style—that is, its focus on *entertainment*—undermines the possibility of restrained, measured, and empirically based policy discussion.

Further, as discussed above, the media now simply shift the same "machinery" and approach among their coverage of stories as disparate in nature as the Columbine High School shootings in Colorado, the murder of JonBenet Ramsey, the deaths of Princess Diana and John F. Kennedy Jr., the trial of Jack Kevorkian, the impeachment of the president of the United States, the Hurricane Katrina disaster, or the controversy surrounding the Schiavo family's most intimate and difficult medical decisions.[9] When the same panels of pundits and reporters discuss such stories in a nearly identical fashion, with little indication as to the relative importance of each and with little context or institutional background, the era of tabloid justice can be seen as seriously undermining the dispassionate discussion required to develop meaningful and workable public-policy solutions to the many intractable legal and political problems that virtually everyone agrees do exist.

Finally, one is left to consider whether there are any broad reforms that could curtail the negative effects of the tabloid justice era. It is not immediately clear that legal or structural reforms emanating from the federal government could counteract any of the trends described in this book. Given the First Amendment and the United States' historic commitment to a free press, most explicit restraints on the mass media would shoulder a heavy burden of constitutional suspicion. Further, the Internet has not even begun to be fully understood in terms of its political, legal, and commercial ramifications.

Thus, attempts by Congress, such as the ill-fated Communications Decency Act of 1998, are at best politically problematic and at worse may actually exacerbate the problems they are intended to address. In the wake of a number of these trials and investigations, there have been calls to ban cameras in courtrooms and to prevent lawyers and other trial participants from speaking with the media. These types of reforms are not likely to result in any significant change in the public's understanding of the judicial process. Again, it is not the amount of coverage that is harmful but rather the style in which these stories are presented. As long as the media pay as much attention to Marcia Clark's hairstyle, JonBenet's pageant outfits, Martha's management style, or Michael's pajamas as they do to the finer points of evidence, the proper role of judges, the nature of due process, and racial and gender equity, the few structural reforms that have been proposed will likely prove to be futile.

The only potentially effective long-term reforms or solutions may lie in the realms of civic education, a greater public awareness of the "problem," and a new sense of propriety on the part of both the citizenry and the media. But given the enormous popularity of "reality-based" programs such as *Fear Factor, Trading Spouses, The Girls of the Playboy Mansion,* and *The Flavor of Love,* a renewed sense of public modesty or self-restraint seems a bit unlikely. For the time being, the American public seems woefully disconnected from its own civic life. That being said, the more pressing concern might be how the media can continue to top themselves. The Menendez brothers trial may have been interesting and provocative in the early 1990s, but now that the network evening news programs have discussed the president's semen in prime time, and repeatedly shown graphic footage of a dying Terri Schiavo, would the mere saga of two rich boys killing their parents have the same level of public appeal?

Any reform efforts that are aimed simply at regulating media behavior or restricting press access to the courts and to police activities undoubtedly would have little impact on the tabloid justice environment. Many of the dynamics of the situation are far more complicated than simply the irresponsible conduct of the news media. Popular culture, commercial imperatives, and a complacent and unengaged citizenry have all converged to produce this set of problems. As news anchor Robert Kovacik's statement that opened this chapter suggests, it is difficult to imagine how we can move toward a relationship between the public and the mass media that is characterized by truly serious news reporting and thoughtful analysis by citizens. In the meantime, we will likely just collectively sit back and anxiously await the next "trial of the century."

Notes

1. Richard Fox interview with Robert Kovacik, January 12, 1999.
2. "Media Cash in on Jackson: The Press and TV Can't Get Enough of the Gloved One's Trial—A Lucrative Spectacular," *Newsday,* February 2, 2005, p. A43.
3. See Doris Graber, *Mass Media and American Politics,* 7th ed. (Washington, DC: Congressional Quarterly Press, 2006), 287–289.

4. Brill's comments are cited in "The Simpson Legacy," *Los Angeles Times Report,* October 8, 1995, p. F5. Also see Alan M. Dershowitz, *Reasonable Doubts: The Criminal Justice System and the O.J. Simpson Case* (New York: Simon and Schuster, 1997). For more recent examples, see Douglas Lee, "Florida Election Case Proved Value of Cameras in the Courtroom," FreedomForum.org, December, 16, 2000, http://www.freedomforum.org/templates/document.asp?documentID=4104 (accessed November 15, 2006); Paula Canning, "Battles for Cameras in Courtrooms Continue," *News Media and the Law,* Spring 2003, http://www.rcfp.org/news/mag/27-2/bct-battlesf.html (accessed November 15, 2006); Al Tompkins, "The Case for Cameras in the Courtroom," *Poynter-Online,* November 28, 2000, http://www.poynter.org/dg.lts/id.5132/content.content_view.html (accessed November 15, 2006); and Amy Ridnour, "The Supreme Court Is Wrong to Ban Camera Coverage," *National Policy Analysis,* November 2000, http://www.nationalcenter.org/NPA317.html (accessed November 15, 2006).

5. In support of this argument, see Barry Brummett, "Mediating the Laws: Popular Trials and the Mass Media," in Robert Hariman, ed., *Popular Trials: Rhetoric, Mass Media, and the Law* (Tuscaloosa: University of Alabama Press, 1990), 179–193.

6. Neil Gabler, "The People's Prince: What JFK Jr. Meant to America," *New Republic,* August 9, 1999, pp. 13–15.

7. Shanto Iyengar and Donald Kinder, *News That Matters* (Chicago: University of Chicago Press, 1987).

8. Robert Entman, *Democracy Without Citizens: Media and the Decay of American Politics* (New York: Oxford University Press, 1989), chap. 7.

9. Gabler, "The People's Prince," 13–15.

APPENDIX A:
DATA COLLECTION

This appendix identifies the exact search terms employed to produce the results in Tables 2.3, 2.5, 2.6, 2.8, 3.7, and 3.8. We also identify our sources and ranges of correct answers in Table 4.4. The first-era searches were conducted in November 1998, and they were reconfirmed on the specific dates listed below for each table. The second-era searches took place in July 2006 on the dates noted below. Results may vary slightly for Lexis-Nexis searches, as this search engine alters publication accessibility. Also, general searches using Yahoo!, Netscape, and Google, as in Table 3.7, will vary, as the presence of Internet websites often changes. Further, Internet searches of almost any type can be imperfect, as they may underestimate the number of references for a particular topic. For instance, an article discussing the O.J. Simpson trial might not employ the usage of "O.J." and therefore would not be included in our total figures in Table 2.3. For each of the searches listed below, we experimented extensively to determine which search phrases produced the most comprehensive findings.

Search Terms by Table

Table 2.3

Source: Lexis-Nexis. Separate searches were conducted using the categories "major newspapers" and "all magazines" for all of the following terms. For magazines, only articles in *Time, Newsweek,* and *US News and World Report* were counted.

Period One Searches

Date Searched	Search Term(s)
7/19/1999	menendez and brothers
7/19/1999	kennedy and smith
7/19/1999	rodney and king
6/23/1999	bobbitt
6/23/1999	o.j. and simpson
7/19/1999	jonbenet and ramsey
6/23/1999	louise and woodward

Period Two Searches

The following searches were used in Lexis-Nexis to determine the number of major newspaper articles

7/15/2006	scott peterson and trial or laci
7/15/2006	michael jackson and trial or molest
7/15/2006	martha stewart and trial or stock
7/23/2006	terri schiavo or michael schiavo

For *Newsweek* and *US News and World Report,* the following Lexis-Nexis searches were used

7/15/2006	scott peterson
7/15/2006	michael jackson
7/15/2006	martha stewart
7/23/2006	terri schiavo

For *Time* magazine, the following searches were used on the EBSCOhost Database

7/15/2006	scott peterson
7/15/2006	michael jackson
7/15/2006	martha stewart
7/23/2006	terri schiavo

Table 2.5

Source: Vanderbilt University TV News Archives, which may be accessed online at http://tvnews.vanderbilt.edu/index.html. Searches on this website must be conducted by year. Searches for O.J. Simpson utilized several search instructions to more fully identify the types of trial coverage in that year. For each year, all "trial" segments were examined to make certain they were legal trials. Story segments that employed the term *trial* but were not about legal cases or issues were dropped from the analysis.

Note: For Table 2.5, we were careful not to include articles that mentioned ABC news anchor Carole Simpson as opposed to O.J. Simpson.

Year(s) Searched	Search Term(s)
1968 through 1993	trial
1994	trial not simpson; simpson and murder
1995	trial
1996	trial
1997	trial
1998	paula and jones not trial; lewinsky not trial; trial
1999	trial
2000	trial
2001	trial
2002	trial; elizabeth smart
2003	trial; michael jackson; kobe not trial; martha and stewart not trial
2004	trial
2005	trial

Table 2.6

Source: Vanderbilt University TV News Archives.

Note: For Table 2.6, we were careful not to include articles that mentioned ABC news anchor Carole Simpson as opposed to O.J. Simpson.

Years Searched	Search Terms
1969–1971	manson and cbs; manson and nbc; manson and abc
1980–1985	bulow and cbs; bulow and nbc; bulow and abc
1994–1997	simpson and murder and nbc; simpson and murder and cbs; simpson and murder and abc not carole
2002–2004	martha stewart and cbs; martha stewart and nbc, martha stewart and abc

Table 2.8

Source: Vanderbilt University TV News Archives. All searches were conducted for the years 1997 and 2003. Each search phrase was conducted for each of the three networks. Thus, each search used the primary search phrase along with *and abc, and cbs,* and *and nbc.*

Year Searched	Search Terms
1997	simpson and civil; jonbenet; cunanan [for Versace murder investigation]; paula and jones; louise and

2003	woodward; cosby and murder; marv and albert; medicare; abortion; affirmative and action; welfare; health and care; social and security; hmo martha stewart; kobe bryant; michael jackson; rush limbaugh; elizabeth smart; scott peterson; unemployment or jobs not tax; medicare; health care not medicare; abortion; tax cuts; gas or oil and prices; affirmative action; budget deficit not tax

Table 3.7

Source: Yahoo! and Netscape were used for first-period cases, Yahoo! and Google were used for second-period cases. These search engines can be accessed at Yahoo.com, Netscape.com, and Google.com. Each search term was employed for each search engine.

Date Searched	Search Terms
November 1998	marv albert; menendez brothers; lorena and john bobbitt; o.j. simpson; louise woodward; jonbenet ramsey
June 2006	michael jackson and molest or trial or scandal; scott peterson or laci peterson; terri schiavo; martha stewart and trial or imclone or prison or stock; natalee holloway

Table 3.8

Blog searches were performed through Google Blog Search. Results represent the number of times each term was mentioned in a blog since approximately June 2005, the date at which Google Blog Search began tracking blog entries.

Date Searched	Search Terms
8/1/2006	william kennedy smith; menendez brothers or lyle menendez or eric menendez; o.j. simpson or oj simpson; louise woodward; jonbenet ramsey; andrea yates; martha stewart and trial or imclone or prison or stock; scott peterson or laci peterson; terri schiavo; natalee holloway; duke and lacrosse or rape

Table 4.4

The correct answer and acceptable range for each question are shown below. Correct answers were determined using the sources designated after each question.

Question	Correct Answer	Range Considered Correct

What percentage of criminal defendants plead
guilty?   90   80–100

Sources: US Sentencing Commission, 2001–2005 Datafiles, USSCFY01–
USSCFY05, Pre-*Booker* Only Cases (October 1, 2004, through January 11,
2005); "A Journalist's Guide to the Federal Courts," *Administrative Office of
the United States Courts,* p. 18, accessed at www.uscourts.gov.

What percentage of criminal defendants have
their cases decided by a jury trial?   3   1–20

Sources: Leigh Jones, "Fewer Trials, More Tribulations," *National Law
Journal,* August 19, 2004, www.law.com/jsp/law/LawArticleFriendly.jsp?id=
1090180363092; "Felony Defendants in Large Urban Counties, 2002," Bureau of Justice Statistics, p. 26, accessed at www.ojp.usdoj.gov/bjs.

What percentage of defendants are acquitted
in jury trials?   15   0–30

Sources: Dan Ackman, "Quattrone Fought Long Odds, and Lost," *Forbes
Online,* September 9, 2004; Linda Seebach, "It Seems Federal Judges, Not Juries, More Likely to Acquit," *Denver Rocky Mountain News,* July 22, 2002, p.
11C.

How many cases does the US Supreme Court
hear in a year?   84   50–130

Source: "US Supreme Court Decisions," *Findlaw,* http://www.findlaw
.com/casecode/supreme.html. The Supreme Court decided an average of 84
cases a year from 2000 through 2005.

What percentage of criminal defendants are
able to hire their own lawyers?   20   10–30

Sources: Stacey L. Reed, "A Look Back at Gideon v. Wainwright After
Forty Years: An Examination of the Illusory Sixth Amendment Right to Assistance of Counsel," *Drake Law Review* 52, 1 (2003); Bill Rankin, "Indigent Defense Rates F," *Atlanta-Journal Constitution,* December 12, 2002, p. 1A.

Is violent crime increasing or decreasing?   decreasing   —

Source: "National Crime Victimization Survey Violent Crime Trends,
1973–2004," *Bureau of Justice Statistics,* http://www.ojp.usdoj.gov/bjs/glance/
tables/viortrdtab.htm. Violent crime has decreased every year from 1994 to
2005.

Question	Correct Answer	Range Considered Correct

Does the United States have a greater, lesser, or about the same percentage of its citizens in jail or prison compared with other democratic countries? — greater — —

Source: Mark Mauer, "Comparative International Rates of Incarceration: An Examination of Causes and Trends," *The Sentencing Project Report,* June 20, 2003.

Who decides what charges will be brought against criminal defendants? — prosecutor — —

Source: Widely acknowledged aspect of the criminal justice system; see David Neubauer, *America's Courts and the Criminal Justice System.* 7th ed. (Belmont, CA: Wadsworth, 2002), chap. 13.

APPENDIX B:
POLLING METHODOLOGY

Two national polls were described in Chapters 4 and 5. The first was conducted between April 1 and June 15, 1999. The second poll was conducted between September 15 and December 15, 2005. All respondents were contacted by phone and were selected through a random sampling of listed residential telephone numbers for the United States. We recognize that a sample of listed numbers is not as reliable as a telephone poll conducted through random digit dialing. Thus, in our sample we did not have access to people without listed phone numbers. This may have excluded respondents with certain types of occupations that are less likely to list their home phone numbers (such as doctors or police officers). Nevertheless, we note that there is no research that suggests that random digit dialing produces drastically different poll results, particularly for a general audience survey such as that used in this book. We chose to utilize only listed numbers primarily as a cost-saving measure, as this increases the chances of calling a willing respondent and thus reduces the overall number of calls necessary. We conducted our surveys on a somewhat limited budget.

The first poll was administered by the Brentwood Group, a national polling firm located in Albany, New York. This firm's callers are professionally trained in carrying out survey research. The second poll was administered by the Indiana State University Sociology Research Laboratory, under the direction of Dr. Thomas L. Steiger. Callers were undergraduate and graduate students who had completed a training session and were enrolled in a related sociology course. Callers were supervised either by Professor Steiger or by a trained graduate student. They were also given a set of instructions on how to handle respondents who asked questions concerning the survey items, so as to ensure consistent interaction with those in our survey pool. The total samples for the polls were 1,003 and 1,034, respectively.

What follows is a brief listing of the general demographics of the samples, which enables our pool of respondents to be compared with other national samples. The sample size for each category of demographic characteristics does not necessarily add up to 1,003 (or 1,034), as a number of the respondents (as is often the case) were unwilling to answer questions about race, education, and income.

Demographic Group	Poll One % of Responses	Poll Two % of Responses
Race		
White	83	82
Black	9	8
Hispanic	2	4
Asian/Pacific Islander	1	4
Other	2	4
Refused to state	4	1
Gender		
Men	45	41
Women	55	59
Age		
18–29	12	15
30–39	19	16
40–49	22	22
50–59	17	21
Over 60	29	26
Refused to state	1	0
Education level		
Did not complete high school	5	4
High school diploma	27	20
Some college	35	37
Four-year college graduate	32	39
Refused to state	2	0
Household income		
0–$14,999	8	7
$15,000–29,999	18	11
$30,000–49,999	27	17
$50,000–74,999	20	18
Over $75,000	15	25
Refused to state	12	19
Party identification		
Democrats, including "leaners"	41	30
Republicans, including "leaners"	37	34
Independents	13	20
Other/refused to state	9	15
Total sample size	1,003	1,034

Assessing the Quality of the Samples

In many ways, the samples for both polls do a good job of mirroring the US public, although there are a few areas where the samples do not quite capture an accurate demographic breakdown. The sample for the first poll slightly overrepresents women, older citizens, more highly educated citizens, and white citizens. The sample for the second poll also overrepresents women, older citizens, the highly educated, and white citizens while also overrepresenting Republicans. Overall, although our samples slightly over- and underestimate some demographic groups, we believe they are adequate for evaluating public attitudes toward the tabloid justice trials. As is shown in the data presented in Chapters 4 and 5, for a number of the demographic factors there is no significant impact on views of the justice system. Further, for the variables we wanted to make comparisons with, the sample sizes were sufficient.

Variations in the Survey Instrument

There were two versions of the survey instrument used in each poll. We moved some of the questions around to determine whether topic order altered how respondents answered. For half of the surveys (in each year), we put the general questions about confidence in the criminal justice system and other various parts of the system at the beginning. For the other half, we placed these questions toward the end. This was done in an attempt to determine if first recalling the specific cases made the respondents think of the criminal justice system more negatively. The results of this experiment were discussed in Chapter 4.

In another experiment conducted with the first survey, we placed the questions about the O.J. Simpson case at the beginning of half of the surveys. In the other half of the surveys, Simpson was the final case that we asked about. We moved this case around to see if reaction to the Simpson events would in any way change how people responded to the other questions. We found that the placement of the Simpson questions had no influence on how the respondents answered the questions, and we thus ignored this aspect of the survey in presenting the results. What follows is an abbreviated version of both surveys. In the second survey we do not show all of the demographic questions or any of the questions that were repeated in both surveys.

Tabloid Justice Survey One

Hello, may I speak to _____? Hello, I am _____. I am working on a national poll being conducted by the Brentwood Group for Union College, and I would like very much to get your opinion on a number of current events from the past few years. We are surveying a large number of Americans to assess their attitudes about various issues that have been in the news. Your opinions are very important to us and the survey will take about eight to ten minutes. Is that okay?

Question 1: How much confidence do you have in the following aspects of the criminal justice system in the United States? Would you say you have complete confidence, a great deal of confidence, some confidence, little confidence, or no confidence at all in:

	Complete	A Great Deal	Some	Little	No
The police	1	2	3	4	5
The jury system	1	2	3	4	5
Judges	1	2	3	4	5
Defense attorneys	1	2	3	4	5
Prosecuting attorneys	1	2	3	4	5

When you learn of the verdict in a criminal case, whether in the news or through talking with friends and family, how confident are you that the criminal justice system made the correct verdict?
[ ] Complete confidence
[ ] A great deal of confidence
[ ] Some confidence
[ ] Little confidence
[ ] No confidence

Question 2: How familiar are you with the facts surrounding the following criminal cases? Would you say you are very familiar, somewhat familiar, somewhat unfamiliar, or very unfamiliar with:

	Very Familiar	Somewhat Familiar	Somewhat Unfamiliar	Very Unfamiliar
The trial of Louise Woodward (also called the nanny trial)	1	2	3	4
The criminal trial of O.J. Simpson	1	2	3	4
The investigation into the death of JonBenet Ramsey	1	2	3	4
The first trial of the officers who beat Rodney King	1	2	3	4
The trials of the Menendez brothers	1	2	3	4
The rape trial of William Kennedy Smith	1	2	3	4
The Senate impeachment trial of Bill Clinton	1	2	3	4

Question 3: First, I would like you to think about the criminal trial of O.J. Simpson. Does the O.J. Simpson trial make you feel more, the same, or less confident in the criminal justice system, generally?

	More	Same	Less	Don't Know the Trial
The criminal justice system	1	2	3	4
As a result of this trial are you more, the same, or less confident:				
in the work of police	1	2	3	4
in the jury system	1	2	3	4
in the work of judges	1	2	3	4
that the criminal justice system treats women fairly	1	2	3	4
that the criminal justice system treats African Americans fairly	1	2	3	4
that the criminal justice system treats people fairly regardless of whether they are rich or poor	1	2	3	4

Question 4: Now I would like you to think about the Louise Woodward trial, also known as the "nanny trial" or the "au pair trial." Does the Louise Woodward trial make you feel more, the same, or less confident in the criminal justice system, generally?

	More	Same	Less	Don't Know the Trial
The criminal justice system	1	2	3	4
As a result of this trial, are you more, the same, or less confident:				
in the jury system	1	2	3	4
in the work of judges	1	2	3	4
that the criminal justice system treats women fairly	1	2	3	4
that the criminal justice system treats people fairly regardless of whether they are rich or poor	1	2	3	4

Question 5: Now I would like you to think about the investigation into the murder of JonBenet Ramsey. Does the JonBenet Ramsey murder investigation make you feel more, the same, or less confident in the criminal justice system, generally?

	More	Same	Less	Don't Know the Trial
The criminal justice system	1	2	3	4
As a result of this investigation, are you more, the same, or less confident:				

	More			
in the work of police	1	2	3	4
that the criminal justice system treats people fairly regardless of whether they are rich or poor	1	2	3	4

Question 6: Now I would like you to think about the rape trial of William Kennedy Smith. Does the William Kennedy Smith trial make you feel more, the same, or less confident in the criminal justice system, generally?

	More	Same	Less	Don't Know the Trial
The criminal justice system	1	2	3	4
As a result of this trial, are you more, the same, or less confident:				
in the jury system	1	2	3	4
in the work of judges	1	2	3	4
that the criminal justice system treats women fairly	1	2	3	4
that the criminal justice system treats people fairly regardless of whether they are rich or poor	1	2	3	4

Question 7: Now I would like you to think about the trials of Erik and Lyle Menendez. Do the trials of the Menendez brothers make you feel more, the same, or less confident in the criminal justice system?

	More	Same	Less	Don't Know the Trial
The criminal justice system	1	2	3	4
As a result of these trials, are you more, the same, or less confident:				
in the work of police	1	2	3	4
in the jury system	1	2	3	4
in the work of judges	1	2	3	4
that the criminal justice system treats people fairly regardless of whether they are rich or poor	1	2	3	4

Question 8: Now I would like you to think about the first trial of the officers charged with beating Rodney King. Does the Rodney King trial make you feel more, the same, or less confident in the criminal justice system?

	More	Same	Less	Don't Know the Trial
The criminal justice system	1	2	3	4

As a result of this trial are you more, the same,
or less confident:

in the work of police	1	2	3	4
in the jury system	1	2	3	4
in the work of judges	1	2	3	4
that the criminal justice system treats African Americans fairly	1	2	3	4
that the criminal justice system treats people fairly regardless of whether they are rich or poor	1	2	3	4

We have only a few questions left and the survey will be completed. Thank you for your patience.

Question 9: As a result of the criminal trials and investigations that we have been discussing, we are interested in knowing whether these cases have changed your personal feelings about the criminal justice system.

a. As a result of these cases, how interested are you in serving as a juror?
[ ] More interested
[ ] Less interested
[ ] No change in interest

b. As a result of these cases, how knowledgeable do you feel about the criminal justice system?
[ ] More knowledgeable
[ ] Less knowledgeable
[ ] No change in knowledge

c. As a result of these cases, are you more or less confident that you or a family member would be treated fairly by the police if arrested as a suspect for a crime?
[ ] More confident
[ ] Less confident
[ ] No change in confidence

d. As a result of these cases, are you more or less confident that you or a family member would be treated fairly by prosecuting attorneys if arrested as a suspect for a crime?
[ ] More confident
[ ] Less confident
[ ] No change in confidence

e. As a result of these cases, are you more or less confident that you or a family member would be treated fairly by a judge if you had been arrested and were standing trial for a crime?

[ ] More confident
[ ] Less confident
[ ] No change in confidence

f. As a result of these cases, are you more or less confident that you or a family member would be treated fairly by a jury if you had been arrested and were standing trial for a crime?
[ ] More confident
[ ] Less confident
[ ] No change in confidence

g. As a result of these cases, are you more or less confident that the laws surrounding the criminal justice system would protect your rights?
[ ] More confident
[ ] Less confident
[ ] No change in confidence

Question 10: News habits. How often do you:

	Every Day	Several Times a Week	Several Times a Month	Rarely	Never
read the newspaper?	1	2	3	4	5
watch world/national news programs?	1	2	3	4	5
watch the channel MSNBC?	1	2	3	4	5
watch the Fox News Channel?	1	2	3	4	5
watch the channel CNN?	1	2	3	4	5
watch the channel Court TV?	1	2	3	4	5

Question 11: Background questions.
a. Sex: interviewee identification: [ ] Male [ ] Female

b. State of respondent: _____ [ ] Rural [ ] Urban

c. Would you tell me your age bracket?
[ ] 18–24
[ ] 25–29
[ ] 30–39
[ ] 40–49
[ ] 50–59
[ ] Over 60

d. What race do you consider yourself? [record verbatim]

e. What is your religious preference? Is it Protestant, Catholic, Jewish, some other religion, or no religion?
[ ] Protestant
[ ] Catholic
[ ] Jewish
[ ] Other
[ ] None

f. Which of the following describes your own educational background?
[ ] Did not complete high school
[ ] High school graduate
[ ] Some college
[ ] Graduate of a two-year college
[ ] Graduate of a four-year college
[ ] Attended postgraduate or professional school but did not graduate
[ ] Completed a postgraduate or professional school degree

g. Additionally, we need to know which one of the following broad categories covers your total expected family income for this year—that is, 1999.
[ ] 0–$14,999
[ ] $50,000–$74,999
[ ] $15,000–$29,999
[ ] Over $75,000
[ ] $30,000–$49,999

h. Generally speaking, do you usually think of yourself as a Republican, Democrat, Independent, or what?
[ ] Republican
[ ] Democrat
[ ] Independent
[ ] Other

If a Republican or Democrat: Would you consider yourself a strong (Republican/Democrat) or not a very strong (Republican/Democrat)?
[ ] Strong
[ ] Not strong

If Independent or no preference: Do you think of yourself as closer to the Republican or Democratic Party?
[ ] Republican
[ ] Democratic
[ ] Neither

Thank you for your participation and have a good day.

Tabloid Justice Survey Two

Hello, my name is _____. I am calling from Indiana State University. I'm not selling anything or doing any kind of fund raising. We're calling about a study we are conducting about current events in the United States. I was hoping to conduct a short interview with someone in this household.

Are you a member of this household? Do you live in this household on a regular basis? Do you live here at least six months out of the year? Are you at least 18 years old?

Before we begin, let me tell you that this study is sponsored by Indiana State University and Union College. The data will be used by the investigators to better understand public opinions regarding the legal system.

This interview is anonymous and your answers will be kept completely confidential. Your participation is voluntary, and if there are any questions you don't feel comfortable answering, please let me know and we'll move on. The survey should take, depending on your answers, between 9 and 12 minutes to complete. Now if I have your permission, we'll begin.

Question 1: How much confidence do you have in the following aspects of the criminal justice system in the United States? Would you say you have complete confidence, a great deal of confidence, some confidence, little confidence, or no confidence at all in:

	Complete Confidence	A Great Deal of Confidence	Some Confidence	Little Confidence	No Confidence
the criminal justice system	1	2	3	4	5
the police	1	2	3	4	5
the jury system	1	2	3	4	5
judges	1	2	3	4	5
defense attorneys	1	2	3	4	5
prosecuting attorneys	1	2	3	4	5
media coverage of the legal system	1	2	3	4	5

What is the biggest problem, if any, with the US legal system?

Question 2: How familiar are you with the facts surrounding the following legal cases? Would you say you are very familiar, somewhat familiar, somewhat unfamiliar, or very unfamiliar with:

	Very Familiar	Somewhat Familiar	Somewhat Unfamiliar	Very Unfamiliar
the trials of O.J. Simpson	1	2	3	4
the Michael Jackson trial	1	2	3	4
the Martha Stewart trial	1	2	3	4
the Scott Peterson trial	1	2	3	4
the Terri Schiavo case	1	2	3	4

Question 3: I would like you to think about the criminal trial of O.J. Simpson. Does the O.J. Simpson trial make you feel more, the same, or less confident in:

	More	Same	Less	Don't Know the Trial
the criminal justice system	1	2	3	4
the work of police	1	2	3	4
the jury system	1	2	3	4
the work of judges	1	2	3	4
that the criminal justice system treats women fairly	1	2	3	4
that the criminal justice system treats African Americans fairly	1	2	3	4

Question 4: Now please think about the Michael Jackson trial. Does the Michael Jackson trial make you feel more, the same, or less confidence in:

	More	Same	Less	Don't Know the Trial
the legal system	1	2	3	4
the jury system	1	2	3	4
the work of prosecutors	1	2	3	4
the work of police	1	2	3	4

Question 5: Now please think about the Scott Peterson trial. As a result of this trial do you have more, the same, or less confidence in:

	More	Same	Less	Don't Know the Trial
the legal system	1	2	3	4
the work of police	1	2	3	4
the jury system	1	2	3	4
media coverage of the legal system	1	2	3	4

Question 6: Now please think about the Martha Stewart trial. As a result of this trial do you have more, the same, or less confidence in:

	More	Same	Less	Don't Know the Trial
the legal system	1	2	3	4
the work of prosecuting attorneys	1	2	3	4
the work of judges	1	2	3	4

Question 7: Now please think about the Terri Schiavo case. As a result of this case do you have more, the same, or less confidence in:

	More	Same	Less	Don't Know the Case
the legal system	1	2	3	4
the work of judges	1	2	3	4
media coverage of the legal system	1	2	3	4
the US Congress	1	2	3	4
the president of the United States	1	2	3	4

Question 8: In general did you agree or disagree with the outcome of the following cases?

O.J. Simpson criminal trial	[ ] Agree	[ ] Disagree	[ ] Don't Know	[ ] Refused
Michael Jackson trial	[ ] Agree	[ ] Disagree	[ ] Don't Know	[ ] Refused
Scott Peterson trial	[ ] Agree	[ ] Disagree	[ ] Don't Know	[ ] Refused
Martha Stewart trial	[ ] Agree	[ ] Disagree	[ ] Don't Know	[ ] Refused
Terri Schiavo case	[ ] Agree	[ ] Disagree	[ ] Don't Know	[ ] Refused

Question 9: As a result of the legal cases that we have been discussing, we are interested in knowing whether these cases have changed your feelings about the legal system.

a. As a result of these cases, how interested are you in serving as a juror?
[ ] More interested
[ ] Less interested
[ ] No change in interest

b. As a result of these cases, how knowledgeable do you feel about the criminal justice system?
[ ] More knowledgeable
[ ] Less knowledgeable
[ ] No change in knowledge

c. As a result of these cases, are you more or less confident that you or a family member would be treated fairly by the police if arrested as a suspect for a crime?

[ ] More confident
[ ] Less confident
[ ] No change in confidence

d. As a result of these cases, are you more or less confident that you or a family member would be treated fairly by prosecuting attorneys if arrested as a suspect for a crime?
[ ] More confident
[ ] Less confident
[ ] No change in confidence

e. As a result of these cases, are you more or less confident that you or a family member would be treated fairly by a judge if you had been arrested and were standing trial for a crime?
[ ] More confident
[ ] Less confident
[ ] No change in confidence

f. As a result of these cases, are you more or less confident that you or a family member would be treated fairly by a jury if you had been arrested and were standing trial for a crime?
[ ] More confident
[ ] Less confident
[ ] No change in confidence

g. As a result of these cases, are you more or less confident that the laws surrounding the criminal justice system would protect your rights?
[ ] More confident
[ ] Less confident
[ ] No change in confidence

Question 10: We are interested in your experience with the legal system. Which of the following have you experienced?

Serving on a jury	[ ] Yes	[ ] No
A member of your family being charged with a crime	[ ] Yes	[ ] No
Testifying in a trial	[ ] Yes	[ ] No
Filing a lawsuit or being sued	[ ] Yes	[ ] No
Employed in the legal system	[ ] Yes	[ ] No
What did you do in the legal system?		

Question 11: Which of the following sources do you most rely upon for your legal information? I'll read you a list and then you'll pick one.
[ ] Talk radio

[ ] Cable news (such as Fox News, CNN, or MSNBC)
[ ] National nightly news (hosted by Peter Jennings, Brian Williams, or Bob Scheiffer)
[ ] Newspapers
[ ] The Internet or World Wide Web
[ ] Local TV news

How often do you listen to/visit/read [answer to the preceding question]
[ ] Daily
[ ] Once a week or more
[ ] Once a month or more
[ ] Less than once a month

Question 12: Law dramas have become popular on television, shows like *CSI, Law & Order, Cold Case,* and so on. Which of the following shows, if any, have you watched in the last two weeks?
[ ] *Law & Order*
[ ] *CSI*
[ ] *Cold Case*
[ ] *Without a Trace*
[ ] *Close to Home*
[ ] *Criminal Minds*
[ ] *Crossing Jordan*
[ ] *The Law Firm*
[ ] *Medium*
[ ] *Cops*

Please tell me whether you strongly agree, agree, disagree, or strongly disagree with the following statement: A person can learn about the law and legal system by watching shows like we just named.
[ ] Strongly agree
[ ] Agree
[ ] Disagree
[ ] Strongly disagree

Question 13: We are in the final stretch. Thank you very much for your patience. These last questions have to do with your impressions of the legal system. Generally speaking, do you think violent crime is going up, down, or staying about the same in the United States?
[ ] Going up
[ ] Going down
[ ] Staying the same

Give me your best guess, what percentage [1–100] of defendants:
  have their cases decided by a jury trial?
  are able to hire their own lawyers?
  are found not guilty in jury trials?
  plead guilty?

Give me your best guess, about how many cases [0–500] does the US Supreme Court decide in a year?

Give me your best guess, who decides what charges will be brought against a criminal defendant?
  [ ] Judge
  [ ] Prosecutor
  [ ] Police

Compared to other democratic countries, do you believe that the US has a greater, lesser, or about the same percentage of its citizens in jail or prison?
  [ ] Greater
  [ ] Lesser
  [ ] About the same

Thank you very much for your time and help. The results of this survey will be published in a book titled *Tabloid Justice*. If you have any questions about the survey, please contact Professor Tom Steiger at Indiana State University. Would you like his phone number?

    If you have any questions about your rights and welfare as a participant in this study, please contact Beth Loudermilk of the Indiana State University Institutional Review Board. Would you like that phone number?

    Good bye.

Note: The demographic questions from the first survey were also asked in the second survey.

BIBLIOGRAPHY

Abernathy, Joe (1993). "Casting the Internet: A New Tool for Electronic News Gathering." *Columbia Journalism Review* 31 (January/February): 56.

Abraham, Henry (1998). *The Judicial Process.* 7th ed. New York: Oxford University Press.

Acorn, Linda (1989). "Crime in Prime Time: New Shows Capture Audiences." *Corrections Today* (February): 44–46, 54.

Aho, Karen (2003). "TV and the Supreme Court: Broadcasters Want Access, but Will They Deliver Serious Coverage?" *Columbia Journalism Review* 42 (September/October): 63.

Altheide, David L. (1984). "TV News and the Social Construction of Justice." In Ray Surette, ed., *Justice and the Media.* Springfield, IL: Charles C. Thomas, 292–304.

Anderson, Philip S. (1999). "Time to Open the Electronic Eye." *ABA Journal* (June): 85.

Ansolabehere, Stephen, Roy Behr, and Shanto Iyengar (1993). *The Media Game.* New York: Macmillan.

Bagdikian, Ben (1997). *The Media Monopoly.* 5th ed. Boston: Beacon.

——— (2004). *The New Media Monopoly.* Boston: Beacon.

Bailey, F. Lee, with Harvey Aronson (1971). *The Defense Never Rests.* New York: Stein and Day.

Bandura, Albert (1994). "Social Cognitive Theory of Mass Communication." In Jennings Bryant and Dolf Zimmerman, eds., *Media Effects: Advances in Theory and Research.* Hillsdale, NJ: Lawrence Erlbaum, 61–90.

Barak, Gregg, ed. (1994). *Media, Process, and the Social Construction of Crime: Studies in Newsmaking Criminology.* New York: Garland.

Barber, Susanna (1987). *News Cameras in the Courtroom: A Free Press–Fair Trial Debate.* Norwood, NJ: Ablex.

Barker, David C. (2002). *Rushed to Judgment.* New York: Columbia University Press.

Bartlett, Katharine R., and Rosanne Kennedy, eds. (1992). *Feminist Legal Theory: Readings in Law and Gender.* Boulder, CO: Westview.

Baum, Lawrence, and James Boyd White (2006). *Judges and Their Audiences.* Princeton, NJ: Princeton University Press.

Belknap, Joanne (1991). "Women in Conflict: An Analysis of Women Correctional Officers." *Women and Criminal Justice* 2: 89–116.

Bennett, Lance W. (2006). *News: The Illusion of Politics.* 7th ed. New York: Longman.

Bennett, Lance W., and David L. Paletz, eds. (1994). *Taken by Storm.* Chicago: University of Chicago Press.

Bennett, Stephen Earl (1986). *Apathy in America.* Dobbs Ferry, NY: Transnational.

Berger, Arthur Asa (1996). *Manufacturing Desire.* New Brunswick, NJ: Transaction.

Binion, Gayle (1993). "The Nature of Feminist Jurisprudence." *Judicature* (November/December): 140–143.

Boland, Barbara, Paul Hahanna, and Ronald Stones (1992). *The Prosecution of Felony Arrests.* Washington, DC: US Department of Justice, Bureau of Justice Statistics.

Boritch, Helen (1992). "Gender and Criminal Court Outcomes: An Historical Analysis." *Criminology* 30: 293–325.

Brass, Kevin (2004). "Trial and Error?" *American Journalism Review* 26: 52–57.

Brummett, Barry (1990). "Mediating the Laws: Popular Trials and the Mass Media." In Robert Hariman, ed., *Popular Trials: Rhetoric, Mass Media, and the Law.* Tuscaloosa: University of Alabama Press, 179–193.

Bryant, Jennings, and Dolf Zimmerman, eds. (1994). *Media Effects: Advances in Theory and Research.* Hillsdale, NJ: Lawrence Erlbaum.

Bugliosi, Vincent, with Curt Gentry (1974). *Helter Skelter: The True Story of the Manson Murders.* New York: W. W. Norton.

Buzawa, Eve S. (1996). *Women as Victims.* Thousand Oaks, CA: Sage.

Caldeira, Gregory (1986). "Neither the Purse Nor the Sword." *American Political Science Review* 80: 1209–1226.

"Cameras in Court Gain Support, but Lose in Wyoming Trial." (1999). *News Media and the Law* 23: 30–31.

Cannon, Lou (1997). *Official Negligence: How Rodney King and the Riots Changed Los Angeles and the LAPD.* New York: Times.

Cantril, Albert H. (1991). *The Opinion Connection.* Washington, DC: Congressional Quarterly Press.

Chaloupkia, William (1999). *Everybody Knows: Cynicism in America.* Minneapolis: University of Minnesota Press.

Chamallas, Martha (1999). *Introduction to Feminist Jurisprudence.* New York: Aspen Law and Business.

Chase, Alston (2004). *A Mind for Murder: The Education of the Unabomber and the Origins of Modern Terrorism.* New York: W. W. Norton.

Chiasson, Lloyd, Jr., ed. (1997). *The Press on Trial.* Westport, CT: Praeger.

———— (2003). *Illusive Shadows: Justice, Media, and Socially Significant American Trails.* Westport, CT: Greenwood.

Christian, John, and William Turner (1978). *The Assassination of Robert Kennedy.* New York: Random House.

Christianson, Stephen G., Edward W. Knappman, and Lisa Olson Paddock, eds. (2002). *Great American Trials.* 2d ed. Detroit: Gale Group.

Cohn, Majorie, and David Dow (2002). *Cameras in the Courtroom: Television and the Pursuit of Justice.* Lanham, MD: Rowman and Littlefield.

Conway, M. Margaret, Gertrude A. Steuernagel, and David W. Ahern (1997). *Women and Political Participation.* Washington, DC: Congressional Quarterly Press.

Craft, Stefanie, and Wayne Wanta (2005). "US Public Concerns in the Aftermath of 9/11: A Test of Second Level Agenda-Setting." *International Journal of Public Opinion Research* 16: 456–463.

Crenshaw, Kimberle, ed. (1996). *Critical Race Theory: The Key Writings That Formed the Movement.* New York: New Press.

Da Marshall, P. (2006). *Celebrity Culture Reader.* New York: Routledge.

Darden, Christopher A., with Jess Walter (1996). *In Contempt.* New York: ReganBooks.

Dautrich, Kenneth, and Thomas H. Hartley (1999). *How the News Media Fail American Voters: Causes, Consequences, and Remedies.* New York: Columbia University Press.

Davis, Richard (1994). *Decisions and Images: The Supreme Court and the Press.* Englewood Cliffs, NJ: Prentice-Hall.

———— (1996). *The Press and American Politics.* 2d ed. Upper Saddle River, NJ: Prentice-Hall.

———— (1998). *The Web of Politics: The Internet's Impact on the American Political System.* New York: Oxford University Press.

Davis, Richard, and Diana Owen (1998). *New Media and American Politics.* New York: Oxford University Press.

Davison, W. Phillips (1983). "The Third-Person Effect in Communication." *Public Opinion Quarterly* 47 (Spring): 1–15.

Delgado, Richard, ed. (1995). *Critical Race Theory: The Cutting Edge.* Philadelphia: Temple University Press.

Delgado, Richard, and Jean Stefancic (2001). *Critical Race Theory: An Introduction.* New York: New York University Press.

Dershowitz, Alan M. (1986). *Reversal of Fortune.* New York: Random House.

———— (1994). "Court TV: Are We Being Fed a Steady Diet? Yes: Its Commercialism Hides Its Potential." *ABA Journal* (May): 46.

———— (1997). *Reasonable Doubts: The Criminal Justice System and the O.J. Simpson Case.* New York: Simon and Schuster.

———— (2004). *America on Trial: Inside the Legal Battles That Transformed Our Nation.* New York: Warner.

Didion, Joan (2006). "The Case of Theresa Schiavo." *New York Review of Books* 52 (10).

Dionne, E. J. (2004). *Why Americans Hate Politics.* New York: Simon and Schuster.

Dominick, Joseph (1978). "Crime and Law Enforcement in Mass Media." In Charles Winick, ed., *Deviance and Mass Media.* Thousand Oaks, CA: Sage, 105–128.

Dwyer, William L. (2002). *In the Hands of the People: The Trial Jury's Origins, Triumphs, Troubles, and Future in American Democracy.* New York: St. Martin's.

Dye, Thomas R., L. Harmon Zeigler, and S. Robert Lichter (1992). *American Politics in the Media Age.* 4th ed. Fort Worth, TX: Harcourt Brace.

Entman, Robert (1989). *Democracy Without Citizens: Media and the Decay of American Politics.* New York: Oxford University Press.

———— (1997). "Modern Racism and Images of Blacks in Local Television News." In Shanto Iyengar and Richard Reeves, eds., *Do the Media Govern?* Thousand Oaks, CA: Sage, 283–286.

Epstein, Lee (1998). *Contemplating Courts.* 2d ed. Washington, DC: Congressional Quarterly Press.

Ericson, Richard. (1993). "Television and the Drama of Crime: Moral Tales and the Place of Crime in Public Life." *Contemporary Sociology* 22: 855–857.

Feinman, Clarice (1994). *Women in the Criminal Justice System.* Westport, CT: Praeger.

Franklin, Charles, and Liane Kosacki (1995). "Media, Knowledge, and Public Evaluations of the Supreme Court." In Lee Epstein, ed., *Contemplating Courts.* Washington, DC: Congressional Quarterly Press, 352–375.

Friedman, Lawrence (1986). *A History of American Law.* 2d ed. New York: Simon and Schuster.

Gabler, Neil (1998). *Life: The Movie.* New York: Alfred Knopf.

Galligan, Denis (2006). *Law in Modern Society.* New York: Oxford.

Gans, Herbert J. (1979). *Deciding What's News: A Study of CBS Evening News, NBC Nightly News, Newsweek, and Time.* New York: Vintage.

Garrison, Jim (1988). *On the Trail of Assassins.* New York: Sheridan.

Geis, Gilbert, and Leigh B. Bienen (1998). *Crimes of the Century.* Boston: Northeastern University Press.

Gersh, Debra (1992). "Crime Victims and the Media: Press Coverage Has a Lasting Impact on Their Lives." *Editor and Publisher* 125 (September): 12–14.

Gilliam, Franklin D., Jr., Shanto Iyengar, Adam Simon, and Oliver Wright (1997). "Crime in Black and White: The Violent, Scary World of Local News." In Shanto Iyengar and Richard Reeves, eds., *Do the Media Govern?* Thousand Oaks, CA: Sage, 287–295.

Goldfarb, Ronald L. (1998). *TV or Not TV: Television, Justice, and the Courts.* New York: New York University Press.

Goldstein, Leslie F. (1992). *The Difference Debate: Feminist Jurisprudence.* Lanham, MD: Rowman and Littlefield.

Goode, Stephen (1979). *Assassination! Kennedy, King, Kennedy.* New York: Watts.

Graber, Doris (1980). *Crime News and the Public.* Westport, CT: Praeger.

——— (1997). *Mass Media and American Politics.* 5th ed. Washington, DC: Congressional Quarterly Press.

——— (2005). *Mass Media and American Politics.* 7th ed. Washington, DC: Congressional Quarterly Press.

Graysmith, Robert (1997). *Unabomber: A Desire to Kill.* Washington, DC: Regnery.

Greek, Cecil (1998). "Crime and the Media Course Syllabus and Lectures," Florida State University. www.fsu.edu/~crimdo/grade&m.html#lectures (accessed December 1, 2006).

Hallin, Daniel C. (1986). *The "Uncensored War": The Media and Vietnam.* New York: Oxford University Press.

Haltom, William (1998). *Reporting on the Courts: How the Mass Media Cover Judicial Actions.* Chicago: Nelson-Hall.

Harris, David A. (1993). "The Appearance of Justice: Court TV, Conventional Television, and Public Understanding of the Criminal Justice System." *Arizona Law Review* 35: 785–827.

Harwood, Richard (1999). "Searching for Facts in a Sea of Speculation." *Nieman Report* 53 (Summer): 61.

Hemmens, Craig, Kristin Strom, and Elicia Schlegel (1997). "Gender Bias in the Courts: A Review." Paper presented at the Academy of Criminal Justice Sciences, Louisville, KY.

Hill, Kevin (1998). *Cyberpolitics: Citizen Activism in the Age of the Internet.* Lanham, MD: Rowman and Littlefield.

Hoekstra, Valerie, and Jeffrey A. Segal (1996). "The Shepherding of Local Public Opinion: The Supreme Court and Lamb's Chapel." *Journal of Politics* 58: 1079–1102.

Holbrook, R. Andrew, and Timothy G. Hill (2005). "Agenda-Setting and Priming in Prime Time Television: Crime Dramas as Political Cues." *Political Communication* 22: 277–295.

Holmes, Su, and Sean Redmond, eds. (2006). *Framing Celebrity: New Directions in Celebrity Culture Reader.* New York: Routledge.

Imrich, Dorothy J., Charles Mullin, and Daniel Linz (1995). "Measuring the Extent of Prejudicial Pretrial Publicity in Major American Newspapers: A Content Analysis." *Journal of Communication* 45 (Summer): 94–117.

Iyengar, Shanto (1991). *Is Anyone Responsible? How Television Frames Political Issues.* Chicago: University of Chicago Press.

Iyengar, Shanto, and Donald Kinder (1987). *News That Matters.* Chicago: University of Chicago Press.

Iyengar, Shanto, and Richard Reeves, eds. (1997). *Do the Media Govern?* Thousand Oaks, CA: Sage.

Jacoby, Jacob, and Wayne D. Hoyer (1982). "Viewer Miscomprehension of Televised Communications: Selected Findings." *Journal of Marketing* 46 (Fall): 12–26.

Jamieson, Kathleen Hall, and Karlyn Kohrs Campbell (1998). *Interplay of Influence: News, Advertising, Politics, and the Mass Media.* 4th ed. Belmont, CA: Wadsworth.

——— (2000). *Interplay of Influence: News, Advertising, Politics, and the Mass Media.* 5th ed. Belmont, CA: Wadsworth. ·

——— (2005). *The Interplay of Influence: News, Advertising, Politics in the Internet Age.* Belmont, CA: Wadsworth.

Jordan, Tim (1999). *Cyberpower: The Culture and Politics of Cyberspace and the Internet.* New York: Routledge.

"Judicial Conference Nixes Cameras in Courtrooms." (2000). *Defense Counsel Journal* 67: 429–535.

Kadri, Sadakat (2005). *The Trial: A History, from Socrates to O.J. Simpson.* New York: Random House.

Kairys, David (1998). *The Politics of Law: A Progressive Critique.* 3d ed. New York: Basic.

Kappeler, Victor, Mark Blumberg, and Gary W. Potter (1996). *The Mythology of Crime and Criminal Justice.* 2d ed. Prospect Heights, IL: Waveland.

Katz, Burton S. (1998). *Justice Overruled: Unmasking the Criminal Justice System.* New York: Warner.

Kerbel, Matthew Robert (1994). *Edited for Television.* Boulder, CO: Westview.

Knappman, Edward W., ed. (1995). *American Trials of the 20th Century.* Detroit: Visible Ink.

——— (1995). *Remote and Controlled.* Boulder, CO: Westview.

——— (2004). *Great American Trials: 201 Compelling Courtroom Dramas from Salem Witchcraft to O.J. Simpson.* New York: Barnes and Noble.

Knight, Alfred H. (1996). *The Life of the Law: The People and the Cases That Have Shaped Our Society, from King Alfred to Rodney King.* New York: Oxford University Press.

Kovach, Bill, and Tom Rosenstiel (1999). *Warp Speed: America in the Age of Mixed Media.* New York: Century Foundation.

Krajicek, Richard (1998). *Scooped.* New York: Columbia University Press.

Kuklin, Bailey, and Jeffrey W. Stempel (1994). *Foundations of Law: A Jurisprudential Primer.* St. Paul, MN: West.

Kurtz, Howard (1995). *Hot Air.* New York: Basic.

Lanoue, David J., and Peter Schrott (1991). *The History, Impact, and Prospects of American Presidential Debates.* Westport, CT: Greenwood.

Lassiter, Christo (1996). "The O.J. Simpson Verdict: A Lesson in Black and White." *Michigan Journal of Race and Law* 1 (Winter): 69–118.

Laufer, Peter (1995). *Inside Talk Radio.* New York: Birch Lane.

Lehman, Godfrey D. (1997). *We the Jury: The Impact of Jurors on Our Basic Freedoms: Great Jury Trials of History.* Amherst, NY: Prometheus.

Lehrer, Jim (1999). "Blurring the Lines Hurts Journalism." *Nieman Report* 53 (Summer): 65.

Lenz, Timothy O. (2003). *Changing Images of Law in Film and Television Crime Stories.* New York: Peter Lang.

"Let the People See the Court." (2006). *Chicago Tribune,* May 3, p. 26.

Levit, Nancy, and Robert R.M. Verchick (2006). *Feminist Legal Theory: A Primer.* New York: New York University Press.

Libby, Eileen (1994). "Court TV: Are We Being Fed a Steady Diet of Tabloid Television? No: Tacky or Not, It Helps Bring the Law to Life." *ABA Journal* (May): 47.

Lipschultz, Jeremy H., and Michael L. Hilt (2002). *Crime and Local Television News: Dramatic, Breaking, and Live from the Scene.* Mahwah, NJ: Lawrence Erlbaum.

Lipsitz, George (1997). "The Greatest Story Ever Sold: Marketing and the O.J. Simpson Trial." In Toni Morrison and Claudia Brodsky Lacour, eds., *Birth of a Nation'hood: Gaze, Script, and Spectacle in the O.J. Simpson Case.* New York: Pantheon, 3–29.

Littleton, Cynthia (1995). "Verdict Propels Tabloid Ratings." *Broadcasting and Cable,* October 1, p. 8.

Lock, Schmuel T., Robert Y. Shapiro, and Lawrence R. Jacobs (1999). "The Impact of Political Debate on Government Trust: Reminding the Public What the Federal Government Does." *Political Behavior* 21: 239–264.

Lotz, Roy Edward (1991). *Crime and the American Press.* Westport, CT: Praeger.

Macchiarola, Frank (1997). "Finding the Truth in an American Criminal Trial: Some Observations." *Cardozo Journal of International Comparative Law* 5 (Spring): 97–113.

Maisel, Louis Sandy, and Darrell M. West, eds. (2004). *Running On Empty? Political Discourse in Congressional Elections.* Lanham, MD: Rowman and Littlefield.

Mandrese, Joe, and Thomas Tyler (1995). "Simpson Shakes New TV Season." *Advertising Age,* October 16, p. 8.

Martin, Elaine (1993). "Women on the Bench: A Different Voice?" *Judicature* 77: 126–128.

Martin, Susan Ehrlich, and Nancy C. Jurik (1996). *Doing Justice, Doing Gender: Women in Law and Criminal Justice Occupations.* Thousand Oaks, CA: Sage.

Matsaganis, Matthew D. (2005). "Agenda Setting in a Culture of Fear: The Lasting Effects of September 11 on American Politics and Journalism." *American Behavioral Scientist* 49: 379–392.

McCombs, Maxwell (1994). "News Influence on Our Pictures of the World." In Jennings Bryant and Dolf Zimmerman, eds., *Media Effects: Advances in Theory and Research.* Hillsdale, NJ: Lawrence Erlbaum, 1–16.

McGlen, Nancy E., Karen O'Connor, Laura van Assendelft, and Wendy Gunther-Canada (2004). *Women, Politics, and American Society.* New York: Prentice-Hall.

Miller, Joanne, and Jon A. Krosnick (1997). "Anatomy of News Media Priming." In Shanto Iyengar and Richard Reeves, eds., *Do the Media Govern?* Thousand Oaks, CA: Sage, 258–275.

Morgan, David (1978). *The Capitol Press Corps: Newsmen and the Governing of New York State.* Westport, CT: Greenwood.

Morrison, Toni, and Claudia Brodsky Lacour, eds. (1997). *Birth of a Nation'-hood: Gaze, Script, and Spectacle in the O.J. Simpson Case.* New York: Pantheon.

Murphy, Walter E., C. Herman Pritchett, and Lee Epstein (2005). *Courts, Judges, and Politics.* 6th ed. New York: McGraw-Hill.

Murphy, Walter F., and Joseph Tanenhaus (1968). "Public Opinion and the Supreme Court." *Law and Society Review* 2 (February): 357–382.

Neubauer, David W. (2002). *America's Courts and the Criminal Justice System.* 7th ed. Belmont, CA: Wadsworth.

Neuman, Russell W. (1991). *The Future of the Mass Audience.* New York: Cambridge University Press.

Nye, Joseph S., Jr. (1997). "The Media and Declining Confidence in Government." *Harvard International Journal of Press and Politics* 2 (Summer): 4–9.

Nye, Joseph, Philip Zelikow, and David C. King (1997). *Why People Don't Trust Government.* Cambridge, MA: Harvard University Press.

Oates, Joyce Carol (1999). "The Mystery of JonBenet Ramsey." *New York Review of Books,* June 24, pp. 31–37.

Oates, Sarah, Diana Owen, and Rachel Kay Gibson (2005). *The Internet and Politics: Citizens, Voters, and Activists.* New York: Taylor and Frances.

Page, Benjamin I., Robert Y. Shapiro, and Glenn R. Dempsey (1987). "What Moves Public Opinion." *American Political Science Review* 81 (March): 23–43.

Paletz, David L. (1999). *The Media in American Politics.* New York: Longman.

Parenti, Michael (1986). *Inventing Reality.* New York: St. Martin's.

Patterson, Thomas (1993). *Out of Order.* New York: Knopf.

———— (1988). *The Mass Media Election: How Americans Choose Their President.* 3d ed. Westport, CT: Praeger.

Paul, Angelique (1997). "Turning the Camera on Court TV: Does Televising Trials Teach Us Anything About the Real Law?" *Ohio State Law Journal* 58: 655–694.

Postman, Neil (1986). *Amusing Ourselves to Death: Public Discourse in the Age of Show Business.* New York: Penguin.

Protess, David L., and Maxwell E. McCombs, eds. (1991). *Agenda Setting.* Hillsdale, NJ: Lawrence Erlbaum.

Purvis, Hoyt (2001). *Media, Politics, and Government.* Ft. Worth, TX: Harcourt.

Quindlen, Anna (2002). "Lights, Camera, Justice for All." *Newsweek,* January 21.

Rapping, Elayne (2003). *Law and Justice as Seen on TV.* New York: New York University Press.

Reiman, Jeffrey (1995). *The Rich Get Richer and the Poor Get Prison: Ideology, Class, and Criminal Justice.* Boston: Allyn and Bacon.

Robinson, John P., and Dennis K. Davis (1990). "Television News and the Informed Public: An Information-Processing Approach." *Journal of Communication* 40: 106–119.

Robinson, Michael (1976). "Public Affairs Television and the Growth of Malaise." *American Political Science Review* 70: 409–432.

Rogers, Everett M., William B. Hart, and James W. Dearing (1997). "A Paradigmatic History of Agenda-Setting Research." In Shanto Iyengar and Richard Reeves, eds., *Do the Media Govern?* Thousand Oaks, CA: Sage, 225–236.

Ryan, John Paul, Allan Ahman, Bruce Sales, and Sandra Shane Dubow (1980). *American Trial Judges.* New York: Free Press.

Sabato, Larry J. (1993). *Feeding Frenzy.* New York: Free Press.

Schachner Chanen, Jill (2004). "Stay Tuned." *ABA Journal* (October): 45–48, 56–58.

Scheb, John M., and William Lyons (2000). "Public Perception of the Supreme Court in the 1990s." In Eliot E. Slotnick, ed., *Judicial Politics: Readings from Judicature.* Chicago: American Judicature Society.

Schlessinger, Philip, and Howard Tumber (1994). *Reporting Crime: The Media Politics of Criminal Justice.* Oxford: Clarendon.

Selnow, Gary (1998). *Electronic Whistle-Stops: The Impact of the Internet on American Politics.* Westport, CT: Praeger.

Shaw, Donald, and Maxwell McCombs (1977). *The Emergence of American Political Issues*. St. Paul, MN: West.

Shenk, David (1998). *Data Smog: Surviving the Information Glut*. San Francisco: Harper.

Sherry, Suzanna (1986). "Civic Virtue and the Feminine Voice in Constitutional Adjudication." *Virginia Law Review* 72: 543–591.

Sisk, Gregory, Michael Heise, and Andrew P. Morriss (1998). "Charting the Influences on the Judicial Mind: An Empirical Study of Judicial Reasoning." *New York University Law Review* 73: 1377–1500.

Slotnick, Elliot E., ed. (1992). *Judicial Politics: Readings from Judicature*. Chicago: American Judicature Society.

Smith, Douglas (1997). "Structural and Functional Aspects of the Jury: Comparative Analysis and Proposals for Reform." *Alabama Law Review* 48 (Winter): 441–581.

Smith, Eric R.A.N. (1989). *The Unchanging American Voter*. Berkeley: University of California Press.

Smith, Patricia, ed. (1994). *Feminist Jurisprudence*. New York: Oxford University Press.

Spill, Rorie L., and Zoe M. Oxley (2003). "Philosopher Kings or Political Actors: How the Media Portray the Supreme Court." *Judicature* 87 (July/August): 22–29.

Stabile, Carol (2006). *White Victims, Black Villains: Gender, Race, and Crime News in US Culture*. New York: Routledge.

Stempel, Guido H., III, and John Windhauser (1991). *The Media and the 1984 and 1988 Elections*. Westport, CT: Greenwood.

Strickland, Ruth Ann, and Richter H. Moore Jr. (1994). "Cameras in State Courts: A Historical Perspective," *Judicature* 78 (November/December): 128–135.

Sunstein, Cass (1988). "Feminism and Legal Theory." *Harvard Law Review* 101: 826–848.

Surette, Ray (1989). "Media Trials." *Journal of Criminal Justice* 17: 293–308.

——— (1991). "Methodological Problems in Determining Media Effects on Criminal Justice: A Review and Suggestions for the Future." *Criminal Justice Policy Review* 6: 291–310.

——— (1998). *Media, Crime, and Criminal Justice: Images and Realities*. 2d ed. Belmont, CA: Wadsworth.

——— (2007). *Media, Crime, and Criminal Justice: Images, Realities and Policies*. 3d ed. Belmont, CA: Wadsworth.

Thaler, Paul (1994). *The Watchful Eye: American Justice in the Age of the Television Trial*. Westport, CT: Praeger.

Thomas, Sue (1994). *How Women Legislate*. New York: Oxford University Press.

Thompson, Ellia (2004). "Courtroom Cameras: Issues Move In and Out of Focus." *The Quill* 92: 7.

Tolchin, Susan J. (1995). *The Angry American.* Boulder, CO: Westview.

Toobin, Jeffrey (1997). *The Run of His Life: The People v. O.J. Simpson.* New York: Touchstone.

Tyler, Tom R. (2006). "Viewing *CSI* and the Threshold of Guilt: Managing Truth and Justice in Reality and Fiction." *Yale Law Journal* 1050 (March): 115.

Vago, Steven (2004). *Law and Society.* 7th ed. Upper Saddle River, NJ: Prentice-Hall.

Vinson, C. Danielle, and John S. Ertter (1999). "Entertainment or Education: How Do Media Cover the Courts?" Paper presented at the Midwest Political Science Association, Chicago, April 15–18.

Walgrave, Stefaan, and Peter Van Aelst (2006). "The Contingency of the Mass Media's Political Agenda Setting Power: Toward a Preliminary Theory." *Journal of Communication* 56: 88–109.

Watson, Tex (1978). *Will You Die for Me?* Old Tappan, NJ: Fleming Revell.

Wattenberg, Martin P. (1990). *The Decline of American Political Parties: 1952–1988.* Cambridge, MA: Harvard University Press.

Wilkes, Roger, ed. (2006). *The Mammoth Book of Famous Trials.* New York: Carroll and Graf.

Williams, Bruce A., and Michael X. Delli Carpini (2004). "Monica and Bill All the Time and Everywhere." *American Behavioral Scientist* 47: 1208–1230.

Wilson, Barbara, et al. (1997). *National Television Violence Study.* Vol. 1. Thousand Oaks, CA: Sage.

Wilson, Theo (1997). *Headline Justice.* New York: Thunder's Mouth.

Wright, William (1983). *The Von Bulow Affair.* New York: Delacorte.

Yioutas, Julie, and Ivana Segvic (2003). "Revisiting the Clinton/Lewinsky Scandal: The Convergence of Agenda Setting and Framing." *Journalism and Mass Communication Quarterly* 80: 567–582.

Zaller, John R. (1992). *The Nature and Origins of Mass Opinion.* New York: Cambridge University Press.

Zaller, John, and Stanley Feldman (1992). "A Simple Theory of the Survey Response: Answering Questions Versus Revealing Preferences." *American Journal of Political Science* 36: 579–616.

Zeigler, L. Harmon, and William Haltom (1989). "More Bad News About the News." *Public Opinion* (May/June): 50–52.

INDEX

ABOUT THE BOOK

This new edition of *Tabloid Justice* reveals that, although the media focus on high-profile criminal trials is thought by many to have diminished in the years since the September 11 terrorist attacks, the polarized, partisan coverage of these trials has in fact continued unabated. The authors investigate the profoundly negative impact of the media's coverage of the criminal justice system—coverage that frequently highlights and aggravates the deepest divisions in US society.

Features of the new edition include results of a recent national poll, richer demographic data, and discussion of the Internet's rising significance. Thorough analysis of recent tabloid cases (featuring Kobe Bryant, Michael Jackson, Terri Schiavo, Scott Peterson, and Martha Stewart) provides a contemporary window on the tactics of a media driven by profit to the detriment of political and legal principles.

Richard L. Fox is associate professor of political science at Loyola Marymount University. He is coauthor of *It Takes a Candidate: Why Women Don't Run for Office* (with Jennifer Lawless). **Robert W. Van Sickel** is assistant professor of political science at Indiana State University. He is author of *Not a Particularly Different Voice: The Jurisprudence of Sandra Day O'Connor*. **Thomas L. Steiger** is professor of sociology at Indiana State University. His publications include *Life's Social Journey* (with Diana Grimes) and *Rethinking the Labor Process* (coedited with Peter Meiksins).

DATE DUE

WITHDRAWN

DEMCO 38-296